PRAISE FOR
King John

"Stephen Church has written the most convincing account we have of England's most reviled monarch. This lively, readable book will appeal both to general readers and to scholars."

—Robert Stacey, Professor of Medieval History and
Dean of the College of Arts and Sciences, University of Washington

"Deep, solid, and vivid, this book is as precise with facts as it is subtle in their interpretation. Stephen Church penetrates the complexity of John's character; Church offers the keys to understanding his failures and his follies, and the cruel actions he took with his entourage. This fascinating book does not pretend to be an impossible rehabilitation of John, but is rather a successful attempt at comprehending his character, the aristocracy, townsmen, and clergy he had to deal with, and the troubled times he could never change."

—Martin Aurell, Professor of Medieval History,
University of Poitiers, *Institut Universitaire de France*

"Very well written, with a clear and precise style. This is a notable work of research. *King John* will change many of our traditional negative views concerning one of the more underestimated kings of English history. Stephen Church has taken a great step forward in giving us a more balanced understanding of John, his personality and reign, and also of the Angevin dynasty."

—Manuel Rojas Gabriel, Professor of Medieval History,
University of Extremadura, Spain

King John

ALSO BY STEPHEN CHURCH

The Household Knights of King John

King John: New Interpretations (ED.)

KING
JOHN

And the

ROAD *to*

MAGNA CARTA

Stephen Church

BASIC BOOKS

A MEMBER OF THE PERSEUS BOOKS GROUP

New York

Books published by Basic Books are available at special discounts for bulk
purchases in the United States by corporations, institutions, and other
organizations. For more information, please contact the Special Markets
Department at the Perseus Books Group, 2300 Chestnut Street, Suite 200,
Philadelphia, PA 19103, or call (800) 810-4145, ext. 5000, or e-mail special
.markets@perseusbooks.com.

First published in 2015 by Macmillan
an imprint of Pan Macmillan, a division of Macmillan Publishers Limited
Pan Macmillan, 20 New Wharf Road, London N1 9RR

Designed by Timm Bryson

Library of Congress Cataloging-in-Publication Data
Church, S. D.
  King John : and the road to Magna Carta / Stephen Church.
     pages cm
  Includes bibliographical references and index.
  ISBN 978-0-465-09299-4 (hardcover)—ISBN 978-0-465-04070-4 (e-book)
1. John, King of England, 1167–1216. 2. Great Britain—Kings and rulers—
Biography. 3. Great Britain—History—John, 1199–1216. 4. Magna Carta. I.
Title.
  DA208.C55 2015
  942.03'3092—dc23
  [B]
                             2014041884

10 9 8 7 6 5 4 3 2 1

To Ann Williams

CONTENTS

LIST OF ABBREVIATIONS

Angevin Acta Project • *The Angevin Acta Project at the University of East Anglia*, ed. N. C. Vincent, J. C. Holt, R. Mortimer, M. Staunton and J. Everard (forthcoming). This work includes the acts of Henry II, Count Richard, and Count John and until publication is accessible from Prof. Vincent at the University of East Anglia

Annales Monastici • *Annales Monastici*, 5 vols, ed. H. R. Luard, Rolls Series (London, 1864–9)

Chronica Magistri Rogeri de Houedene • *Chronica Magistri Rogeri de Houedene*, 4 vols, ed. W. Stubbs, Rolls Series (London, 1868–71)

Chronicle of Richard of Devizes • *The Chronicle of Richard of Devizes*, ed. J. T. Appleby (London, 1963)

Coggeshall • *Radulphi de Coggeshall Chronicon Anglicanum*, ed. J. Stevenson, Rolls Series (London, 1875)

Curia Regis Rolls • *Curia Regis Rolls of the Reigns of Richard I, John and Henry III Preserved in the Public Record Office*, (London, 1922, ongoing)

English Episcopal Acta • *English Episcopal Acta*, cited by volume number and diocese, published by the British Academy (Oxford, ongoing)

EHR • *English Historical Review*

Epistolae Cantuarienses • *Epistolae Cantuarienses* in *Chronicles and Memorials of the Reign of Richard I*, 2 vols, ed. W. Stubbs, Rolls Series (London, 1864–5), volume i

Expugnatio Hibernica • *Giraldus Cambrensis, Expugnatio Hibernica. The Conquest of Ireland*, ed. A. B. Scott and F. X. Martin (Dublin, 1978)

Foedera • *Foedera, Conventiones, Litterae et cuiuscunque generis Acta Publica*, ed. T. Rymer, new edn, vol. I, part i, ed. A. Clark and F. Holbrooke (Record Commission, London, 1816)

Giraldus Cambrensis, Opera • *Giraldus Cambrensis, Opera*, 8 vols, ed. J. S. Brewer, J. F. Dimock and G. F. Warner, Rolls Series (London 1861–91)

Gervase of Canterbury • *The Historical Works of Gervase of Canterbury*, 2 vols, ed. W. Stubbs, Rolls Series (London, 1879–80)

Gesta Regis Henrici Secundi • *Gesta Regis Henrici Secundi Benedicti Abbatis*, 2 vols, ed. W. Stubbs, Rolls Series (London, 1867)

Gillingham, *Richard I* • J. B. Gillingham, *Richard I* (New Haven, CT, 1999)

Histoire des Ducs de Normandie • *Histoire des Ducs de Normandie et des Rois d'Angleterre*, ed. F. Michel (Société de l'histoire de France, Paris, 1840)

Historical Works of Ralph de Diceto • *The Historical Works of Master Ralph de Diceto*, 2 vols, ed. W. Stubbs, Rolls Series (London, 1876)

History of William the Marshal • *History of William the Marshal*, 3 vols, ed. A. J. Holden, S. Gregory and D. Crouch, Anglo-Norman Texts Society (London, 2002–6)

Itinerary of Richard I • *The Itinerary of King Richard I*, ed. L. Landon (Pipe Roll Society, new series, 13, London, 1935)

Layettes du Trésor des Chartes • *Layettes du Trésor des Chartes*, 4 vol. in–4°, tome I: 755–1223, A. Teulet (Paris, 1863–1902)

Letters of Innocent III to England and Wales • *Letters of Innocent III Concerning England and Wales* (1198–1216), ed. C. R. Cheney and M. Cheney (Oxford, 1967)

Liber Feodorum • *Liber Feodorum. The Book of Fees Commonly Called Testa de Neville*, 3 vols (London, 1920–31)

Matthew Paris, *Chron. Maj.* • *Matthaei Parisiensis, Monachi Sancti Albani, Chronica Majora*, 7 vols, ed. H. R. Luard, Rolls Series (London, 1872–83)

Memoranda Roll 1 John • *The Memoranda Roll for the Michaelmas Term of the First Year of the Reign of King John, 1199–1200*, ed. H. G. Richardson (Pipe Roll Society, new series, 21, 1943)

Pipe Rolls • Citations to Pipe Rolls are to the regnal years of the reigning kings and published by the Pipe Roll Society, London

Rigord • Rigord, *Gesta Philippi Augusti*, in Œuvres de Rigord et de Guillaume le Breton, ed. H. F. Delaborde, i (Paris, 1882)

Roger of Wendover, Flores Historiarum • *Rogeri de Wendover, Chronica sive Flores Historiarum*, 5 vols, ed. H. O. Coxe, English Historical Society (London, 1841–5)

Rot. Chart. • *Rotuli Chartarum in Turri Londinensi Asservati*, ed. T. Duffus Hardy (Record Commission, London, 1837)

Rot. Cur. Reg. • *Rotuli Curiae Regis: Rolls and Records of the Court held before the King's Justiciars or Justices*, 2 vols, ed. F. Palgrave (Record Commission, London, 1835)

Rot. de Fin. • *Rotuli de Oblatis et Finibus in Turri Londinensi Asservati*, ed. T. Duffus Hardy (Record Commission, London, 1835)

Rot. de Lib. • *Rotuli de Liberate ac de Misis et Praestitis Regnante Johanne*, ed. T. Duffus Hardy (Record Commission, London, 1844)

Rot. Litt. Claus. • *Rotuli Litterarum Clausarum in Turri Londinensi Asservati*, 2 vols, ed. T. Duffus Hardy (Record Commission, London, 1833, 1844)

Rot. Litt. Pat. • *Rotuli Litterarum Patentium in Turri Londinensi Asservati*, ed. T. Duffus Hardy (Record Commission, London, 1835)

Rot. Norm. • *Rotuli Normanniae in Turri Londinensi Asservati*, ed. T. Duffus Hardy (Record Commission, London, 1835)

Selected Letters of Pope Innocent III • *Selected Letters of Pope Innocent III Concerning England (1198–1216)*, ed. C. R. Cheney and W. H. Semple (London, 1953)

Walter of Coventry • *Memoriale Fratris Walteri Coventria*, 2 vols. ed. W. Stubbs, Rolls Series (London, 1872–3)

William of Newburgh • *William of Newburgh, Historia Rerum Anglicarum* in *Chronicles and Memorials of the Reign of Richard I*, 2 vols, ed. R. Howlett, Rolls Series (London, 1884)

William the Breton • William the Breton, *Gesta Philippi Augusti* in Œuvres de Rigord et de Guillaume le Breton, ed. H. F. Delaborde, i (Paris, 1882)

THE FAMILY OF KING JOHN

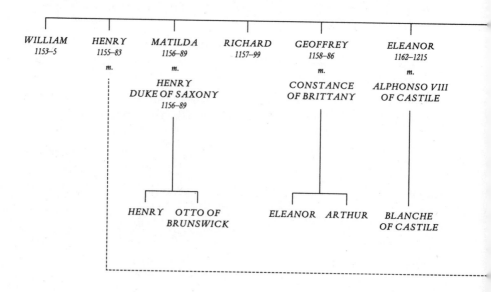

WILLIAM	HENRY	MATILDA	RICHARD	GEOFFREY	ELEANOR
1153–5	1155–83	1156–89	1157–99	1158–86	1162–1215
	m.	m.		m.	m.
		HENRY DUKE OF SAXONY 1156–89		CONSTANCE OF BRITTANY	ALPHONSO VIII OF CASTILE
		HENRY OTTO OF BRUNSWICK		ELEANOR ARTHUR	BLANCHE OF CASTILE

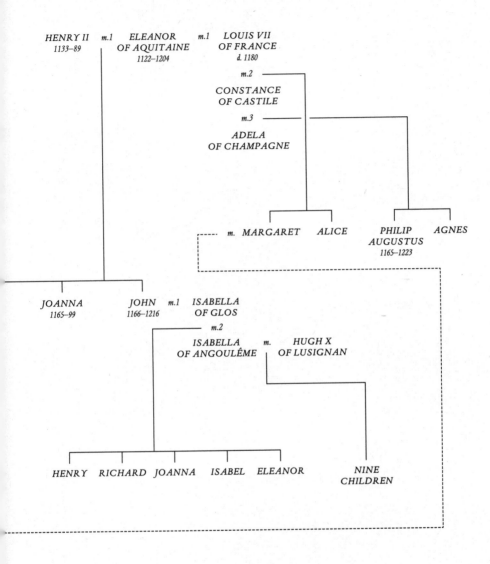

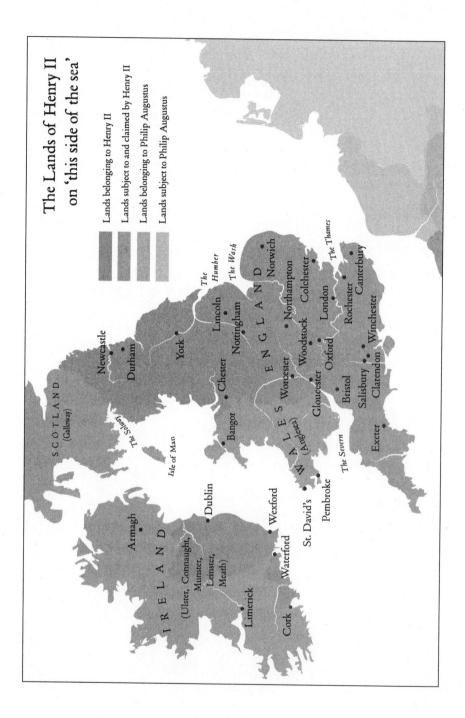

The Lands of Henry II
on 'this side of the sea'

Lands belonging to Henry II

Lands subject to and claimed by Henry II

Lands belonging to Philip Augustus

Lands subject to Philip Augustus

SCOTLAND
(Galloway)

The Solway

The Humber

The Wash

Newcastle

Durham

York

Lincoln

Nottingham

Chester

Bangor

WALES
(Anglesea)

Worcester

Gloucester

ENGLAND

Northampton

Woodstock

Oxford

Norwich

Colchester

London

The Thames

Rochester

Canterbury

Winchester

Bristol

Salisbury

Clarendon

Exeter

The Severn

Isle of Man

IRELAND

(Ulster, Connaught,
Munster,
Leinster,
Meath)

Armagh

Dublin

Wexford

Waterford

St. David's

Pembroke

Cork

Limerick

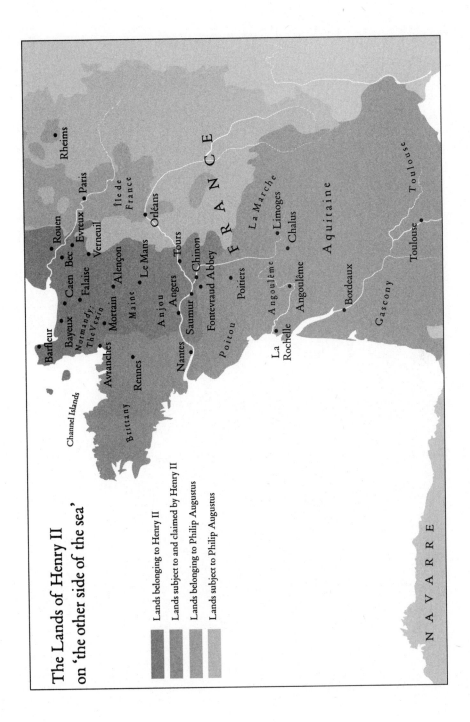

The Lands of Henry II on 'the other side of the sea'

Lands belonging to Henry II

Lands subject to and claimed by Henry II

Lands belonging to Philip Augustus

Lands subject to Philip Augustus

Barfleur

Rheims

Rouen

Paris

Caen Bec Evreux

Bayeux

Falaise Verneuil

Île de France

Normandy The Vexin

Mortain Alençon

Orléans

Avranches

Maine Le Mans

Tours

Rennes

Chinon

Angers

Anjou

Saumur

Fontevraud Abbey

Nantes

Poitou

Poitiers

La Marche

Limoges

Chalus

Brittany

La Rochelle

Angoulême

Angoulême

Aquitaine

Bordeaux

Gascony

Toulouse

Toulouse

F R A N C E

Channel Islands

N A V A R R E

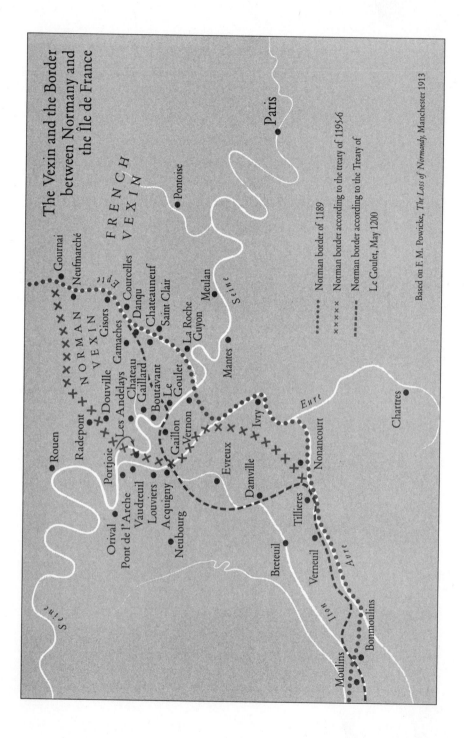

The Vexin and the Border
between Normany and
the Île de France

F R E N C H
V E X I N

Paris

Pontoise

Gournai
Neufmarché

Épte

Courcelles
Gisors
Danqu
Gamaches
Chateauneuf
Saint Clair
N O R M A N
V E X I N
La Roche
Guyon
Meulan

Douville
Chateau
Gaillard
Boutavant
Le
Goulet

Rouen

Radepont
Les Andelays
Portjoie
Gaillon
Vernon

Mantes

Seine

Orival
Pont de l'Arche
Vaudreuil
Louviers
Acquigny
Neubourg

Evreux
Damville

Ivry

Eure

Nonancourt

Chartres

Seine

Breteuil
Tillieres

Verneuil

Avre

Iton

Moulins

Bonnmoulins

Norman border of 1189

Norman border according to the treaty of 1195-6

Norman border according to the Treaty of
Le Goulet, May 1200

Based on F. M. Powicke, *The Loss of Normandy*, Manchester 1913

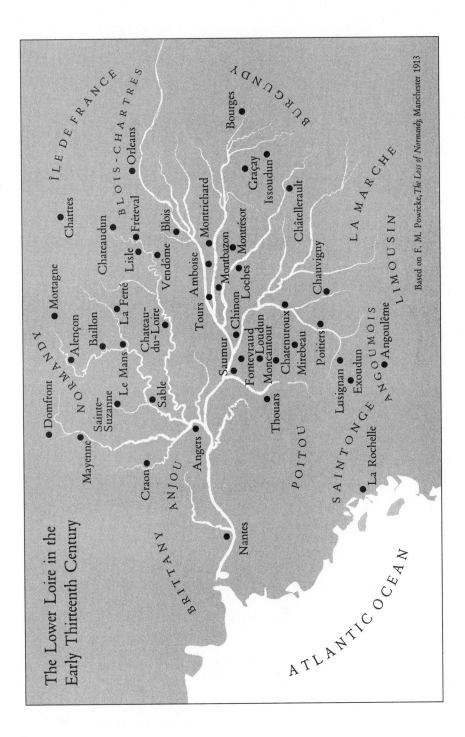

The Lower Loire in the
Early Thirteenth Century

ÎLE DE FRANCE

BLOIS - CHARTRES

BURGUNDY

NORMANDY

BRITTANY

ANJOU

POITOU

SAINTONGE

ANGOUMOIS

LIMOUSIN

LA MARCHE

ATLANTIC OCEAN

Chartres
Mortagne
Alençon
Baillon
Chateaudun
La Ferté
Lisle
Fréteval
Blois
Vendôme
Montrichard
Montbazon
Montrésor
Graçay
Issoudun
Bourges
Orleans
Châtellerault
Chauvigny
Amboise
Tours
Loches
Chinon
Saumur
Fontevraud
Loudun
Moncantour
Chatenuroux
Mirebeau
Poitiers
Exoudun
Lusignan
Angoulême
La Rochelle
Thouars
Nantes
Angers
Craon
Sablé
Le Mans
Sainte-Suzanne
Mayenne
Domfront
Chateau-du-Loire

Based on F. M. Powicke, *The Loss of Normandy*, Manchester 1913

King John's effigy at Worcester. Carved between 1228 and
1232, and here seen as drawn by C. A. Stothard between
Sept. 27 and Oct. 3, 1813. (British Museum Prints and
Drawings, 1883.7.14.493)

PREFACE

The Angevins were an aristocratic family who controlled large tracts of land in the British Isles and France, which brought them extraordinary wealth and power. For fifty years, between the mid-1150s and the early years of the thirteenth century, they were the dominant force in northwestern European politics. They brought within their control not only their ancestral homelands of Anjou, Normandy and England, but also many of the territories that surrounded them, including Aquitaine, Brittany, Scotland, Ireland and Wales. No one in late twelfth-century Europe could ignore an Angevin ruler, and the rulers whose lands stood closest to those of the Angevins had to deal constantly with an aggressively expansionist neighbor.

This book examines the life of King John, the last of the Angevins to rule these wide territories, and who became, in 1204, the first king for more than half a century to permanently reside in England. It is, therefore, in part a study in failure, the failure of a ruler to retain control over the continental lordships that had descended to him by right of inheritance. It is also a study in the crisis of English kingship. The processes that began with the Norman Conquest of 1066 set in train the principles by which English kings would rule during the twelfth century. John would test these principles, such as the right of a king to determine the inheritance patterns of his magnates' property and the right to determine appointment to senior ecclesiastical positions, to destruction.

He managed his kingdom to a point where many of those over whom he ruled decided to gather themselves together behind a set of principles (outlined in the document we call Magna Carta) firstly to force John to rule according to the terms of a written constitution and then, when that failed, to unseat him from his throne and offer it to another.

John died in the midst of civil war while facing an invasion of his kingdom from French royal forces led by the son of the king of France. This was a catastrophic end for a man who had started his life and lived it with extraordinary optimism. As a near contemporary commentator put it when summing up John's life, "he was a great prince, though not a happy one, who, like Marius, experienced both good and bad fortune."[1] Gaius Marius was an apposite choice for the chronicler to use. The subject of a life by Plutarch, Marius was one of the greatest consuls of the Roman world, a strong and brave soldier, popular with his own men, but quite unskilled in the realm of politics, and, in the end, unable to take his aristocracy with him. Marius had other faults that could also be laid at John's door: he was ambitious to the point of it becoming a fault and had an inferiority complex that made him capriciously cruel. By the time of his death, Marius, like John, was embattled and keenly aware that he had not achieved in his lifetime the things that he ought to have done. Marius's death, like John's death, was welcomed "with great rejoicing and a confident hope that [they] were rid of a grievous tyranny." And Marius, like John, "died before he had satisfied and completed his desires."[2]

But this book starts on an optimistic note. John was not a villain capable of the worst venality we can imagine; he was a man placed, by accident of birth, the vagaries of life and his own ambition, into a position of power for which he proved himself to be ill suited. And at the outset of his reign over the Angevin dominions, he was full of hope for a successful future. According to Adam of Eynsham in his *Life of St Hugh of Lincoln*, in April 1199 John was with the saint at Fontevraud Abbey, where Richard the Lionheart, John's brother and predecessor, was to be buried. There the two were waiting to be admitted by the nuns to the church when Hugh sought to warn the soon-to-be king about the dangers faced by his immortal soul as he took up the reins of government:

> Fix your mind always on the howls and perpetual torment [of the damned], and let your heart dwell upon their unceasing punishment; by frequently recalling their misfortunes you will learn the great risks that those incur who are set over others as rulers for a short space of time, and who, by not ruling themselves, are eternally tortured by demons.[3]

As he spoke, Hugh pointed above the door of the abbey to the sculptured tympanum, now lost, which showed the Last Judgment. As Christ sat in majesty, the souls of the departed were being separated into those who would be saved and those who would suffer the eternal anguish of damnation, among them kings in full majestic regalia about to hear the words "Go ye cursed into everlasting fire." John's response was to draw the sainted bishop to the opposite wall and point to him those kings, made conspicuous by their splendid crowns, who were being conducted joyously by angels to the king of Heaven. "My lord bishop," he said, "you should have shown us these, whom we intend to imitate and whose company we desire to join." John did not deliberately set out on a path leading to his ruin; and so I have written this biography with that thought uppermost.

My purpose in this book is not to attempt to rehabilitate King John but to accept that, in the eyes of many of his contemporaries, he ended his days as a tyrant confronted by his subjects for his tyranny. How John came to be seen as a tyrant is at the heart of this account. It is a story, however, that is not constrained by the knowledge that his life would end in disaster, but which examines his life as though it was not foreordained that it would end in Magna Carta and civil war. At each juncture in John's life there was the potential for him to succeed. I have tried to reveal the complexity of the man who became the notorious figure of popular legend, to see his life unfold—in so far as it is possible to do so—as it unfolded and not to place on it the burden of hindsight. Whether I have succeeded or not will be for the reader to judge.

This book has been a long time in the making and during that time I have incurred numerous debts. My first is to the departed, Allen Brown, who first introduced me to the sources on which this book is founded. Allen showed me the extraordinary depth and variety of late twelfth- and early thirteenth-century documents, and his teaching has left me with a lasting appreciation of their wonderful complexity.

Since Allen's death, I have enjoyed the kindness and support of many scholars. David Carpenter, Susan Reynolds, Christopher Harper-Bill, Diana Greenway, John Gillingham, Michael Prestwich and David Crouch provided inspirational early guidance. My colleagues at the University of East Anglia have provided a constant source of advice: Mark Bailey, Julie Barrau (now at Cambridge), David Bates, Sarah Churchwell, Peter Crooks (now at TCD), Hugh Doherty, Tom Licence, Gesine Oppitz-Trotman and Nicholas Vincent. Others, too, have been generous with their time and expertise, including my students, especially Hetty Kaye and Rich Daines, both of whom took on the task of reading complete drafts of this book. My thanks also go to my friends Des Seal and Louise Turff, who both read a draft of the work, much to mine and my readers' profit. Matthew Strickland, Alheydis Plassmann, Elizabeth Tyler and Colin Veach all contributed to the process of refining my ideas on John. George Morley at Macmillan firmly, professionally and kindly guided me through the finishing stages of this book. My greatest debt is to Ann Williams, who taught me how to be a medieval historian. She has proved a constant friend and supporter for the whole of my academic career, and so this book's dedication belongs to her.

INTRODUCTION

O N JULY 17, 1797, the tomb of King John was opened. It had lain in the choir of Worcester Cathedral since 1232, and although the body had been exposed for two days in 1529, the skeleton that was within was remarkably intact.* The man who had been interred in the tomb had been about 5 feet 7 inches tall; when he had been laid to rest, he had been wrapped in his coronation robes with his head covered in his coronation cap, which he had worn for seven days after he had been anointed with holy oil on the day of his coronation, Ascension Day, May 27, 1199.[1]

John had died on the night of October 18/19, 1216, as a storm raged around Newark Castle where he had come to rest after travelling from Lynn in Norfolk, and there could have been no doubt at all in the minds of those who placed his body in its tomb that their king had died an abject failure. He had started his reign as the de facto ruler of not only England but also large parts of what would become the kingdom of France. He was duke of Normandy and of Aquitaine, and count of Anjou. In addition, he enjoyed rulership of the kingdom of Ireland, overlordship of Wales, Scotland and Brittany, and claimed overlordship of the county of

---

* It is quite likely that Henry III looked on his father's face at least once in 1232. It was certainly the habit of his own son, Edward I, to have Henry's tomb opened regularly (D. A. Carpenter, "The burial of King Henry III, the *Regalia* and royal ideology," in his *The Reign of Henry III* (London, 1996), 427–61). In the modern era, John's tomb was opened in 1529 and its contents possibly seen by John Bale (J. H. P. Pafford, "King John's Tomb in Worcester Cathedral," *Trans. Worcestershire Archaeological Society*, new series, 35 (1958), 58–60).

I

Toulouse. By 1204, he had lost Normandy, Anjou and the northern part of Aquitaine (called Poitou and centered on Poitiers), though he still held the southern part (called Gascony and centered on Bordeaux). By his death, John had lost control of London (his capital city), of Westminster (where his Exchequer sat), of the south of England (to the French who had invaded under the leadership of Louis, son of the French king), and he had enemies in the north and in the east of his kingdom. He was buried at Worcester in part because there was nowhere else suitable for him to be interred since so much of his kingdom was in enemy hands, whether those of the French or of his own barons.*

No king's reputation can survive such a disastrous end to his reign. Within a decade of John's death, the chronicler Roger of Wendover had made John not only a failed king but also one who was positively evil; by the time Roger's successor, Matthew Paris, in his "Great Chronicle," came to augment Roger's work a decade after that, John had become the very worst of rulers who, when released from the fetters of the sensible counsel of Geoffrey fitz Peter, his justiciar, was prepared to give up his kingdom and people into Muslim servitude in pursuit of war:

> King John sent secret messengers . . . to the emir of Morocco to tell him that he would voluntarily give up himself and his kingdom and also abandon the Christian faith, which is considered false [in return for an alliance against his enemies] . . .

According to Matthew's account, the emir contemptuously refused John's proposal and when he inquired as to the nature of the king from one of those sent to propose the alliance, he heard what he suspected to have been true.

------

* Worcester had long had connections with the royal family. In 1158, when he decided to stop the habit of wearing his crown on the great feasts of the Christian calendar, as a symbol of his determination to break with custom, John's father, Henry II, gave his crown to Worcester.

John was a tyrant rather than a king, a destroyer rather than a governor, an oppressor of his own people, and a friend to strangers, a lion to his own subjects, a lamb to foreigners and those who fought against him; for, owing to his slothfulness, he had lost Normandy and, moreover, was eager to lose the kingdom of England or destroy it; he was an insatiable extorter of money, and an invader and destroyer of the possessions of his own natural subjects . . . he had violated the daughters and sisters of his nobles; and was wavering and distrustful in his observance of the Christian religion.[2]

The emir's view of John (as recounted by Matthew) is very much our own: we see John as being irreligious, a man who was willing to stoop to any level to achieve his goals yet a slothful man who let his lands be lost to another; we see him as a sexual predator and a ruler who was despised by his contemporaries; and although some historians have applied their ingenuity to attempting to reform our perceptions of this man in the popular imagination they have done so with little success.[3]

The popular view of King John is almost wholly a later concoction. To begin with, to call him "Prince" John is an anachronism based on the later habit of calling the sons of English monarchs "princes." In twelfth-century England, this practice had yet to take hold. In John's world, only some Welsh rulers, the earls of Chester, and some of the rulers in the Holy Land were beginning to call themselves *principes*.[4] Occasionally, political commentators used the word *principes* to refer to rulers in general, but no one called the sons of Henry II and Eleanor of Aquitaine princes. During his early years, John was, simply, "the king's son," and sometimes "John Lackland"[5]; later, when he assumed direct control of Ireland in 1185, he was "John, son of the lord king of England and lord of Ireland"; after Richard's accession in 1189, he was "count of Mortain" (his title in Normandy) and when issuing documents relating to Ireland, he was also "count of Mortain and lord of Ireland." In this book, therefore, before his accession to Richard's throne in 1199, he is referred to as "John" or "Count John," but never "Prince John." And neither did this Count John have anything to do with the legendary character of Robin Hood. That relationship, too, is a wholly later invention; it was suggested first by John Major in his 1521 *History of Greater Britain*, on no grounds whatsoever, but became popular through Anthony Mundy's *The Downfall of Robert Earl of Huntingdon* and his *The Death of Robert Earl of Huntingdon*, both published in 1598.[6]

That many of John's contemporaries saw John at the end of his reign as a tyrant is beyond doubt. While twelfth-century kings were regularly subject to rebellions and plots on their lives, no king before John faced a community of the realm that was determined to set limits on his power. In forcing John to concede the terms of Magna Carta and then in deciding to unseat him and his dynasty from the throne of England, John's barons went further in their rebellion against their king than any of their predecessors. What they did in 1215 was unprecedented. To be sure, kings had been forced to concede charters to their subjects promising the reform of their realm, most notably at the outset of their reigns. Henry I, for example, set out a series of improvements to royal rule in his coronation charter, issued in 1100. This charter would go on to inform those who drew up the terms of Magna Carta, but it was fundamentally different from Magna Carta because it had been issued as a statement that the new king would rule differently from his discredited brother, William Rufus.[7]

The charter with which Magna Carta has most in common is the charter of King Stephen, issued in November 1153, which marks the moment when the war with the future Henry II came to an end. The king agreed to recognize Henry as his heir, disinheriting his own surviving son, William. The charter, however, was equally clear that Stephen's accession to the kingdom and his continued hold over it was also legitimate, for if it were not, then Henry could not inherit the kingdom from him. The charter was a concession generously given by a magnanimous king determined to find a solution to the war that had scarred his kingdom. In reality, however, Stephen and Henry had been forced to these terms by their barons, who were no longer willing to fight in the war that raged between them.[8] John, too, would be forced by his barons to come to a peace settlement the details of which were to be laid out in the form of a charter granted by the king. Magna Carta, like the charter of 1153, maintained the myth that the king was master of his kingdom even when, quite patently, he was not. His barons banded together to bring John's tyranny to an end by tying the royal beast to the tether of Magna Carta.

No individual in medieval societies warranted the attention of his contemporaries more than the king. He was the fount of all power within the realm (at least in terms of how power was imagined even if not how it was exercised in reality) and he was the person in whom the polity invested its identity. As a result, men tried to read the king's motives into his actions, and those who had power over the written word left us their reflections on what drove the king to act in any given way. Their thoughts are those of men who watched John in action, either up close (as Gerald of Wales did on the Irish expedition of 1185) or from a distance in place (as Ralph of Coggeshall did from his Cistercian monastery in Essex) or from a little remove in time (as Roger of Wendover did from his abbey at St Albans in the 1220s and 1230s). Each, in his own way, has taken the events of John's life and tried to fit them into his understanding of the man. But in the case of John we can in fact dive into sources that reveal the king's very own thoughts, sources that were unavailable even to contemporary chroniclers.

The most remarkable fact about studying John is that we get closer to the man who was King John than any other monarch before him, and many after him, too. There are a number of reasons for this happy state of affairs. Firstly, it was at the beginning of John's reign that the king's writers, his Chancery clerks, began the habit of recording a good portion of their outgoing correspondence. Why they chose to do so has been a matter of debate for a very long time,[9] but the fact that they did means that we have the day-to-day correspondence of government for most of

John's reign.* Not all letters were recorded, of that we can be certain, but enough were for us to have a worm's eye view into the daily machinery of the government of the Angevin lands before 1204 and of the kingdom of England thereafter.

Secondly, these documents came into existence at time when royal government was conducted by the king himself along with his domestic servants. Medieval society should be imagined not as a monolithic state but as a series of centers of power consisting of individual men or family groups surrounded by their supporters. It was these supporters who constituted the medieval household. Amongst the names that contemporaries gave to this group was the Latin word *familia*, from which we get our word "family," but which meant, in the twelfth century, the wide group of individuals who supported their lord and who relied on him for their daily bread and wine, not just those who were related to him by blood. This made the lord's domestic officers his key administrative officers, too. The butler, the constable, the steward (there were two sorts, the seneschal and the dapifer), and the chamberlain were the central officials in any household, from the very smallest to the very greatest in the land, including the king's household, which was only different in scale from those of his secular and ecclesiastical contemporaries.[10]

Thirdly, John involved himself not only in great matters of state but also in the day-to-day organization of his household.[11] Cheek by jowl in the Close rolls (the records on which the correspondence addressed to individuals was enrolled), for example, are letters authorized and witnessed by the king for the mundane purchases of wax candles for the royal household and fine colored cloths for the queen's dresses, together with matters of great state business, such as the carriage of treasure from

---

* Sometimes the rolls fail us, at which point we are forced to become reliant on the views of outsiders to the charmed circle of royal servants on the stock-in-trade of the early medieval historian—the chronicle. The Close Rolls, on which this book is particularly reliant, survive from 1200–1 (in part), 1201–2 (in part), 1202–8 (in full), 1212–17 (in full). The Patent Rolls survive from 1201 to 1205 (in full), 1205 to 1206 (in part), 1206 to 1210 (in full), 1212 to 1217 (in full).

England into Poitou and the closure of English ports against emissaries from the pope.[12] These are revealing insights into the mind of the king at work and reveal something of John's personal preoccupations.

This is not, however, a claim to be able to see and therefore show the inner John, nor to reveal what John felt; but we are able to uncover much about what happened in John's life and, most importantly of all, explain something about the world he inhabited. And through understanding that world, it is possible to begin to understand John. I hope to show that his life takes on a different hue when placed against the backdrop of the tumultuous historical events of his life and reign, culminating in the production of the most important symbolic document of the Middle Ages, Magna Carta, the 800th anniversary of which is marked in 2015. In 2009, UNESCO, inscribing Magna Carta in its Memory of the World Register, described it as "the cornerstone of English liberty, law and democracy" with a "legacy that has had and continues to have enduring worldwide influence." The fact that in 1215 those who drew up Magna Carta could not have imagined the ways in which it would contribute to the future is irrelevant compared to the essential point that they created a text that was to resonate throughout the next 800 years. The life of King John is the context from which Magna Carta arose.

The twelfth and early thirteenth centuries were an extraordinary time for the English monarchy. The effects of the Norman Conquest in 1066 were still unresolved and three of its legacies had a profound impact on the way English kings ruled. The first of these was that the English king was richer in lands by a margin so great that no mere baron could challenge the king for power. Unlike their predecessors of the eleventh century, who had to answer to great men such as Earl Harold, and unlike their successors of the fifteenth century, who had to bow to men such as Warwick the Kingmaker, twelfth- and thirteenth-century English kings were so much richer than their aristocratic contemporaries that no one individual could contest their authority (though collectively they might and sometimes did). This overwhelming command of resources made the Angevin kings dangerous men, since there seemed no way in which their decisions might be challenged.

The second legacy was the legal view that all land in England belonged to the king and that everyone else, from the richest to the poorest, whether layman or ecclesiastic, held his land from the king, whether directly as a tenant-in-chief or indirectly as a tenant of one of the king's tenants-in-chief. This gave the king the right to determine who held what land, and although notions of the correct forms of inheritance were fast developing in the twelfth century, English kings could, and did, interfere in the land rights of their tenants. The extent of royal interference in the dynastic politics of aristocrats came to have a particular twist in John's reign, resulting in the first crucial clauses of Magna Carta, which encapsulate the key complaints of the barons about royal misrule.

The third legacy of the Norman Conquest was that it gave English kings a lasting interest in the continent of Europe, an interest made all the more significant with the accession of Henry II. When Henry came to the throne in 1154 he brought with him the duchy of Normandy, the county of Anjou and, in right of his wife, Eleanor, the duchy of Aquitaine. The consequences of this lasting interest were an absentee king who demanded significant sums of money to conduct his overseas business and the development of governmental structures in England to deal with that problem.

All three of these legacies combined to make the Angevin kings vastly powerful, so much so that they could rule almost as despots with little to challenge either their power or their authority in England. But for the emerging community of the realm, which was being infected by the twin ideas that the kingdom should be run for the public good and that the king had a duty to take counsel, a king accountable only to God was increasingly unacceptable.[13] Magna Carta was a direct consequence of the conflict between a king bent on ruling as he wished and a community of the realm determined to limit the king's freedom of action, and not only that, but also to limit his successors' freedom of action. Magna Carta signaled the beginnings of English constitutional monarchy.

The idea that men might rule as tyrants and that tyranny was a form of behavior to be discouraged and, eventually, checked certainly had currency in the twelfth century. John of Salisbury, writing in the 1150s, had much to say on the subject, classifying tyrants as private (the head of the family), ecclesiastical (a bishop, for example), and public (a king or other secular ruler). The public tyrant was the man who ruled by his "will" rather than by "law,"[14] who failed to heed the teachings of the Church, and failed to "love justice." This type of tyrant deserved "to be cautioned and eventually slain."[15] The evidence for King John ruling by his "will and wish" litters the sources, and it was in an attempt to ensure that King John ruled justly and by law that men forced on him the terms of Magna Carta, and when that failed to curb his rule, they moved to remove him from power.[16] This is the story of how that came about.

I

LACKLAND

J OHN WAS BORN AT the end of 1166, or early 1167, at the Tower of
London,* the youngest son of King Henry II and his queen, Eleanor of Aquitaine, the most charismatic couple of mid-twelfth-century
Europe. Henry ruled a territory that stretched from the Pyrenees in the
south of France to the very borders of Scotland, and he dominated the
rulers of the British Isles as well as large swathes of the French kingdom
that were notionally bound to the French king. He was the greatest ruler
in Western Europe in the second half of the twelfth century, challenged in
the east only by the power of the Emperor, Frederick Barbarossa.

Yet there was a very real fragility to Henry's rule. Henry may have
been a single human being only capable of being in one place at any one
time, but in legal terms he was four separate and distinct individuals.
He was king of the English in England, and when dealing with English
matters he had no superior but God. This legal reality held true when
he took his armies into Wales or into Ireland or menaced the king of the
Scots. But in his French territories, Henry had a different legal standing. In Normandy, he was duke of the Normans, and when he invaded

---

The date of John's birth is traditionally set as December 24, 1167, at Oxford (*Handbook
of British Chronology*, ed. E. B. Fryde et al. (London, 3rd edn, 1986), p. 37), but this is
wrong on almost every count. At the page-proof stage of this book, Thomas N. Bisson, the
editor of the new edition of Robert of Torigny's chronicle, kindly shared his thoughts with
me on the subject of the date of John's birth. I am deeply grateful to him. See also A. W.
Lewis, "The birth and childhood of King John: some revisions," in *Eleanor of Aquitaine:
Lord and Lady*, ed. B. Wheeler and J. C. Parsons (London, 2002), 159–75.

Brittany and brought it under his dominion, he did so under the banner of the duke of the Normans, with the claims that the Norman dukes had traditionally enjoyed over the Bretons since before the eleventh century. In Aquitaine, he was duke of the Aquitainians in right of his wife, Eleanor, and when he pressed his claims over the county of Toulouse, he did so as Eleanor's husband; and it was with the rights claimed by Eleanor's ancestors that he demanded the submission of the county's ruler. In no instance on the continent could he press any claim as king because in the territories of western Frankia there was but one family entitled to bear the name king: the Capetians.

The Capetian kings of France, Louis VII (ruled 1137–80) and Philip Augustus (1180–1223) were the inheritors of the royal title that had formerly belonged to the Carolingian kings of tenth-century western Frankia (the area which came to be called France). No one else in those lands might call himself king. More importantly, these Capetian kings consistently pressed their claim to be the overlords of the whole of France. By the time that Henry II came to inherit his French lands, most other rulers (the dukes and counts of the various provinces of France) had come to accept, too, that they owed homage (the act of giving oneself into the care of a lord) to the king of France. The king might have been politically and militarily weak, but all still accepted that he was their lord, even if he was not their military superior.[1] What this legal nicety meant in practice varied depending on circumstances, but it had profound implications for Henry and his sons.

In January 1169, Henry made the Treaty of Montmirail, which brought to a conclusion a long-running conflict with King Louis VII of France. In it, Henry agreed to divide his lands between his sons, rather than attempting to pass them on intact. For Louis, the hope was, therefore, that the French Crown would, after Henry's death, face a weakened and divided Angevin family holding on the continent.[2]

According to the treaty, Henry II's eldest son, also named Henry, was to receive the kingdom of England, the duchy of Normandy and the county of Anjou. Richard was to inherit his mother's lands, Aquitaine, which he would hold from the king of France. He was also betrothed to Louis' daughter, Alice. Geoffrey was to have Brittany in right of his wife to be, Constance, daughter and heir of its duke, Conan, and to do homage for it to his elder brother, Henry, as duke of Normandy.

A year later, on June 14 at Westminster Abbey, the younger Henry was crowned as king of England. This was a unique event: no future king of England had ever been crowned in his father's lifetime, though it had become the practice of the Capetian kings of France to have their eldest sons sanctioned as their successors by the act of coronation. There were precedents, therefore, but they did not lie in England, and the consequences of the Young King's coronation were so unfortunate that, when he died in 1183 while in the throes of his second major rebellion, Henry II did not seek to repeat the experiment. Nor did any of his successors.

In all these arrangements, John was ignored, unsurprisingly perhaps, since in January 1169, he was just two years old. While his parents were no doubt concerned to provide for him in due course, they were experienced enough at childrearing to know that a two-year-old boy might easily not make adulthood. The terms of the Treaty of Montmirail, moreover, were about the situation as it stood, and although those who drew up the agreement had an eye to the future, John was not part of their plan, thus earning the sobriquet "Lackland," given to him by his father in what would now be seen as a less than supportive jibe. The well-attested verbal cruelty of Henry's court can perhaps be ascribed in origin to the man at the very heart of power: the king himself.[3]

As is the way with medieval men and women, we know very little about John's upbringing, but we do know some things that help us understand his development. At some point early in his childhood, John was sent to the monastery of Fontevraud, near Chinon, though it is unlikely that he was intended for a career in the Church.[4] The act of oblation—the giving of a child by his parents to a monastery—was one that was fast running out of fashion by the time of John's entry into Fontevraud, and it is quite possible that claims that John was oblated by his father is an overstatement of what is more likely to have been a period spent in the abbey's school.[5]

Fontevraud was founded by Robert of Arbrissel, a hermit whose charismatic preaching attracted a following of mostly women of all social classes, including members of the high nobility as well as prostitutes and beggars, and which, in about 1100, he was required to regularize. The community at Fontevraud became the special concern of the counts of Anjou, and the community remembered not only Robert as its founder but them also.[6] The structure of the monastic community was distinct. It was a mixed house with both men and women living in it but was unique in that the women were dominant. The men were not monks but canons regular who labored on the nuns' estates and acted as their chaplains, in order that the nuns might enjoy the rituals of the monastic life. The men lived in one part of the monastery, while the women lived in several cloisters, separated by function and by class. It was the aristocratic women who ruled.[7] When it came to the decision-making process, in the world of Fontevraud, it was class that mattered, not gender. The community followed the Rule of St Benedict, and by the time that John is said to have been a member of the community, it was still being strictly observed.

No other monastic community, whether long established or part of the new movements in monasticism of the twelfth century, had a structure in which religious women governed religious men. Like other orders that succeeded in the twelfth century, Fontevraud attracted imitators, and thus became the mother house of a large number of dependent communities, including, after the accession of Henry II, three in England.[8] The community had a special place in the hearts of the Angevins, and under Henry II Fontevraud took on the character of a royal mausoleum. It was here that Henry was to be buried, to be followed by his son, Richard the Lionheart, his daughter, Joanna, queen of Sicily, and his wife, Eleanor of Aquitaine—her grandfather had had a hand in supporting the founder of Fontevraud, so the community had Aquitainian connections that satisfied Eleanor.[9]

John, in the company of his sister, Joanna, had therefore been placed in a matriarchy for the purposes of learning his letters.[10] Quite when he entered Fontevraud is difficult to say. He certainly could not have been there in his teenage years (nuns did not teach teenage boys), and it is unlikely that John had been placed in the community as an infant (nuns were not in the habit of wet-nursing babies).[11] In 1170, aged three, John had been handed over to the care of his eldest brother, the Young King, for him to promote and support, so we can suppose that John was not at Fontevraud until after that time.[12] John emerges from the records as an individual in about the year 1177, so the simple deduction has to be that John's time at Fontevraud occurred between 1172 and 1177.

But it would be wrong to see this period in John's life as one during which he was abandoned. On the contrary, he was at the spiritual home of the Angevin dynasty, nurtured by women who would have been friends and relations of his own family. There were few better locations for a boy to learn the basics of his literate education even if it was an unsuitable place for a boy to learn how to fight. It was normal, too, for all boys of John's class to spend their formative years away from the family home, and a period of education in a monastic community, especially a nunnery, before the age of puberty was not unusual for boys who were less suited to war than those with more bellicose instincts.[13]

John was the recipient of a privileged education, the best that his world could give, and in a place that he could recognize as home. He may have been denied his mother's attentions (she was in prison from 1174 after her capture by Henry II during the revolt she led against him) and his father, too, must have been a distant figure, but none of that was unusual. Where John's education did stand out as different was in relation to his brothers. His three elder brothers, Henry (b. 1155), Richard (b. 1157) and Geoffrey (b.1158), had all had tutors assigned to them and all learned the skills of the knight. Throughout the second half of the 1170s, the young Henry earned himself a reputation as a chivalrous benefactor on the European tournament circuit, where he supported a large retinue that was successfully led by one of the greatest knights of the day, William

Marshal.[14] Geoffrey of Brittany was also a successful tournament knight as well as a bellicose ruler of Brittany. Indeed, Geoffrey was to meet his end as a result of injuries sustained in a tournament held outside Paris in August 1186. And while Richard did not engage in tournaments, he was the epitome of the knight-ruler, leading his troops by brave example.* John, on the other hand, missed out on the rough and tumble of knightly instruction. Until the age of ten, John was given an education more like that imparted to his sisters, Eleanor (b. 1163) and Joanna (b. 1165), than that provided for his brothers.[15]

John, therefore, was perhaps more cosseted and more softened than his elder brothers. He certainly approached the world differently from them. When the contemporary commentator Gerald of Wales came to describe the boys, he thought that John was less prepared in martial affairs than any of his elder brothers. This did not mean that John was destined for the Church: legitimate children were far too valuable for the purposes of diplomacy. Henry only directed his illegitimate children to ecclesiastical appointments (three of his four known bastards went into the Church). But it might explain why, of all his brothers, John was the least martial and the least successful in dealing with other men.

P ROVIDING FOR HIS YOUNGEST son proved to be a constant headache for Henry. Having excluded him from the arrangement of 1169, the king felt the need to make sure that his son was not left entirely destitute and at the mercy of his elder brothers. In 1173, when he was six, John was betrothed to Alice,[16] the heiress of Humbert III, count of Maurienne and Savoy. In the context of the politics of the south, this union made good diplomatic sense for Henry II. Had it come off, it would have given the king easy access to northern Italy, and the importance of the marriage agreement can be gauged by the fact that the count of Toulouse and the king of Aragon were both drawn into

---

* Gillingham, *Richard I*, 140 describes an impromptu tournament in Cyprus that ended in a brawl between Richard and William des Barres.

its negotiations.[17] As duke of Aquitaine in right of his wife, Henry II claimed overlordship of Toulouse, and the kings of Aragon also had an interest in the lands of southern France. John was, therefore, to play a central role in the politics of a region vital to Henry's ambitions, and was to be "lackland" no longer. But while the proposed union of the two children might have made good diplomatic sense, the marriage proposal sparked civil war of catastrophic proportions within Henry II's realm. This was John's first introduction into what it meant to be a member of the Angevin family.

The War Without Love,[18] which raged over Henry II's lands between 1173 and 1174, was one of the defining moments of his reign. For more than a year, Henry was confronted by the rebellion of his three sons, the Young King, Richard and Geoffrey, as well as his wife, Eleanor of Aquitaine, and a very great number of his subjects. Aligned against him, too, were the king of France, Louis VII, and the king of the Scots, William the Lion. It was a coalition that presented a most formidable opposition. That Henry survived is testament to his abilities as a military commander and the loyalty of the core of his administration, but it was a near-disastrous event for both him and the lands over which he ruled. At the conclusion of it, Queen Eleanor was cast into prison for her role in fomenting rebellion. There she was to remain under close confinement until 1183, and then, less strictly confined but still under close guard, until her vengeful husband died in July 1189. John's relationship with his mother must therefore have been more distant than that enjoyed by his older siblings.

I N 1174, A YEAR after their betrothal, John's young fiancée died. Whether the marriage would have gone ahead after the debacle of the civil war is to be doubted: the terms of the marriage agreement stipulated that should Alice die, then her younger sister, Sophie, would become John's bride. That she did not suggests that, for Henry II, the ardour had gone out of the match. Instead, Henry decided to use the defeat of his sons' rebellion as another opportunity to provide for John. As part of the settlement, estates were set aside from the Young King's inheritances in England, Normandy, Anjou, the Touraine and Maine.*

The following year, Reginald, earl of Cornwall died. One of Henry I's many bastards, Reginald had produced only daughters, three of them, who immediately became wards of the king.[19] Wardship was one of the perquisites of lordship in the post-Conquest period and it meant that the king—as the lord of the kingdom—had the right to control the heirs of all who held land directly of him and who were under age. This was a lucrative business, giving the king something like a dozen wardships a year, two of which would be of baronial size. And of these dozen or so wardships, almost two-thirds would involve heirs below the age of consent, thus giving the king the right of marriage, as long as the heir had not already been betrothed.[20] In fact, so much of an issue was wardship to the king's tenants-in-chief that when they came to draw up the terms of Magna Carta in 1215, concerns over inheritance took up seven of the first eight clauses of the text.[21] Death, and especially what happened after death to their heirs and properties, was at the forefront of the minds of every man of consequence in the age of the Angevins.

The case of Reginald, earl of Cornwall brings this point into stark relief. Sometime in midsummer 1175, the earl died and was carried to Henry I's mausoleum, at Reading, to be interred in the abbey close to his father. He had ruled Cornwall as an independent territory, taking its revenues for himself and not answering to the Exchequer. It was a royal appanage, set aside for the earl and largely free of royal control, or even oversight. The earl's three daughters had reserved to them a small portion of their father's estates and each made good marriages, but the lion's share of the county went to service John's needs.[22] The girls had been disinherited, despite custom dictating that they should share the inheritance

---

* A thousand pounds' worth of land in England, including the castles of Nottingham and Marlborough, and the county of Nottinghamshire; a thousand pounds' worth in Angevin money of renders in Normandy along with two castles of Henry II's choosing; a thousand pounds' worth in Angevin money of renders in the county of Anjou; and one castle each in Anjou, Touraine and Maine (*Gesta Regis Henrici Secundi*, i, 78).

amongst themselves. Custom may have pointed in one direction, but when an Angevin king set his mind against custom, the Angevin king got his way.[23]

Further provision was made for John in 1176 when he was betrothed to Isabella, the youngest of the three daughters of William, earl of Glouces- ter. Here again Henry II intended that William's daughters should be disinherited, except for a small portion set aside for them, and that John should inherit the whole estate to go with his bride. This was part of the settlement by which Earl William bought Henry's goodwill after the War Without Love, but it was a high price for his two elder daughters to pay.[24]

The following year, 1177, at a council in Oxford, celebrations were held for the establishment of John as king of Ireland, a move that was, supposedly, approved by Pope Alexander III (though the fact that Alex- ander consistently denied John the crown of Ireland would suggest that the pope was less enthusiastic about the idea than our source suggests). The council was a great event, at which Henry II received the submission of a number of Welsh rulers and then, turning his attention to Ireland, gave a series of grants in the island to be held of himself and of his son, John, an event that one chronicler saw as a "partition of the island."[25]

Henry's interests in Ireland went back as far as 1155, when he had gathered a council at Winchester for the express purpose of discussing the possibility of the conquest of the kingdom of Ireland so that it might be given to his brother, William. According to a contemporary report, Henry's plan was put to one side when his mother, the Empress Matilda, expressed her disapproval of the project.[26] But although the plans for William were shelved, Henry still sent a mission to the papal curia with the intent of acquiring from Adrian IV, the English pope, his blessing for any campaign that Henry might launch.[27]

The English incursions into Ireland began in earnest during Henry's reign, and although not undertaken directly at Henry's behest, he was quick to take advantage of the situation. In the autumn of 1171, Henry journeyed to Ireland, where he received the submission of the incomers and of the native Irish rulers, and by the summer of 1172, he was again petitioning the pope to sanction his activities. In September 1172, Alexander III had three letters drawn up, one to the kings and princes of Ireland, one to the legate and the archbishops of Ireland, and one to Henry II, in which he acknowledged the fact that Henry had subjected Ireland to his rule.[28] And it was not long before Henry began to see Ireland as affording an opportunity to provide further for John.

After restoring the estates of Hugh, earl of Chester (confiscated as a result of the earl's decision to side with the Young King in the War Without Love), in May 1177, Henry, according to the contemporary commentator Roger of Howden, "sent Hugh to Ireland to prepare the way for John to whom he had conceded the island, for he had acquired from Alexander III license to crown his son and make him king of Ireland."[29] Later that month, at a council held at Oxford, Henry, "before his bishops and the magnates of his realm, appointed his youngest son John as king of Ireland," after which he distributed land to his followers "to be held of himself and of his son swearing to both the king and to John allegiance and fidelity against all men for the lands in Ireland."[30] Although John would not visit his new kingdom until 1185, he was, by 1177, finally in possession of landed resources commensurate with his status. In Ireland, John was to be king in his own right without, in so far as we can see, the oversight of his brother, the Young King, even when in the fullness of time the boys would succeed to their father. So he was never made to perform homage for Ireland to the younger Henry (as king of England), unlike Geoffrey, who was required to perform homage for Brittany to the younger Henry (as duke of Normandy).

John appears to have been with his father at the Christmas festivities of 1176 (home from school for the holidays),[31] and he must have been at Oxford in May 1177 to receive the homage of the men of Ireland at the Council of Oxford: these things had to be done in person. He was ten years old, and perhaps this is the moment he emerged from the care of the nuns. For the first time, we begin to see some of John's expenses being paid out of the royal estates, which suggest that he was starting to incur the costs of maintaining his own following.*[32] In March 1178, John was to be found in the company of his half-brother, the illegitimate Geoffrey, bishop of Lincoln, when they crossed from Southampton to Normandy. At Christmas that year, John was at Winchester with his father and his legitimate brother Geoffrey, and then crossed to the continent with his father early in 1179.[33] By this time the young man had the beginnings of his own household, including a steward, two chamberlains and two washerwomen, Millicent and Isabelle.[34] John's father was using the windfall revenues that came from confiscated monastic lands to fund his son's gradually forming household, even if he was too young to start ruling his western territories in person.

In 1179, aged twelve, John joined the household of Ranulf de Glanville, where he was to remain until his education was complete.[35] The apprenticeship in the household of Ranulf must have had a profound impact on John. Ranulf was the king's justiciar in England between 1180 and Henry II's death in 1189, which meant that he was the most powerful man in the realm after the king, and, since the king was often absent on the continent, the justiciar was, for most purposes, the power in the land.†[36] He sat at the Exchequer, which was not only one of the key ways in which the king collected revenue but was also a branch of the king's court to which appeals might be made while the king was absent. As the king's alter ego, the justiciar also acted as a military commander. Ranulf led, for example, an English army against the Welsh in 1182, and he presided over royal councils in his master's absence. In short, Ranulf was king in all but name, so he was an ideal tutor for John, who was expected to rule Ireland and play his part in the government of England through his estates in the West Country.

---

* Part of the cost of his maintenance, along with the cost of buying two palfreys (the standard horse on which a man of quality would travel), were met by the revenues of the lands of the abbot of Peterborough, during the vacancy following the abbot's death.

† Richard fitz Nigel, Ranulf's contemporary, in his treatise on the Exchequer, describes the justiciar as "top man in the kingdom."

It has been argued that there were few better ways for a ruler in waiting to witness the business of government. But Glanville had some unpleasant lessons to teach. One cause célèbre surrounded the events of 1184, when Glanville used his position to trump up charges of rape against Gilbert of Plumpton because he wished to give Gilbert's wife in marriage to Reiner, his steward. The abuse of office caused such an outrage that the people of Worcester rushed to the gibbet to try to save the man, but in the end it was only the actions of the bishop of Worcester that prevented Gilbert's execution, though the poor man was left to rot in prison for the remainder of Henry II's reign.[37] Roger of Howden tells the story because its hero, Bishop Baldwin, then became archbishop of Canterbury, but for us the tale provides an insight into how justice under Ranulf de Glanville might really have worked. Nothing illustrates more clearly the importance of the twelfth-century aphorism "be in court when your friends are present and your enemies are absent."[38] The consequence of ignoring that advice was life-threatening.

Ranulf de Glanville left us a monumental manual of administrative procedure, "The Treatise on the Laws and Customs of England."[39] Whether Ranulf wrote this text himself is a matter of contention, but what is certain is that it came from the circle of which Glanville was at the heart. A work of remarkable cogency and clarity, it deals in particular with the holding of land and succession to it.[40] Since John's own methods of rulership revolved around this very theme, it is not too far fetched to imagine that he was influenced by the text we know as *Glanvill*.

John was certainly taught how to play chess, a noble pursuit and one that occupied idle moments throughout his life. Chess was an aristocratic game and an ability to play it was considered one of the essential knightly skills, a skill that was not expected of lesser individuals. Indeed, the ability to play chess was a recurrent motif of the courtly literature of the period. Characters such as Tristan, Lancelot and Alexander were all competent players, and in the epic *Ruodlieb*, written in southern Germany in the middle years of the eleventh century, chess is made to represent the complexities of the negotiations with which his master charged the eponymous hero.[41] Chess playing had associated with it the qualities that made a knight good: "cunning; calculation; the ability to bend the rules without dishonourably breaking them."[42]

Gerald of Wales, in his *On the Instruction of Princes*,[43] thought that the sons of Henry and Eleanor were unskilled in letters, but his standards for what made a well-educated ruler were high. When talking of the Young King Henry, John's eldest brother, Gerald called him another Hector son of Priam, like Hector "a terror to his enemies," and again like Hector a man of noble and courtly manners. He was a "Julius Caesar in genius . . . an Achilles in strength, an Augustus in conduct, a Paris in beauty."[44] These delightfully hyperbolic descriptors were meant to indicate to the reader that the qualities that were to be found in these ancient heroes were also to be found in the Young King. John had none of these attributes.[45]

But John could certainly read Latin and French. We know that in later life the king had his own copy of Pliny the Elder's *Natural History*,[46] a vast encyclopedia covering topics such as astronomy, geography, anthropology and biology, as well as pieces on farming and gardening, medicine and drugs, the properties of metals and stone, and art and painting. No doubt John dipped into the work as it suited him (as Pliny had encouraged his readers to do in his Preface), but it is interesting to note the sort of information John would have had at his fingertips. He also owned a copy of Augustine's *City of God*, a standard text, but one that requires the reader to have a good command of Latin and philosophy.[47] Amongst other texts, John had a copy of Hugh of St Victor's *On the Sacraments of the Faith*. While Augustine's work had been standard fare for highly educated readers for five hundred years, Hugh's book, written in the 1120s, is a theological and mystical work that was being taught in the schools of Paris to the top minds of John's generation. In addition, he owned a copy of a *Romance History of England*, written in French and presumably meant for his edification and entertainment.

Each of these texts comes to our attention because the king ordered them to be delivered for his use. And we have good reason to assume that he read them, not least because the texts he ordered in 1208 were directly relevant to his conflict with Pope Innocent III. In order to comprehend them, John must have had a highly sophisticated education. His library is also evidence of eclectic interests, ranging from French romances, through encyclopaedias of general knowledge, to highly sophisticated theological, mystical and philosophical texts in Latin. John was amongst the most highly educated secular men of his age.[48]

IT WAS IN 1183 that John emerged into the political limelight. He was sixteen years old and his brothers, the Young King Henry, Richard of Aquitaine and Geoffrey of Brittany, were once again in open rebellion. At the Christmas court in 1182, held at the king's palace in Caen, Normandy, Henry II was joined by his sons along with other luminaries, including Henry the Lion and his wife, Henry II's daughter, Matilda.[49] John appears to have been in England at this point, still in Glanville's household and enjoying the festivities with the justiciar, rather than with his father, sister and brothers. According to one eyewitness account of the events at Henry's court, a dispute arose between the brothers during the journey from Caen to Le Mans. At Le Mans, Henry II ordered Richard and Geoffrey to do homage to the Young King for their lands, and although Geoffrey acquiesced, Richard refused. He held Aquitaine directly from the French king and he saw his father's demand as being both unreasonable and unlawful: he was right.[50]

Nevertheless, in an attempt to mollify his father, Richard later offered his homage to the Young King, but he, in his turn, refused to receive it.[51] The Christmas feast was quickly turning into a Christmas farce. Richard, in high dudgeon, withdrew from the court without his father's permission, pursued by the Young King and by Geoffrey: the boys were making war on one another. Indeed, it emerged that the Young King and Geoffrey had been conspiring with the nobles of Aquitaine to undermine Richard and that the events that ensued at the Christmas court were wrapped up in these intrigues; then Henry and Geoffrey turned against their father. The resultant conflict threw the Angevin lands into turmoil again, a turmoil only resolved when the Young King died on June 11, 1183.

T HE DEATH OF HIS eldest brother was the catalyst for the sixteen-year-old John to make the transition to a central role in Henry's plans for his sons. He now had a place to play in his father's territories. Soon after the Young King's funeral, John was summoned to meet his father. It rapidly emerged that Henry wanted to lever Richard out of Aquitaine and give him the Young King's position as his heir apparent in England, Normandy and Anjou, while John was to succeed Richard in Aquitaine. In the summer of 1183, therefore, Henry II's intention was once again to present his youngest son with a possible future in the south of France.[52]

But while Henry II had a clear idea about how he wished to distribute his lands after his death, his eldest surviving son, Richard, did not see things in quite the way his father did. Richard had been accepted as duke of Aquitaine by both its people and by its overlord; Richard had done homage for Aquitaine to Louis VII (d. 1180) and then again to his successor, Philip Augustus. Aquitaine belonged to him, and there was no way in which he could be persuaded to give up the duchy to his brother, John. Richard argued that he could take the place of the Young King while also retaining control of Aquitaine; it was not in Henry II's gift to simply take it away from the legitimately constituted duke. It must have seemed to both Richard and to the French king that Henry II, at his own whim, was attempting to ride roughshod over the seignorial structure of Aquitaine and the legitimate relationship between the French king and his duke.[53] Father and son were obdurate in their positions; Richard removed himself from court and fled to Poitou, where he prepared himself for the inevitable retribution that his father would visit upon him.[54] In the winter of 1183–4, as John began his eighteenth year, the king authorized his two younger sons, Geoffrey and John, to make war on Richard.

It seems that the Young King's death made Henry II abandon his plan to create a western kingdom based on Cornwall, Gloucester and Ireland for John and choose instead a solution that made more sense (to Henry if not to Richard). And perhaps it is the speed with which Henry decided to abandon the western plan with John being placed in Aquitaine that shows it was cobbled together into an inchoate whole; it could never have been more than second best when compared with giving John a compact territory of his own.

But unfortunately for John, Richard was too well entrenched in his southern lands to be dislodged by his younger brothers' military exploits or, indeed, by his father's intimidating words or sweet entreaties.[55] By the autumn of 1184, Henry seems to have given up the idea that John should succeed to Aquitaine, either in whole or in part, and he summoned his three sons to England, where they were brought together at Westminster during a Church council over which Henry was presiding. Part of the business was to choose a new archbishop of Canterbury, which was duly done. The king received from the archbishop the kiss of peace and Richard, Geoffrey and John all received it likewise. This was a public display of unity on the grandest of stages.

Keeping Richard and John with him, the king sent Geoffrey into Normandy,[56] perhaps making the point that Richard would not automatically fill the Young King's now empty shoes.[57] Richard and John seem to have accompanied their father throughout December and beyond the Christmas festivities, held that year at Windsor. A glittering array attended the Christmas court, including the king, his temporarily released queen, Eleanor of Aquitaine, their daughter, Matilda, her children and her husband, Henry the Lion, duke of Saxony, David, brother of the king of the Scots, and numerous secular and ecclesiastical magnates. After Christmas, Henry and his sons went on to Guildford, where the king gave Richard his license to return to Poitou.[58] It was time for Henry to revive the plans he had originally conceived and send John to visit his lands in Ireland to establish himself as its ruler. The hope of Aquitaine having receded into the distance, the western kingdom was back on the agenda for John. His attentions were to be redirected to Ireland.

2

IRELAND, 1185

MATURITY, AND THEREFORE RESPONSIBILITY, came early to men of John's status. By modern standards, life was short, even for the most privileged in society. Of John's brothers, William died in infancy, neither Henry nor Geoffrey reached thirty and Richard was forty-two when he died. Of his three sisters, two died in their early thirties and the third, Eleanor of Castile, just made it into her fifties. Even their father was only in his mid-fifties when he died. John's extraordinary mother lived into her early eighties, but she was exceptional in this as in so many other ways. She saw into the grave two husbands, four sons and four daughters (two from her first marriage to King Louis VII of France). The press of time was felt keenly by those with ambition. By the age of seventeen, John's father had already become duke of Normandy, by eighteen he had added Anjou to his lands, and by twenty he had acquired Aquitaine. Aged twenty-one, in 1154, Henry was crowned king of England. At Christmas 1184, John turned eighteen. If John were to emulate his father, he had much to do.

Preparations for John's Irish expedition had begun in the late summer of 1184 and were confirmed that autumn, after Richard, Geoffrey and John had been brought together by their father to bury their differences.[1] The king was now determined that Ireland would provide the future for his youngest son. Even a plea from the patriarch of Jerusalem that John be allowed to lead an expedition to the east would not sway Henry. The patriarch had arrived in time for Christmas, and over the Christmas table

27

made a spirited attempt to persuade Henry that his duty lay in defending Christ's lands, not in defending what he had in Europe. The counts of Anjou had a claim to the kingdom of Jerusalem as descendants of Fulk V, who had been king-consort of Queen Melisende from 1131 to 1141. Fulk was Henry II's paternal grandfather and, as king of Jerusalem, even more illustrious than his maternal grandfather, King Henry I of England. Yet Henry refused to give up his English kingdom and his continental duchies and counties for Jerusalem, and further forbade his youngest son from taking up the cause, though John was willing to follow his celebrated ancestor eastward. Henry, however, was determined that John should go to Ireland to pick up the reins of government.

IRELAND, IN 1185, WAS a complex place, politically, culturally and linguistically. In 1169, the English had come to Ireland in force and found a fragmented society. The Irish rulers, of whom there were many, spoke Gaelic and, while they might acknowledge the existence of a notional kingdom of Ireland ruled over by a high king, they certainly did not acknowledge that any one family had the right to rule over them. In fact, the high kingship of Ireland was more an idea than a reality.[2]

The geography of the island also made for an inchoate whole. The south-eastern seaboard that faced onto the Irish Sea had come to be dominated by the settlements founded by the Vikings (known in the Irish sources as Ostmen), who had entered Irish society in the eighth and ninth centuries. These places, Dublin, Waterford, Wexford and Cork, along with Limerick in the west, became the trading communities that dominated the economy of the island in the twelfth century and beyond. Dublin, especially, was preeminent and was the key city that the competing Irish rulers needed to control if they wished to enjoy the benefits of overseas trade and to make a claim for the high kingship.[3]

By the time the English arrived, there remained a very real division between the trading communities of the sea's edge and the heartlands of Ireland covered by wood and water, with few roads and fewer bridges.

This was a landscape that was neither easy to traverse nor easy to dominate, whether for homegrown potentate or for ambitious outsider. Ireland was an intensely regional society divided by geography, culture, kindred and by a north–south divide. The economy was overwhelmingly pastoral and a man's wealth was counted in cattle as much as it was in the land that he and his family owned.

The idea that conquering one elite meant conquering the whole island—as the Normans had done in England in 1066—was no more than wishful thinking. The Irish, moreover, were a people well equipped for war, used to the idea of castles, with fleets of ships of their own, and a military caste whose members were capable of sustained and very effective military service. Thus the political landscape was fluid, constantly changing as one powerful leader rose to dominance while another was eclipsed, and it was a landscape in which armed conflict was endemic. Men bore arms as a mark of freedom, and the weapon of choice was the double-headed axe, which the Irish used to devastating effect. The incoming English might have coats of mail, but these were no defense against an axe-wielding warrior with malicious intent.

After his Irish expedition of 1171–2, Henry II established his own men in the island, the most important of whom was Hugh de Lacy. Henry gave him the Irish kingdom of Meath, control of the city of Dublin and the position of justiciar of Ireland, in other words making him the most powerful man after the king. Hugh had to make these grants a reality by force of arms, which he did by displaying the same level of political realism employed by Irish rulers. In the heartlands of Europe, French-inspired Chivalric morals forbade the slaughter of one's aristocratic enemies, but here, on the edge of the world, these rules did not apply, and English men who would have baulked at killing their political rivals in England and France were happy to murder their Irish neighbors at will. Hugh de Lacy threw himself into Irish politics with the enthusiasm of a man born to it, and he made his control of Meath and of Leinster so successful that by 1185 his position was unassailable. When John entered

Ireland he had not only the native Irish and English settlers with whom
to negotiate, he also had to deal with a man who had imposed himself as
the dominant force in Irish politics over the previous decade.[4]

The relationship that John enjoyed with Ireland was also a complex
one. His father had made him king of Ireland in 1177, but there had been
no coronation because successive popes had refused to sanction the move.
Even in his own backyard a king such as Henry II still had to admit that
in certain matters the pope's power was supreme. In the matter of making a king of the whole of Ireland, Henry needed papal sanction and he
did not have it. John was therefore "Lord of Ireland," though there is no
doubt that in his own mind John went there to rule his kingdom.

John's Irish campaign began in earnest in September 1184 when the
trusted royalist commander, Philip of Worcester,[5] was sent to Ireland to
relieve Hugh de Lacy of his role as the king's senior representative. That
summer, too, John Cumin, the English-born archbishop of Dublin, was
instructed to prepare the way for John. At Christmas 1184, further plans
were made between Henry and his sons, and then, on Sunday March 31,
1185, John's father knighted him at the royal castle at Windsor. The knighting ceremony marked an aristocratic man's entry into adulthood, and in
John's case the event signaled to the assembled witnesses that the boy was
now a man, ready to meet the military demands of his new position in the
world.*[6] Three weeks later, John had mustered his troops at the departure
point at Milford Haven in South Wales. There, on the evening of April 24,
three days after Easter Sunday, he set sail for Ireland. He arrived at Waterford at lunchtime the following day, brimmed with confidence, though in
reality he was about to shove his sword into a hornet's nest.

Part of the problem lay in John's own attitudes toward the island and
its inhabitants, both native Irish and English incomers. His actions toward the Irish in particular were extremely provocative. Soon after he arrived at Waterford, John was met by certain native Irish lords (unnamed

---

* Roger of Howden has John being sent by Henry immediately after the ceremony
and he further says of John that he had been made king of the island by Henry ("*eum inde
regem constituit*").

in the sources), who were roundly abused by some in John's entourage: "they were treated with contempt and derision, and showing them scant respect, some of them were pulled about by their beards."[7] It was a glum start. Not surprisingly, the maltreated left John's camp and joined the opposition to his rule.

There was a widespread view in Western Europe that the native Irish were barbarians. Gerald of Wales, one of the most prolific writers of the age, who had family connections amongst the incomers and accompanied John in 1185, wrote two works concerning Ireland. In the first, *A History and Topography of Ireland*, written for Henry II in about 1188, Gerald saw in the native Irish a barbarous people, with uncut beards, black dress and with a habit of fighting without armor in open battle. In the second, *The Conquest of Ireland*, written for Richard as duke of Aquitaine in about 1189, Gerald lambasts the Irish for their willingness to break oaths and break the peace, and yet resort to anger when those with whom they had made an agreement broke their oaths. They were, in his view, an unreliable people, who had to be governed severely.

This opinion had the very best of authorities. Bernard of Clairvaux, writing his life of St. Malachy of Armagh in about 1149, characterized the Irish as "beasts" who were "shameless in regard of morals," "unclean" and "stubborn in regard of discipline." Indeed, Bernard claimed the Irish as pagans. His *Life of St Malachy* had a profound effect on how the Irish were perceived in western Christendom and played its part in influencing the way in which the papal authorities came to see them. The language used by Pope Alexander III in granting Henry the right to interfere in Irish matters characterized the natives as godless.[8] By coming to Ireland, the English were bringing God as well as civilization to the peoples at the edge of the world. Given his actions, there is little doubt that John went to Ireland with a view of the native Irish that was guaranteed to provoke a hostile reaction. That reaction, and John's response to it, made his first foray into Irish affairs a disaster.[9]

The failure of the expedition is often explained as the result of John's inexperience, and his reliance on the advice of other youths of equally shallow character. Yet Henry II had sent his son to Ireland with men of experience.[10] These men occupied the principal roles in John's household and ought to have been able to provide him with good advice had he been willing to listen. Four of its key members emerged directly out of Henry II's cadre of elite administrators. Alard fitz William had been employed by John's father since 1175.[11] Alard was John's chamberlain during the Irish expedition, assuming authority for the very living space in which John occupied his time, and thus was constantly at John's side during the expedition.[12]

Gilbert Pipard was another of Henry's men who went to Ireland with John.[13] He had been sheriff of Gloucestershire since 1168, so he, too, was no mere youth. He had been an itinerant justice[14] and was high in royal favor, having the best part of a £1,000 debt written off by the king's good will.[15] As custodian of the lands of the earl of Chester from 1181 until 1185, he controlled one of the richest estates in the kingdom,[16] the revenues of which in part funded John's expedition.[17] In 1185, the earldom of Chester was handed to Bertram de Verdun, another of Henry II's stalwarts (he had been in Ireland with Henry in 1171), who also joined John's household.[18] He became John's steward, the key role in any medieval household, having control of the hall and also responsibility for the management of his lord's resources. And in Bertram, John had a right-hand man who had fifteen years of high-level administrative experience under his belt.*[19] John's second steward was William Wenneval (seemingly a lesser steward than Bertram de Verdun), who was a long-term royal servant, since at least 1173.[20] The experience was there for John to draw on, but it seems that he preferred to listen only to the young bloods in his circle.

During his early youth, John had been raised in the household of Ranulf de Glanville, and it was here that he met some of the other men who were to play a crucial part in the next few years of his life.[21] These

---

* Bertram de Verdun had been sheriff of Warwickshire and Leicestershire since 1170, when he took over the county farms in the wake of the wholesale removal of English sheriffs instigated by Henry II in response to widespread criticism of them.

were the youngsters of John's entourage, the men to whom John was too willing to listen, brought up on the example of the brutality of Ranulf's rule as justiciar. Ranulf's nephew, Theobald Walter, was John's teenage friend in Glanville's household, and when John went to Ireland, so, too, did Theobald. At Waterford, perhaps as his very first act, since Waterford was where John made landfall in March 1185, John gifted to Theobald and to Ranulf de Glanville jointly five and a half cantreds of land in Limerick. It was a massive grant of land (a cantred was an administrative subdivision of a county), which made sure that the young Theobald would be a man of real consequence in Ireland—so long as he could take it, since much of the land had yet to be prized out of the hands of the Irish. It was a license for Theobald to make his fortune, but to do so at the expense of others; by 1199 he had done so. Theobald's troops were the authors of the massacre of Diarmait Mac Carrthaig, king of Desmond, and his men, killed while they were gathered for a peace conference. The Ostmen of Cork were also involved in the slaughter, so the blame did not lie fully at John's feet. But the key to Henry II's success in Ireland during his sojourn in 1171–2 had been his ability to move above the politics of the native Irish and incoming English. John and the young men of his court, it seems, had not learned that lesson and were acting in concert with particular factions in order to pursue their own agendas.

It was a sign of good lordship to reward one's followers, and the young John wanted to be seen as a good lord; as his charters show, he willingly rewarded those who were close to him. But Ireland was not an empty land waiting for a new ruler to come and parcel it out. Granting land to his followers meant that John had to disinherit others amongst the native Irish and the settlers alike who had made their lives in the island in the wake of the events of 1169. Philip of Worcester, for example, was given a speculative grant in Southern Tipperary, but he had to make good his title by force.[22] This behavior won John few friends in Ireland.

John failed in Ireland because of youthful folly. He had wise men around him, placed there by his father, but he was incapable of listening to them. Instead, John listened to the advice of those who shared his own enthusiasm to dominate his new lands and to reward those who served him. And rather than staying in Ireland to push through with his plans, by the autumn of 1185 he decided to return to England. Enduring an Irish winter might not have suited his temperament, but it would have been the sensible course of action to take. His father planned to send him back to Ireland in the summer of 1186—plans that were thwarted by events—but he should not have needed to do so. John lacked the resolve to make his rule of Ireland a reality. He was back in England in time for Christmas.

The English commentators were disappointed. They saw in John's return a failure to manage his resources correctly. He had, it was said, failed to pay his stipendiary troops, and so many had deserted him. He was, to them at least, a laughing stock, thoroughly humiliated by his lack of success. The Irish annalists saw in John's retreat the actions of a man who could not stand up to the power of the earlier incomers, in particular to Hugh de Lacy, who no doubt resented John's presence in a land he had made his own. More importantly, though, everyone now knew that, in his first attempt to show the sort of ruler he might be, John had failed.

Uncannily, it was exactly at this moment that news came to England that the new pope, Urban III, as one of his first acts after his consecration, had finally agreed that Henry might make one of his sons king of Ireland. Roger of Howden preserves two versions of the story, the first in his *Deeds of King Henry II*, a contemporary narrative, which simply has the pope sending Henry a gold crown as a symbol of the young man's promotion; the second in his *Chronicle*, written late in Richard's or early in John's reign, in which he supposed that the gold crown sent by Urban was topped by the plumage of a peacock.[23] One can but hope that the second version was a scurrilous rumor designed to throw scorn on John; popes did not send peacock-feathered crowns to anyone, even those they did not take seriously. But despite Pope Urban's change of heart, John never wore the crown of Ireland. Henry, and later Richard, did not allow it; and when in 1199 John might have taken the crown for himself, he chose not to do so: he remained lord of the kingdom of Ireland, as did his successors.

A FTER THE EXPEDITION TO Ireland, John drops back into ob-scurity. But in 1186, there were two events of equal significance for Henry's youngest child. The first was the death of Hugh de Lacy on July 26, assassinated by an axe-wielding man of Meath, nicknamed "the youth without bowels," which is presumed to refer to his slimness rather than his lack of courage. He was able to outrun his pursuers and so lived to tell his side of the tale.[24] Henry II was delighted at the news of Hugh's death and made plans to send John back to Ireland. But while waiting for a favorable wind to take him there, another piece of news changed everything. On August 19, less than a month after Hugh's death, John's elder brother Geoffrey died. Henry's plans for Ireland were brought to a halt, and John was recalled to his father's side.

Geoffrey's death precipitated a renewed crisis within the Angevin family. Philip Augustus used the opportunity to demand that Geoffrey's duchy of Brittany be given up to the French or, should he not get what he wanted, he would invade Normandy. In these circumstances, Ireland receded into the background; all focus was on ensuring that Henry's continental possessions remained under his control. For the next three years, Henry's attentions were directed first on Philip and then on his son, Richard, who was determined to force his father to designate him as heir to all his lands. Richard suspected that Henry was minded to dis-inherit Richard in favor of John. It is unlikely that Henry either could or indeed wished to do so, but nonetheless Richard feared it. He tried to insist that John should take the cross and join him on crusade (Richard had been the first great ruler to promise to go on crusade after news of the fall of Jerusalem to Saladin in 1187 reached Europe), so as to make sure that should Henry die while the crusaders were in the Holy Land, John could not take full advantage of the situation.[25] By early 1189, when Henry had only a few months to live, there was open warfare between the king and his eldest son. Henry died on July 6, 1189, with Richard and

Philip Augustus arrayed against him. It is said that, on his deathbed, he asked for the names of those who were against him to be read out to him. The first name on the list was John.* The youngest of his sons had gone the way of all the others and had turned against his father.

Henry ii's death came as no real surprise. As early as May 12, the men of Holland, Lincolnshire, working on the assumption that the king was already dead, started a dispute over marshland belonging to Crowland Abbey, using force to gain entry to the abbey's lands.[26] The (supposed) death of the king had created an opportunity for the use of violence: the king was dead, the king's peace was therefore at an end and would remain absent until the new king was crowned. The men of Holland had, of course, jumped the gun by some two months; but it is an indication that the death of the aged king was not unexpected.

The moment of a king's death was fraught with danger for two very good reasons. Firstly, as the marshland case indicates, with the death of the king, so, too, died the king's peace. Men used the absence of royal rule as an opportunity to settle old scores and to redress wrongs by the use of violence. There was, for example, a general release of all royal prisoners after the king's death on the grounds that, since the old king had died, offences against him had lapsed. For the same reason, religious corporations, whose title to land and property relied on grants made to them by previous (often long-dead) kings, quickly sought confirmations of the charters recording the grants made to them. And while the new king recognized that he had little choice but to confirm those titles to land,[27] the recipients were glad enough to pay the fee required for their new charters, which they might then use to defend their property rights against aggressors.

Secondly, there was no automatic succession. There was usually a choice about who would be the next king. The old king might have

---

* The story comes from the *History of William the Marshal*, which was written in the 1220s.

expressed his view and his view might carry weight, but the man who would be king needed more than the old king's approval. Henry had attempted to negate the potential dangers of both the interregnum and the succession disputes when he had had his son Henry crowned king in 1170, but that had proved disastrous, since he had in effect created a political rival with the same sanction from God as himself. He did not seek to repeat that mistake with Richard.

In July 1189, however, there was no doubt in the minds of those who determined the succession: Richard would succeed his father in all the Angevin lands. Richard was present at Henry's funeral at Fontevraud (though John was not); shortly thereafter, the brothers met and travelled to Normandy in each other's company where, we are told, they were both welcomed warmly because it was expected that the two would band together to reform the kingdom.[28]

The author of this comment was Roger of Howden, who had been a member of Henry II's court since 1173 and now transferred his allegiance to Richard. He was also to accompany Richard on crusade, so he gives us an insider's view of court politics and intrigue that is far superior to any of his contemporaries. It is instructive, therefore, that in this man's opinion there was a widely held belief that the brothers would work in harmony. Everyone knew that Richard had taken the cross and was determined to go to the Holy Land, so it must have seemed natural that, in these circumstances, John would be his brother's principal representative during the king's absence.

The way that Richard treated his brother in the immediate aftermath of his accession would suggest that Richard, too, saw John as a lynch-pin in the arrangements he made for his absence. After his investiture as duke of Normandy on July 20, Richard granted to John the possessions that had been given to John by their father, which, in England, amounted to some £4,000-worth of land, and, in Normandy, the county of Mortain, part of which included the Channel Islands; Richard also confirmed John's betrothal to Isabella of Gloucester, which had been arranged in 1176, and thus his rights to her inheritance.[29] If this was not enough, once the brothers had landed in England (they travelled separately as a precaution against them both being killed by shipwreck), a second tranche of grants was awarded to John. Richard made his brother custodian of the counties of Cornwall, Dorset, Somerset, Nottingham, Derby and Lancaster, as well as commissioning him with the castles of Marlborough and Ludgershall, with the forests that were attached to them.[30]

Quickly thereafter, Richard handed to John custody of the honors of Wallingford, Tickhill and Eye, and he gave him the Peak and Bolsover in the north. And on August 29, John was married to Isabella, thus making him the dominant force in the west of England with a reach that spanned from Ireland to Normandy. The only problem was an interdict* placed on John's lands by the archbishop of Canterbury, who deemed John and Isabella to be too closely related and had, therefore, opposed the marriage.

At twenty-two John was at last a man of substance, and he seemed to enjoy the confidence of the new king. On the eve of Richard's coronation it must have looked for all the world as though the brothers would rule in harmony, and that in the event of Richard dying on crusade, John would succeed to the Angevin inheritance: certainly one contemporary left his view in writing that he thought that Richard "did not intend to return to his realm."[31]

Richard's coronation ceremony took place at Westminster Abbey on September 3. We have, through the eyewitness account of Roger of Howden, a most remarkable description of the event, the first time in English history that anyone had thought to set down in writing what he had seen. At the heart of the inauguration ritual was, of course, Richard and his anointing with holy oil on his head, on his chest and on his hands. John also had a part to play in the ceremony, carrying before the king one of the three golden swords that represented the public authority invested in the king. According to another eyewitness to the occasion, John and Eleanor of Aquitaine stood by Richard as he was crowned.[32] The day after the ceremony, John, along with great men of England, laymen and

---

* A ban on the performance of the rituals of the Church.

ecclesiastics alike, gave his homage and fealty to King Richard, and, first amongst the laymen, witnessed the charter that the new king gave to Hugh du Puiset, bishop of Durham, confirming his grant of Sedbergh, Cumbria. In it John is styled "the Lord John, the king's brother."[33] His preeminent place in Richard's regime was thus affirmed.

3
Brother in Arms

RICHARD'S DECISION TO LEAVE on crusade left his lands vulnerable. Kingdoms, duchies and counties needed their rulers because in medieval societies ultimate authority was vested in them, at least in theory, and their absence created a power vacuum. But Richard had made plans to ensure the security of his lands, with his brother John playing a major role, especially within the kingdom of England. And it was on the political landscape of England that the dramas of the next few years of John's life were to be played.

Within days of his coronation, Richard appointed William de Mandeville, earl of Essex, and Hugh du Puiset, bishop of Durham, both men of exceptional merit and of considerable age, as co-justiciars to rule England during his absence.[1] At the same time, he put his brother John at the head of an army and sent him into South Wales to force Rhys ap Gryffydd, king of South Wales, to come to terms.[2] The next month, October, John issued a safe conduct to Rhys to come to a conference at Oxford.[3]

In November, John witnessed the charter by which Richard confirmed the king of the Scots in his English possessions, after which Richard gave John yet more lands. The grant added the county of Devon to those territories that John already enjoyed,[4] and to add luster to John's situation, the papal legate lifted the interdict that had been placed on his lands by Archbishop Baldwin.[5] By the beginning of December, John was still riding high in royal favor, and the vision of the brothers jointly bringing peace to the kingdom held strong.[6] That Christmas, Richard crossed to the continent, holding his Christmas court at Lyons-la-Forêt, Normandy, while John and his mother remained in England, the pair only crossing the Channel in the second week of February in the company of Alice, the French king's sister. It was at this point that Richard began to experience doubts about his brother's loyalty.

We simply do not know why Richard began to turn against John: perhaps others had influenced him at court, men who saw the younger sibling as a threat to their own position. The prime candidate is William de Longchamp. William knew Richard well. He had been his chancellor throughout the 1180s and so, as the bearer of Duke Richard's seal, was at the heart of the regime in Aquitaine. When Richard became king, William moved effortlessly into the royal chancery to take up the same post. Within days of Richard's coronation, William was elected to the see of Ely, where he was consecrated as bishop on December 31, 1189. Throughout the early months of the reign, William was fully expecting to follow his master to the Holy Land, but then events intervened. On December 12 one of the two co-justiciars, William de Mandeville, died. Richard had to make a decision: should he replace William or not. By December 17, he had made up his mind to appoint William de Longchamp as Mandeville's replacement.[7]

William of Newburgh, an Augustinian canon and chronicler of the reigns of Henry II and Richard, declared the appointment of William de Longchamp as one of the two key errors that Richard made before his departure to the Holy Land, and although this view was expressed after William's disastrous period as co-justiciar, there is some justification to it. In trusting William de Longchamp to keep the peace in England, Richard had made an obvious blunder. Within days of William's appointment, the new co-justiciar was in dispute with his fellow office holder, Hugh du Puiset, and as time went on even before Richard left Europe, it became increasingly clear that William could not work in concert with anyone. He was a one-man operation in a situation that demanded a conciliar approach to government.

There was something else unresolved in the early months of 1190: the question of the succession. Richard was undertaking a perilous enterprise, and there was open speculation about the likelihood that he would die on crusade. In the event of his death, however, no one yet knew who would be his heir. Henry II had expended extraordinary amounts of energy in attempting to prevent a succession dispute on his death so it cannot have escaped Richard's notice that he needed to make provision for that eventuality, too. But even by early 1190, the king had not declared his position, and this delay must have caused his younger brother some disquiet. There were at least two nephews who had a claim to Richard's inheritance, one of whom, Arthur of Brittany, according to developing rules of inheritance, had a better claim to Richard's lands than John. Arthur was aged just two and a half in early 1190, but he could still pose a threat to John's hopes. The rather late commentator (and somewhat dubious authority) Roger of Wendover, writing in the 1220s, thought that Richard had named Arthur his heir between mid-March and the beginning of June 1190.[8] Whether Richard had done so or not, he had certainly not declared for John, a point that must have been obvious to everyone who gave the matter any thought, including John himself.

In February 1190, therefore, when he was summoned to the continent, it must have looked to John as though all were conspiring to keep him from the inheritance he thought should be his. The high favor that he had enjoyed in the autumn of 1189 seemed to be ebbing away, and the extensive grants of land Richard had conceded to him were beginning to look like inducements to buy his acceptance that the Angevin territories were destined not for him, but for the next generation. And at the heart of the conspiracy against him was William de Longchamp, royal chancellor, bishop of Ely, and also soon-to-be papal legate.

THE MEETING IN NORMANDY between John and Richard in February must have been tense. The king had rearranged matters in England to make William de Longchamp chief justiciar and had removed Hugh du Puiset from his co-justiciarship to make him simply justiciar of the North. There would no longer be two co-justiciars of equal importance: William was to be in charge. The king then made his younger brother swear on a gospel book that he would not enter England for the next three years, except with Richard's express permission. The chroniclers noticed that this injunction also applied to Geoffrey, archbishop-elect of York, Richard and John's half-brother. William de Longchamp was to have a free hand in England with no danger of interference from the two most significant men of the realm, John and Geoffrey.

Had Richard stood by this decision, then perhaps matters might have worked themselves out differently, but at the moment that the oaths were being uttered, Eleanor of Aquitaine entered the discussion and persuaded her elder son to release John from his oath,[9] so long as he would faithfully serve the king. John was further made to swear that he would treat William de Longchamp as his superior in matters of the kingdom.[10]

Richard's crusade departed on July 15, 1190, and by September 22 he was at Messina, Sicily, where he declared openly that Arthur was his named successor.[11] News of this declaration reached England by early November 1190, at which point, according to William of Newburgh, William de Longchamp, fearing that he would lose power if John succeeded to the throne, enlisted the support of King William of Scots to ensure that Arthur would succeed should Richard die. William of Newburgh also tells us that John heard both of Richard's decision and of Longchamp's determination to put it into effect. John, therefore, in the words of Newburgh, "busied himself in prudently gaining over to his party all whom he could influence."[12] He knew as well as anyone the importance of being ready should the opportunity present itself. Richard's wishes in the matter, once dead, could be set aside.

B Y EARLY 1191, IT was becoming increasingly clear that the real problem at the heart of Richard's regime in England was not Count John, but the chancellor and justiciar, William de Longchamp. Richard had set up William as the senior justiciar in the kingdom in his absence, but he had not established the bishop as the sole authority in the land. In the summer of 1190, however, William had placed the justiciar for the north, Hugh du Puiset, under house arrest. Since, as chancellor, William had custody of the king's seal by which all documents were authenticated, he was now the power in the land. He had a further string to his bow. At Richard's insistence, Pope Clement III had made William a legate of the apostolic see. Legatine authority gave William full papal powers and made him the superior ecclesiastical authority in England. William was thus the alter ego of both the king and of the pope, and he held the trump cards in both the secular and the spiritual realms. It was as close as Richard could get to creating the model substitute king without crowning a new king in his place.

The problem was that William de Longchamp began to act like a king not only in the way that he wielded power but also in the way that he presented himself to the world. After a year of his rulership, many in England were asking themselves what sort of tyrant had been set over them, and by the summer of 1191, there was an open conspiracy seeking to oust William from his post. The criticisms levelled at him were trenchant. In a letter composed by Hugh de Nonant, bishop of Coventry (the man widely seen as the articulate voice of Longchamp's critics), the chancellor was accused of abusing his office to such an extent that

> Whatever property that swam beneath our skies was no longer said to belong to the king, but to him, for there was neither that which is hunted for on land, fished for in the water, or flying in the air, which was not compelled to be at the service of his table, insomuch as he appeared to have shared the elements with God; leaving heaven of heavens alone to God, and reserving the remainder for his use, or rather abuse, and luxurious enjoyment . . . [and worse still] for his own aggrandisement and for the glorification of his name, he was in the habit of getting up songs that he had picked up by begging, and adulatory jingles, and enticed jesters and singers from the kingdom of France by his presents, that they might sing about him in the streets.

William's critics accused him of acting the role of king, and they were doing so in one of the most public forms of the age: letter writing.

Letter writing in late twelfth-century northern Europe was a vigorous habit, and letters were sent with the expectation that they would be widely circulated and play their part in shaping public opinion. There were no "private letters in the modern sense of the term."[13] Until the widespread use of ciphers emerged in the later Middle Ages, secret messages were transmitted by word of mouth.[14] Letters, then, were designed to be read by many, both in the present and in the future,[15] and as such had to be fit for public consumption. The opening salvo against William was therefore undertaken by written word and the views of those who stood against William were widely circulated; even if they were not copied verbatim into chronicles, the letters visibly influenced the opinion of their authors against William. Amongst the chroniclers of the age, no one had much good to say about William de Longchamp.*[16]

Roger of Howden—a partisan of Hugh du Puiset, so we can see in his criticisms those of his patron—also had strong words of complaint to lay against William for the ostentatious nature of his display as he travelled about the kingdom. While it might be acceptable, or even expected, for a king to travel in extravagant style, it was not tolerable that a base-born official should ape his betters:

> On the authority also of his legateship, he came to take up his lodging at bishoprics, abbeys and priories, and other houses of the religious orders, with such a vast array of men and horses, hounds, and hawks, that a house where he took up his abode for only a single night, was hardly able within three years to recover its former state.

---

* Hugh of Coventry's letter elicited a response from one of the chancellor's supporters, Peter of Blois, a letter writer of extraordinary ability, but in whose hands the chancellor's case could only be defended on the grounds that those who acted against him did so on the grounds of "treachery and ingratitude."

William de Longchamp was making powerful enemies more easily than he was making powerful friends.

One of those enemies was Count John, and the cause of their difficulty lay in the fact that William saw John as a threat. The shock that John had received when he heard that Richard had openly declared for Arthur as his heir presumptive was compounded by William's hasty actions in attempting to ensure Arthur's succession before the fact. John must have brooded over this matter. And when in early 1191 it became clear that Richard was having second thoughts about his chancellor, John must have seen it as an opportunity to undermine William.

Open conflict between the two began in the early spring of 1191, with a struggle for control over certain strategic key castles.[17] On March 4, the two met at a conference in Winchester there to hammer out their differences. Little seems to have been achieved by this meeting and conflict was renewed. Shortly thereafter, William attempted to gain control of Lincoln Castle, allegedly because he wished to enjoy the nearby forests, though this seems unlikely. More plausibly, William was trying to gain strategic castles while simultaneously attacking the property of one of John's chief supporters, Gerard de Canville.[18]

Gerard had been a successful servant in Henry II's entourage, who had been richly rewarded with a marriage to Nicola de Haye, which gave him her inheritance in England and Normandy along with the constableship of Lincoln Castle.[19] Longchamp's forces now lay siege to Lincoln, which was stoutly defended by Nicola while her husband went in person to entreat Count John to intervene. John, whether in response to Longchamp's actions or as part of a wider struggle between them is unclear, seized the castles of Nottingham and Tickhill and then threatened the chancellor with a direct attack on his forces. The chancellor, aware that John had the support amongst the magnates that he lacked, retreated. Round one had clearly gone to Count John, who now saw himself emerging as the one man who could stop the chancellor from acting oppressively.

A second aspect of the developing conflict between John and William emerged as a result of the death of Baldwin, archbishop of Canterbury. Baldwin had joined Richard's crusade but had gone on ahead with an advance party. It was outside the walls of Acre, while his king was still in Sicily, that Baldwin died, and when news of his death reached Richard, he determined to grant the archbishopric to the archbishop of Monreale, Sicily. Richard therefore wrote to John to express his view and entreat his brother to act on his behalf in the matter.[20] Quite what John made of the decision, history does not record, but he did make it his business to convey his brother's wishes to the monks of Christ Church, Canterbury, in whose power the election lay.

We know of some of the detail of the resultant election dispute because the monks of Christ Church preserved many of the letters on the matter that came to their notice. The royal chancery had yet to develop the tradition of recording the king's outgoing correspondence (this would begin in John's reign), so all we have is the material that the monks chose to keep in order to record the outcome of this particular succession struggle, but it is enough to give a clear indication of how the business unfolded. The letter of January 21 in which Richard instructed John to act on his behalf is preserved in this collection, as is a companion letter in which Richard addressed the monks directly asking for their agreement to elect William of Monreale.[21] But, according to the historian of the Canterbury community, Gervase, that letter was not delivered to the convent until May 5. On that day, William de Longchamp met the monks in chapter to deliver the king's message to them.[22] The monks applied to William for a delay to consider the meaning of the king's wishes, which he granted, and he and his delegation withdrew to allow the community to consider its position.

We do not know what William de Longchamp said to the monks, but it might well be that the chancellor was already thinking about putting himself forward for election as archbishop. Certainly, by the end of August, Count John was openly accusing William de Longchamp of having ambitions beyond those intended for him by Richard. John wrote directly to the monks of Christ Church warning them that he had heard that they intended to elect the chancellor and cautioning them to listen to the advice of Walter of Coutances, archbishop of Rouen, concerning the election. A later letter, sent by the prior and convent to Longchamp apologizing for not electing him, confirms that the chancellor had designs on the archbishopric for himself.[23]

The third aspect of the conflict came in the form of Walter of Coutances and the leader of the group of men whom Richard had sent back to England to take charge of a situation that he feared was rapidly running out of control. Walter was an extraordinarily adept politician who had become immensely successful as a result of his ability to pick his way through the intrigues of the court. He came from a Norman family that had settled in Cornwall, and, like many of his contemporaries, this Norman extraction coupled with an English upbringing allowed Walter to bestride the English Channel in his influence and in his interests. We first pick him up in the sources in 1169 as a canon of Rouen cathedral, and he quickly rose in the ranks, becoming, by 1183, bishop of Lincoln and then, in 1184, archbishop of Rouen. Posts such as these only came to the most trusted and most successful of royal servants, and Walter was one of those rare creatures who acquired the trust of all four of the kings he served: Henry II and Richard I, later John and, after the fall of Normandy in 1204, Philip Augustus, king of France. He had a keen sense of loyalty to the office of king that overrode his feelings about the individual who occupied that position.

Walter had taken the cross and joined King Richard on crusade but had reached Messina when news of the difficulties caused by William reached the king. He was sent back to England in the company of William Marshal and Hugh Bardolf to add his weight and wisdom to the good government of the realm. Even before he had left Europe's shores, Richard was beginning to doubt the wisdom of his choice as chief justiciar. Archbishop Walter set foot on English soil at the end of June,[24] though since he, too, was wary around the chancellor, neither he nor those who came with him from Richard had the courage to confront

William at this juncture, the letters remaining sealed and unused but ready to be deployed when the opportunity arose.[25]

Walter was therefore present to witness the next stage in the struggle between William and John. While the chancellor accused the count of plotting to take the kingdom, the count in his turn argued that he was defending the kingdom for his brother against the rapacity of an official gone mad with power. The two met at Winchester on July 28 to further hammer out their differences and the agreement that they reached was enshrined in a treaty, the text of which was deemed so important that it was preserved, in one form or another,[26] by all the main chroniclers of the crisis. The two castles of Nottingham and Tickhill were to be "restored to the king," the first was to be held by William Marshal, the second was to be held by one of Count John's most trusted supporters, his steward William de Wenneval.[27] It is worth emphasizing that both castles were being "restored to the king" and that Count John was deemed to be his legitimate representative. It was a clear acknowledgment that John had a stake in the good government of his brother's realm; as was the fact that both castles were to be rendered to John in the event of Richard's death. William of Newburgh took this part of the agreement to mean that William de Longchamp had been forced to recognize John as Richard's heir.[28]

By the terms of the treaty, other key castles were handed over to principal men of the kingdom, none of whom could exactly be described as Longchamp's friends, but then they were not exactly Count John's friends either. The castle at Wallingford went to the archbishop of Rouen; Bristol went to Richard fitz Nigel, bishop of London; Hugh de Nonant, bishop of Coventry acquired the castle of the Peak and that of Bolsover (should Richard of the Peak decline it), Walter fitz Robert acquired Eye Castle, Roger Bigod took control of Hereford Castle, and Richard Revel took Exeter and Launceston. This marks the point at which power was first wrested from Longchamp's grasp. It would take just one more mistake by the chancellor to pitch the kingdom into the crisis—a crisis that would result in him being ousted from his post.

The spark that ignited the conflagration that consumed William was the arrest of Geoffrey, archbishop of York in September 1191. Unlike John, Geoffrey was still banned from England, and so he had spent the year on the continent. He had been consecrated as archbishop by the archbishop of Tours, and then, perhaps with John's encouragement, he decided to return to England. He landed at Dover on September 14 and went immediately to St. Martin's Priory from which, after a five-day siege, he was bodily dragged, still in his archiepiscopal robes, having just celebrated Mass. The archbishop's biographer, Gerald of Wales, takes up the story in the most vivid of prose:

> The castellan's men grabbed him by the feet and arms, carried the struggling archbishop from the altar and handled him so roughly that his head hit the pavement of the church heavily. And when they came out of the church, they led him to a horse, which he did not wish to mount, but went on foot, carrying his cross in his hands at all times; and so he was brought through the muddy streets of the town to the castle where he was delivered to the constable.[29]

The archbishop's treatment sent shock waves through the upper echelons of English society. Men still remembered that Thomas Becket had been murdered by thugs acting (though he denied it vigorously) on Henry II's wishes, and here was the king's representative, his justiciar, acting in a way that was chillingly similar to that notorious event. Some were prepared to make the link between the two events explicit, no doubt encouraged by Archbishop Geoffrey. After languishing in prison for eight days, he was released, after which he made directly to Canterbury there to pray at the shrine of the holy martyr.[30] Appalled by what he now realized was a dreadful mistake, Longchamp sent representatives to meet Geoffrey to assure him that his arrest had been an error, an error, moreover, in which he had played no part. But neither the archbishop nor the chancellor's critics were prepared to believe him.[31] The fact remained that his officer (who happened to be his brother-in-law, which made William's denial even less plausible) had laid violent hands on the prelate.*[32] It was a disaster; in the view of Roger of Howden, the chancellor had given his enemies the weapon they needed to unseat him, and they ruthlessly pursued him with it.

Medieval kings often found it expedient to arrest and imprison their bishops. Senior ecclesiastics could be troublesome creatures, since they could command the moral and religious authority to challenge the power of kings, and, on the whole, English kings were distrustful of those who stood up to them. The conflict between Henry II and Thomas Becket was the most extreme example of what could happen when a bishop confronted the tyranny of a king; in using violence to deal with a difficult bishop, Henry was not unique.[33] Longchamp, in having Archbishop Geoffrey arrested, was doing no more than English rulers had done before. But Longchamp was not the king. As contemporaries saw it, his greatest fault was that he saw himself as a monarch and behaved as such. Their view was confirmed when Longchamp's officers acted violently toward Geoffrey. There is no doubt that Geoffrey was a problem and his return violated the oath he had given to the king. In coming to England, therefore, he had behaved provocatively; perhaps he had been attempting to goad the chancellor into an unwise move. But what had transpired on Geoffrey's return to England confirmed many people's worst fears about the chancellor.

Spurred on by Hugh de Nonant, bishop of Coventry, Count John led the coalition that determined to bring the chancellor to account. A council was convened at Loddon Bridge, a few miles outside Reading, at which the chancellor was expected to be reconciled with Archbishop Geoffrey: evidently John was taking the lead in attempting to bring about peace between the two.[34] Longchamp failed to attend. His opponents then headed

---

* Gerald of Wales transcribed the letter patent authorizing Geoffrey's arrest, though his status as a notorious forger makes it difficult to accept his testimony. That said, the arrest did occur and Gerald's transcription shows that William's opponents were determined to lay the blame at his door.

for London and, en route, a melee occurred between John's knights and those of the chancellor—an engagement that the count's knights won—which persuaded the chancellor that his life was in danger. He took refuge in the Tower of London.

The following day, October 8, at a Great Council in St. Paul's churchyard Longchamp's record as justiciar was scrutinized.[35] The council concluded that he had "transacted all the affairs of the kingdom according to his own impulse and will," contrary to the instructions that had been left by King Richard.[36] At that point the archbishop of Rouen and William Marshal produced their trump card: the letter that Richard had issued the previous February stating that they were to depose the chancellor if he acted arbitrarily and without council, and that, if he were found guilty, he was to be deposed from office and the reins of government put into the hands of the archbishop of Rouen. In the words of Roger of Howden,

> it seemed good, therefore, to John and all the bishops, earls, and barons of the kingdom, and to the citizens of London, that the chancellor should be deposed, and substituted in his place the archbishop of Rouen, who was willing to do nothing in the kingdom except by the will and consent of his associates, and the sanction of the barons of the Exchequer.[37]

The citizens of London, moreover, agreed to support Count John as Richard's heir should the king die without issue. With that, William de Longchamp was deposed, replaced by Walter of Coutances, a figure of stature and much more pleasing to the great barons of the realm.

THE DOWNFALL OF WILLIAM de Longchamp happened because, in the end, he overplayed his hand. In that sense, his end was of his own making. John certainly played his part in it, but he cannot be seen as the *éminence grise* in the affair, manipulating the leading players so as to maneuver himself into prime position to unseat Richard and to take the kingdom for himself.[38] That would be to read history backward, always an unwise thing to do. John was certainly keen to be designated as Richard's heir, and he was certainly keen to play a leading part in the affairs of the kingdom as Richard's brother and as one of the principal barons of the realm in his own right, but he was not, at this stage, trying to unseat Richard. No one, not even John, could have moved against the chancellor without the support of the king. It was King Richard who gave Archbishop Walter of Rouen and William Marshal the tools with which they could depose the chancellor, and it was these tools that Walter and his associates used at the Great Council at St. Paul's to rid themselves of their unwanted despot.

The new arrangement made Count John the "supreme governor of the whole realm," acting in concert with Walter, archbishop of Rouen, who was chief justiciar and "supreme after the count." They appointed new men as itinerant justices, keepers of the Exchequer and constables of the castles.[39] And John was generally recognized as the heir apparent.[40] According to the chroniclers, there was widespread rejoicing at the deposition of a chancellor who had overstepped the bounds of acceptable behavior both as justiciar and as legate of the apostolic see. He had used his position ruthlessly for the profit of himself, his family and his followers, and he had done so openly and wantonly. To cap it all, his going was one of ignominy. Like many a despot, ancient, medieval and modern, William de Longchamp spluttered his indignation, swore vengeance on his enemies and found it impossible to believe that any fault in his fall lay at his door. His view was that he had been undone by the faithlessness of men who should have been faithful to him; and he went on the offensive.

A pamphlet war ensued, with the bishop of Coventry writing on behalf of those who had deposed the chancellor, and Peter of Blois, writing on behalf of the chancellor. The chancellor was forced to flee the country in the most humiliating of styles (dressed as a woman), and from his continental vantage point, he attempted to win back his exalted position. He appealed to the king, he appealed to the pope, he issued sentences of excommunication against named individuals and generally against all those who had helped in unseating him; he even laid an interdict on his own diocese. In return, the archbishop of Rouen, newly installed as justiciar, excommunicated Longchamp. This was the opportunity for Richard of Devizes to tell another tale to the detriment of the chancellor, one in which he was so callous that he abandoned his flock to the spiritual wilderness for his own political ambitions:

> One day Queen Eleanor was visiting some cottages that were part of her dower in the diocese of Ely. There came before her from all the villages and hamlets men with women and children, a people weeping and pitiful, with bare feet, unwashed clothes, and unkempt hair. They spoke by their tears, for their grief was so great that they could not speak. There was no need for an interpreter, for more than they wanted to say could be read on the open page of their faces. Human bodies lay unburied here and there in the fields because their bishop had deprived them of burial . . . the queen took pity on them, for she was merciful, and immediately dropped her own affairs to go to London [to bring about a reconciliation between the warring parties].[41]

But Longchamp did not want reconciliation. He complained to the king about his treatment, and then to the pope, and on each occasion he sought to lay the blame firmly at John's door.[42] This, however, ignores the fact that there was a widespread conspiracy against William brought on by his inability to work with the chief men of the realm, which is further illustrated by a series of letters that William sent once he had received papal backing.

William wrote to the bishop of Lincoln ordering him to summon the bishops to enact the papal mandate by which the offenders against him should be excommunicated. He told the bishop that while he was content to allow John's sentence to be deferred, he ordered that the sentence against the other conspirators (whom he named) should be enacted at once. The list shows that, amongst those who held power in the kingdom, he had few or no friends. It quickly became apparent, however, that he was attempting to woo an especially powerful friend to his side: Count John.[43] Indeed, William invited John to "repent" and make his peace. It was in December 1191 that John began to think that he could perhaps hasten the end of Richard's reign for his own advantage.

4

TROUBLESOME BROTHER

J OHN SPENT THE CHRISTMAS of 1191 at Howden, Yorkshire, one of
Hugh du Puiset's estates. What was discussed we can only guess at,
but one of the topics of conversation must surely have been the French
king's return from crusade. The Third Crusade was not proving to be
an unqualified success. The German emperor, Frederick Barbarossa, had
died on the journey east, and only a fraction of his troops arrived in the
Holy Land. The ancient city of Acre, besieged since August 1189, was
still holding out against the crusaders. Philip had arrived outside its walls
in April 1191 to be followed by Richard, with the city eventually falling
on July 12. In less than a month, Philip decided to return home, leaving
Richard to assume the undisputed leadership of the crusade. By December
1191, Philip was back in Paris seeking to undermine Richard's position in
Europe. John's decision to start actively working against his brother seems
to stem directly from Philip's resumption of his place in European affairs.

The return of Philip Augustus to Europe transformed the political landscape of the Angevin lands. Although Richard and Philip had
agreed a peace treaty, which was to last until both rulers had returned to
Europe, Philip evidently had no intention of keeping to it. The relationship between them had irrevocably broken down, and since Philip was
Richard's acknowledged overlord for his continental lands, the French
king had a powerful lever in his campaign to bring Normandy under his
permanent control.[1] As soon as the Christmas festivities were complete,
Philip renewed the object of his political ambition.

On January 20, he marched to the traditional meeting place between the kings of France and the dukes of Normandy and demanded that the seneschal of the duchy (and therefore Richard's deputy while he was away) return his sister Alice to his custody, and that he also hand over to him Gisors, the counties of Aumale and Eu.[2] The seneschal was unwilling to acquiesce to King Philip's demand without Richard's express permission. Philip then seriously considered an invasion of Normandy, but Richard's status as a crusader protected the duchy from his immediate attack.

While Philip prepared for war against Richard, it was widely rumored that Count John planned to go over to Philip's side. Only the quick action of Queen Eleanor prevented John from embarking for the continent. Eleanor played a crucial role in her sons' lives, especially Richard's and John's. She had been pivotal in negotiating Richard's arrival in England in 1189, she had been central in the process of securing Berengaria of Navarre as Richard's bride, and now she became crucial in keeping a lid on John's political ambitions.[3] The queen landed in England on February 11 and then called councils at Windsor, Oxford, London and Winchester to which the magnates of the kingdom were summoned and during which, according to Richard of Devizes, by lamentations and entreaties, she persuaded her son John not to cross the Channel to join Philip Augustus.

While he may have decided to remain in England, John did not stop maneuvering himself into an advantageous position. A second part of his plan revolved around establishing himself and his supporters in the key castles of the kingdom. Windsor, which had been in the custody of Hugh du Puiset, was handed to John (perhaps that had been part of the conversation between them over the dinner table that Christmas), as was the castle of Wallingford.

John also now chose to reintroduce William de Longchamp to the English political scene, and so, at his behest, William made landfall in England. In Roger of Howden's account, John's motive for attempting to inveigle the discredited chancellor back into power was prompted by a bribe of £500 of silver, but it seems likely that there was much more to the story than Howden reveals.[4] According to Richard of Devizes, the council meeting in London at that time intended to "speak with John about his assumption of castles," but instead threw itself on his mercy, begging him to attack the former chancellor. John declined to oblige, saying:

> This chancellor does not in the least fear the threats or seek the friendship of any or all of you, if he can have only my favour alone. He is to give me 700 pounds of silver within the week if I will not meddle between you and him. You see I need money.

The count then withdrew and waited for the council to decide on its next course of action that, as John must have thought it would, resulted in the magnates agreeing to find the necessary money to match the chancellor's offer, £500 of it from the king's own coffers. Longchamp withdrew in disarray, threatening his revenge on those who had turned against him.

John was effectively asking each party to bribe him for his support, and some contemporaries were clearly unimpressed by his actions. From John's point of view, however, being given money in return for support was no more than the usual way to rule a kingdom. In the Angevin lands, for example, men and women expected to pay their ruler for his patronage: it was part and parcel of normal everyday business. Men bought the king's largesse, they bought his benevolence, they bought his good will and they paid to have his heart softened in their favor. All of these payments were deemed legitimate, even if the amounts were sometimes thought to be excessive. In taking the promise of money from the former chancellor and then in encouraging a bidding war between him and his enemies, John was merely indulging in normal ruler practice. Certainly Richard had been no less squeamish in extracting money from those of his subjects who came within his sights.

However, it is hard to see the William de Longchamp affair as being about money (though no doubt the money was welcome). It is much more likely that John was testing the strength and resolve of those who were ruling England for Richard. What he seems to have discovered is that while they were weak, they had the support of someone who could encourage them to withstand John—his mother, Queen Eleanor. After Longchamp's second withdrawal from England, we hear little of John's activities, which suggests that he was no longer a threat to the government of the kingdom. It seemed he remained in England, however, in prime position, should events present themselves, to secure the kingdom.

O N OCTOBER 9, 1192, King Richard set sail for home from the Holy Land. His extraordinary journey across Europe, only to be captured near Vienna on December 21 by Duke Leopold of Austria's men and then to be handed over to the new Emperor, Henry VI, is the stuff of history and legend. His imprisonment rocked Europe and was profoundly shocking to those controlling Richard's lands.[5] The triumphant letter that the emperor wrote to King Philip of France, dated December 28, informing him of Richard's capture was widely circulated. Presumably Philip learned of Richard's captivity around Epiphany (January 6, 1193) and John, who was at Cardiff, would have heard a week or so later.

John's reaction was immediate: he not unreasonably calculated that Richard would never be released, and decided that this was his moment to make a serious bid for Richard's lands.[6] By mid-January, John was in Normandy. He went straight to Alençon, where he made the case to the seneschal and the barons of the duchy that they should receive him as Richard's replacement. He found in them, however, an indefatigable group of men determined to remain loyal to Richard while he lived. John then went on to Paris to cement his alliance with King Philip. Here, John was offered the hand in marriage of Philip's sister, Alice, and with her all England and Normandy along with Richard's other continental lands.[7] Philip then assembled a fleet at Wissant with soldiers from Flanders who, according to Gervase of Canterbury, were delighted at the opportunity to invade England.

Once again, Queen Eleanor played a crucial part in the affairs of her sons. She mustered defenses along the Kentish coast and prepared to repel the invaders. In the end, the Flemish fleet never set sail, but it was evidently a time of extreme nervousness for the English political elite. John, in the meantime, came to England, where he attempted to gain the support of the king of the Scots (who refused him) and made preparations for the defense of his castles. By Easter 1193, England was in a state of civil war, which only ended when a peace was brokered by the new archbishop of Canterbury, Hubert Walter, who had been sent from Germany with instructions to ensure that above all else the ransom was raised so that Richard would be released from the captivity in which he was held by the emperor. Meanwhile, Philip launched his troops against Normandy, capturing Gisors Castle, and then laying siege to the ducal capital of Rouen. The city was saved only by the bravery and determination of the citizens, led by the earl of Leicester.[8]

Shortly after midsummer, news reached Richard's lands that the terms of his release had been agreed. In retrospect, John's gamble looked foolish, and he began to behave in a manner that suggests that the prospect of his brother's return was making him panic. He left England and went to Paris, where he was at Philip's side as the terms of the truce between Richard and the French king were agreed. Despite Richard conceding that John's Norman castles should be returned to him, their castellans refused to hand them over, seemingly driving John even further into the French king's camp.[9] As Richard's release date—January 17, 1194—approached, John and Philip became increasingly concerned about what would happen after Richard's return, and they did their best to persuade the German emperor to hang onto his captive. Despite their best efforts, however, on February 4 Richard was released and was free to return home.[10]

RICHARD'S CAPTURE IN DECEMBER 1192 had seemingly presented John with a golden opportunity to succeed to his brother's lands, but John had miscalculated badly when he judged that Richard's officials in England and in Normandy would swing behind his cause. In England, despite the problems arising from William de Longchamp's misrule, by

1193 the new regime was working harmoniously, and in Normandy, John could not persuade its seneschal to break ranks and submit to him. In the duchy and in the kingdom, Richard's officials stood firm against John while they waited to hear what would happen to their master.

John's state of mind in January 1194 is revealed by the preservation of a most remarkable document, one that demonstrates that, far from supinely accepting the inevitability of Richard's release, up until the very last moment John was striving to rule in Richard's stead. A letter patent created according to French royal chancery practice, not Angevin, it is written in John's name and sealed with his seal. Addressed generally, to all who would read it, the letter makes it known that Count John had made an agreement with King Philip concerning his succession to the Angevin lands, whereby in return for Philip's acceptance of John as his heir, John gave to Philip "Normandy on the French side of the river Seine to the English Channel, except the city of Rouen itself and two leagues around." John further conceded to Philip the key strongholds of Le Vaudeuil, Verneuil, Evreux and Chennebrun. John also gave up to Philip and his son Louis other strategic places throughout the Angevin lands in Maine, Anjou, the Touraine and Aquitaine, and he further agreed to hold these continental lands as a baron of the French king subject to, as any other baron would be, the king's court at Paris.[11]

The contents of this letter make for remarkable reading. John was declaring that he was prepared to tear the heart out of the Angevin inheritance. To concede eastern Normandy to Philip was to make a definitive break with his family, and the agreement that the duke of Normandy was to be subject to the French king's court in Paris was to abandon all precedent by which the dukes of the Normans met the kings of the French on the borders of their lands as equals. These two concessions, had they been enacted, would have wrecked Angevin power in the duchy. It was a spectacular blunder.

This was John's last throw of the dice and revealed him to be a risk taker of extraordinary proportions, prepared to chance everything, including the very future of his dynasty, in the hope that he personally would win the Angevin lands. John's mother thought that he had "the shallow mind of an adolescent"[12]: John's brother thought that he "lacked the ability to stand up to someone who opposed him."[13] Both may have been right—they knew the man of whom they spoke—however, the agreement of January 1194 also showed John to be a man all too willing to play at brinkmanship, but who ultimately lacked the fine judgment to know when he had gone too far. Another man would have pulled back from the agreement and prepared to make his peace in the best way he could, but not John. This character trait would emerge again and again throughout the remainder of his life.

THE FIRST MEETING BETWEEN Richard and John was always going to be awkward. Richard's return to England and the final suppression of the resistance (John never entered England again while Richard lived, so it was his deputies who bore the brunt of Richard's retribution) took place at around Easter time. A second coronation held at Winchester on April 17 completed the process by which the king was returned to his former state. Richard knew that John had not only conspired against him but had also conspired to keep him in prison; the emperor, Henry VI, had been kind enough to show Richard the letters by which Philip and John had tried to ensure his continued imprisonment.

With their mother mediating, the brothers first met at Lisieux, where John threw himself at Richard's feet and begged for mercy. When Richard had been reconciled to his father in 1174, he had been made to perform public acts of penance and homage, and was required to shed tears as symbols of his remorse. Such displays of contrition were expected behavior for a penitent rebel and in 1194, John seems to have played his part to the full, perhaps even shedding the requisite tears. The author of the *History of William Marshal*, writing from the distance of the 1220s, sought to place in Richard's mouth the words "John, have no fear. You are a child, and you had bad men looking after you."[14] It was a withering comment from his elder brother, especially as had he succeeded, Richard would have been ruined. John was twenty-seven years old.

From this moment on, John's threat to Richard's rule evaporated. Although Richard forgave John for his actions, it was not until a year later, in 1195, that his anger toward his brother abated and he allowed John to take control of his former properties. John spent twelve months in the political wilderness and it must have cost him dear, financially as well as in terms of his reputation. While he kept the earl's third penny (the right to a third of the Crown profits from the administration of the county) of Gloucestershire throughout the period of his disgrace, that in no way compensated him for the loss of his English castles and shires as well as the loss of the lands and revenues associated with his properties in Normandy, all of which had been confiscated. John was not sent into exile, but for the next year, he receded so far from the center of political events that he neither appears in the chronicles nor in the documentation produced by the king's Chancery.

John's return to the political scene began in May 1195, exactly a year after his reconciliation with Richard (perhaps the length of time is significant), when, we are told, Richard allowed John to take up the reins of control in Mortain and Gloucester. At this point John reappears as a witness to Richard's acts, showing that he had been accepted back into the ranks of the king's entourage. The first of these is dated June 10, 1195, and concerns a grant to a member of the urban community at Rouen.[15] Five days later, John issued a charter to Walter de Lacy granting him the whole of Meath in Ireland, which Walter's father had held before his death in 1186.

The significance of this particular charter lies in John's relationship with Ireland. As lord of Ireland, John had assumed the rulership of the kingdom with no superior but his father. Once Henry II was dead, John was his own man in the island, with the greatest threat to his control being the Anglo-Irish lord Walter de Lacy. Some believed that Walter's father, Hugh, had caused the failure of the 1185 expedition, and so John's relationship with Walter was, understandably, strained.[16] In 1192, John ejected Walter from his Irish lands, but on his return from captivity, Richard sought to reinstall Walter and take from him homage for his

Irish lands, despite having no legitimate rights in Ireland and thus being in no position to exact homage from John's tenants. But on April 8, 1194, Walter received a charter from King Richard for Meath.[17] It is an indication of the extent of Count John's fall that King Richard could act in such a high-handed manner.

Nevertheless, a year later, Richard, it seems, was seeking to rectify matters. The charter that John issued on June 15 to Walter de Lacy was, in effect, a confirmation of his brother's act, although it makes no mention of Richard's grant. On the contrary, the text of John's charter assiduously avoids all mention of Richard, preferring instead to refer to the grant in which "Henry my father gave and by his charter confirmed to Hugh, Walter's father" the land in Meath, and which "I surrendered and granted and by this present charter confirmed" Walter's title to his inheritance.[18] The charter's language marks an important moment in John's rehabilitation, and although he is not named, it is more than likely that Richard witnessed the grant.* Richard had returned Ireland to his brother. There was no fanfare and there was no grand statement, but in June 1195, John was again lord of Ireland in his own right.

By slow degrees John continued to rebuild his relationship with his brother. He acted as a military commander, though admittedly not with unqualified success. He and Earl David of Huntingdon led the men of Rouen against the town of Vaudreuil but were caught by surprise by the French king and had to retreat rapidly in order to avoid capture.[19] In spring 1196, John joined Richard in his army. He was outside the walls of Gamaches in the eastern marches of Normandy in August that year,

---

* The charter to Walter de Lacy was completed by a place and date at the foot of the document. Most of John's charters, as lord of Ireland and count of Mortain, were sealed without a place and date of compilation, which means that we have to work hard to tie down many of his grants to particular points in time. A few of John's charters were dated, however, which seems to have happened when they were drawn up by the royal Chancery scribes, who were used to place-dating the king's charters, a habit they had acquired since Richard's accession in 1189. The charter to Walter, therefore, was drawn up by the royal Chancery, which means that Richard was in the vicinity when the grant was made, though his name was not given as one of the formal witnesses.

which, unlike Vaudreuil the year before, fell to his siege engines, and he campaigned around Gavray in Lower Normandy at the western edge of the duchy in the same year.[20] In May 1197, John was in the company of the infamous Brabançon mercenary Mercadier at Beauvais, where, in a sharp encounter, his troops bested the notoriously militant bishop, who was also King Philip's cousin, and held him captive. It was said that Richard hated the bishop and rejoiced in his captivity, placing him in prison and refusing to ransom him. Richard must have been pleased with his brother, especially as he then went on to play his part in the capture of the fortress at Milly-sur-Thérain.[21]

By July 1197, John's rehabilitation was complete, and he had emerged as Richard's preferred successor in the event of the king dying without legitimate issue. By this time young Arthur of Brittany, whom Richard had designated as his heir in 1190, was at the French court, and it was John, now second only to the king, whose name adorned the treaty between Richard and Baldwin, count of Flanders. The treaty was forged in June or July 1197 and in it John, as Richard's representative, swore that the king would uphold its terms. The second witness was Otto, styled "count of Poitou," who was Richard and John's nephew and who, at one time, had perhaps been Richard's preferred candidate for the throne.[22] It had taken him three long years of hard work, but John had at last managed to undo the damage caused by his actions while Richard was held captive.

John's new position as Richard's favored successor is confirmed by a document issued in his own name on September 8, 1197. It is a letter patent, addressed generally, stating that "were Richard to die without a legitimate heir" he would "not make a truce or a peace with King Philip without the assent of the count of Flanders." It was witnessed by Hubert Walter, Richard's right-hand man, as well as by the vice-chancellor, Bishop Eustace of Ely.[23] The greatest secular magnates of Richard's regime were also witnesses: William Marshal, Earl David of Huntingdon, William fitz Ralph and William de Humet, respectively seneschal and constable of Normandy. The letter was issued from the Norman ducal capital, Rouen, and that Richard himself was present at its granting is suggested by the fact that the king was, according to Gervase of Canterbury, that very day with Baldwin and King Philip between Gaillon and Les Andelys concluding a peace treaty that was to last until January 1199.[24]

A month later, on October 16, 1197, John's place as Richard's preferred successor was reemphasized with another great ceremony at which he confirmed, "at the request of my most dear lord and brother Richard, by the grace of God king of England, duke of Normandy and Aquitaine, count of Anjou,"[25] the exchange between him and the archbishop of Rouen of the manor at Les Andelys on which Richard had built Chateau Gaillard.[26] The exchange was enshrined in two documents, a grant from Richard and John's confirmation of that grant. The witness lists match each other almost exactly and reveal the extent to which the political and ecclesiastical communities of England and Normandy, together with some representatives from further afield, now looked to John as Richard's heir.[27]

But there is one revealing difference between the two lists. John, count of Mortain was the senior lay witness to Richard's grant, whereas Richard appears only by virtue of the fact that John was affirming his brother's grant. Undoubtedly the king was there directing proceedings, but it was John who took precedence. The centrality of Chateau Gaillard to the defense of Normandy must also in part explain why Richard wanted this charter confirmed by John more than any other. It was symbolic of the position that John now held in Richard's regime. And the witnesses, matching as they do the witnesses to King Richard's original charter, were both symbolic of the brothers' unity of purpose and also represented the fact that the key men in the regime, the men who would determine the succession, were now firmly behind John.[28] The hope that had been expressed by Roger of Howden at the outset of Richard's reign that the brothers would rule in harmony was, in 1197, being finally realized.

John recognized the importance of these men to his future and was keen to rebuild his relationships with them. But this was, of course, a two-way process, and Richard's ministers now began to look at John differently, no longer as a troublesome younger brother but as a coruler with Richard and as a potential master of their destiny should the future unfold in a certain way. Richard was almost forty, and he and Berengaria had yet to produce children. He was a brave man who had brushed with death before, and even if he did produce an heir, it would be a long time before that heir was of age. Wise men, therefore, began to look to the future. William Marshal, for example, was accused of "planting vines" with the man who might succeed Richard if it came to it.[29] There are indications that others were equally prudent. On July 31, 1197, at Lyons-la-Forêt, John granted to John, bishop of Worcester "at the petition and request of our reverend father in Christ, Hubert, by the Grace of God, archbishop of Canterbury and John bishop of Worcester," the right to fell trees in the count's forest of Malvern.[30] Hubert, like William Marshal, would have a crucial part to play in John's accession.

5

Winner Takes All

E ARLY IN 1199, JUST as Richard was about to make his way southward to Aquitaine, King Philip told Richard that his brother was
once again in the French camp and, according to Howden, he showed
Richard a document by which the treachery could be proved. Howden
was astonished that anyone should believe that John would turn against
his brother and side with Philip, for John had been a loyal servant since
1194. John, when he heard of the accusation, reacted swiftly and decisively, sending two of his knights to the French court to refute the charge.
According to Howden, no one could be found who would challenge
John's knights, and so John's reputation was restored. In Howden's version of events, John was received "into greater favour" by Richard after
this.[1] John was certainly with Richard at Roche-Turpin near Vendôme
on March 1, where he witnessed a charter to Spalding Priory, and when
the king was on his deathbed a month later, he had no hesitation in des-
ignating John his heir.[2]

The death of King Richard on April 6, 1199 came as a surprise to all.
He was just forty-one years old, he had survived countless military en-
gagements, a crusade and a year in captivity, and there had been no inti-
mations of mortality. His death was caused by gangrene, which poisoned
his system a few days after he had been hit in the shoulder by a crossbow
bolt fired from the battlements of the castle of Châlus-Chabrol in the
Limousin. The mortally wounded king took eleven days to die, during

which he had plenty of time to make provision for his soul and to advise on what should happen to his lands once he was dead.

Richard's backing for John's claim to the Angevin inheritance was evidently important, otherwise there would have been little point in him making provision for the succession. The reality, however, was that, in the case of a disputed succession, powerful interest groups could determine whom their next ruler should be. It took about three weeks for news of Richard's death to reach England, or at least to find its way into the official business of the law.[3] At Easter that year, when news got out that Richard was dead, there were disturbances as men took advantage of the absence of royal rule to engage in direct action that, while the king still lived, they would have hesitated to do.[4]

Theoretically at least, the key men of Normandy and England had already assigned their support to John: that was the import of the events of summer and autumn 1197. But of course, after the death of the king, men could always change their minds. The *History of William Marshal*, for example, gives us an insight into what ensued between Earl William and Archbishop Hubert Walter when they heard of Richard's death. The author's dramatic reconstruction has William at the tower in Rouen Castle, having his boots removed before he clambered into bed, when he received news of the king's death. Pulling himself together, he dashed to the archbishop's quarters, where the two discussed what should happen next. They noted that the late king had nominated John as his successor, but also debated the possibility of throwing their weight behind Arthur of Brittany. The discussion, according to the *History*, revolved around who was the rightful heir to England and Normandy. William Marshal plumped for John on the grounds that he thought a son of Henry II was closer in line to the inheritance than the king's grandson by an elder son (this was Geoffrey), and therefore nephew to King Richard.[5] He was wrong, according to developing laws of inheritance,[6] but that was not the point. What mattered was that while there were a number of legitimate candidates for the succession to a kingdom or duchy, there was always a choice.

Men of power, then as now, are adept at arguing the law to fit their predisposition. And in any case, Richard himself had muddied the waters by declaring for Arthur in 1190 and later for Otto of Brunswick, and later still for John. In England and Normandy, the actions of William Marshal and Hubert Walter, subsequent to their discussions on the night they received news of Richard's death, ensured that John would succeed to the kingdom and the duchy.[7]

In Aquitaine, John's mother, Eleanor, seventy-seven years old but as formidable as ever, guaranteed that the duchy adhered to her son rather than her grandson, but here inheritance custom helped John. In much of greater Poitou, the system of inheritance, known as *droit de viage* or *droit de retour*, gave all male members of a generation joint interest in the family property, with each male succeeding his brother until that generation was exhausted. In the political landscape of Poitou, therefore, no one would doubt John had a better claim than Arthur to succeed to Richard's lands, though of course the consequence of this system of inheritance was that Arthur, if he were to survive, would be John's heir no matter how many sons John might sire. And in Anjou, John himself attempted to force the matter by taking his army directly to Chinon—the location of the Angevin treasury—and persuading the castellan, Robert of Thornham, to release its keys to him.

At the heart of the problem for John was the fact that each of the lands over which Richard ruled had a choice as to which of Richard's relations they might choose as their lord. While he and his advisers wanted to see Richard's lands as a complete entity that he could inherit, it is obvious that others involved did not see it in that way. Certainly Philip of France argued that the lands that Richard held on the continent were not one political unit but many, over which Richard held sway as duke of the Normans or as count of the Angevins or as duke of the Aquitainians. It is evident, too, that the aristocracies of the various lands also held the view that each of their lordships had a separate choice to make about the identity of their ruler. Not surprisingly the men of Brittany chose Arthur, but so, too, in the main part, did the men of Anjou. And it is clear that in

Poitou opinion was divided, though not consistently so; men felt free to change their minds about which candidate to support as the mood took them. Arthur himself, of course, claimed that he was Richard's lawful heir in all Richard's lands, but as it was for John so it was for Arthur. The two had to compete to win the support of the key men in each of the lands over which they wished to rule.

In an odd twist of fate, the two rivals for Richard's inheritance were in each other's company when news of the death reached them: John was being entertained in Brittany by Arthur. Both saw Anjou as crucial, which explains why John, a keen reader of history who understood the lessons that it taught, made his first act to secure the Angevin treasury at Chinon. Arthur chose instead to head for the county capital of Angers where, on Easter Sunday, he had himself invested as count, claiming to enjoy the position "by right of inheritance."[8] Meanwhile, Arthur's mother, Constance of Brittany, along with William des Roches (now appointed Arthur's seneschal of Anjou and Maine), marched to Le Mans where they hoped to lay hands on John, which they failed to do. Probably at Tours (rather than Le Mans, as stated in some sources),[9] Arthur joined his mother, then swore fealty and did homage to the French king, Philip Augustus. He now had the resources of the French monarchy on his side, and it must have looked, at least to some, that John's hold on this central belt of his continental possessions was tenuous indeed.[10]

To counter that threat, a week later, on Sunday, April 25, John had himself invested as duke of Normandy. The ceremony was conducted by the archbishop of Rouen, who, having given John the sword of ducal office, then placed on the new duke's head a golden circlet decorated on top with roses worked in gold.[11] This was an act symbolic of the fact that the duke of Normandy enjoyed regalian powers over his duchy, and it was an attempt, albeit an unsuccessful one, to exclude French royal interference. As soon as he had heard of Richard's death, Philip Augustus had declared war on Normandy, and had already taken the city of Evreux in the Vexin.[12] Meanwhile, John's mother, Eleanor, in the company of

Mercadier, led an army from Poitou into Anjou to attempt to bring the Angevins to heel for her son. In England, at some point after Easter (Easter Sunday fell on April 18 in 1199), Hubert Walter and William Marshal declared the king's peace while John busied himself in Normandy securing his holdings in the duchy.[13] On May 21, John took ship for his new kingdom and, a few days later, on Ascension Day 1199, he was crowned king of England at Westminster.

THE CORONATION RITUAL THAT John underwent had its roots in the entrance rituals of the Catholic Church. The rite of baptism, the ordination of priests and bishops, the consecration of new churches, and the inauguration of kings and queens all had at their heart anointing with holy chrism (olive oil and balsam) by an (arch)bishop, which act signaled the moment when the person was bound in communion with the Christian fellowship.[14] Some kings did not receive unction with holy oil (the kings of the Scots, for example, were not anointed until 1329). But English kings were, from at least the tenth century, consecrated kings: they were most certainly anointed, and it was this that turned them from mere mortals into kings with a direct connection to God.[15] It was not the metal circlet placed on his head that made John king of England, it was being anointed by someone of sufficient standing in the Church. By 1199, that person, by the exclusive right of the Papal Bull *Quanto majorem* issued by Alexander III in 1171, was the archbishop of Canterbury.[16] The act of anointing gave English kingship a sacral nature, and thus gave English kings a special relationship not only with God but with the Church. It also brought added bonuses; for example, it had the benefit of making rebellion against the "Lord's anointed" an act of treason against God, and it was politically decisive in any succession dispute, since only one anointed king might be alive at any one time (the exception of 1170 proving the rule). But what the Church gave with one hand, it took back with another: a man who wished to become king of England must have the sanction of Holy Church. John now had that sanction.[17]

In England, the coronation ritual marked the birth of a new king,*[18] and it also marked the birth of his new government. Apart from the Exchequer (which kept its own accounting year of Michaelmas to Michaelmas, that is September 29 to September 28), the new king's reign marked the beginning of his government. His acts were dated by the regnal year, and the regnal year began on the anniversary of the coronation. Most kings were crowned on a Sunday—the most auspicious day in the weekly calendar—but Ascension Day always falls on a Thursday, though it, too, was seen as a fortunate day, since it marks the moment of the assumption of Christ into heaven. But from an administrative point of view it proved a problematic anniversary as, like Easter, which it follows by forty days, Ascension Day is a moveable feast, which meant that John's regnal years began and ended on different dates in the Julian calendar.† For John no one regnal year lasted exactly twelve months.‡

In the first charters of John's reign that survive to us, the dating clause is always made with reference to the year of his reign as king of England, even when that grant was to a Norman abbey, such as Bec, or to the burgesses of one of his Aquitainian townsmen, such as the men of Saint-Emilion.[19] No attempt was made to date documents by the ducal year or by the comital year. For John, it was his kingship that mattered. So although John did not rule, for example, Normandy as king—there he was duke and his overlord was the king of France—nonetheless, when he issued charters or letters to his men of Normandy, he always styled himself in exactly the same way: he was king of England, lord of Ireland, duke of Normandy and Aquitaine, count of Anjou; when he addressed his letters and charters generally, it was always to his archbishops, bishops, abbots,

---

* Which was no doubt celebrated, as, at Ely for example, the coronation of Richard was remembered in the holding of an eight-day festival each year.

† Except for his third and fourteenth regnal years, which both began on May 3 and ended on May 22 in the following year.

‡ Of John's predecessors, only William the Conqueror was crowned on another day of the week, and that was because he was crowned on an even more favorable date, Christmas Day, which in 1066 fell on a Monday.

counts, barons, justices, vicecounts (in England that meant sheriffs), provosts (or reeves), all his bailiffs and his faithful men.

Most importantly of all, in all John's territories the item that authenticated the document, the seal, was always the same seal. It was inscribed on the obverse with the legend "IOHANNES: DEI: GRATIA: REX: ANGLIE: DOMINVS: HIBERNIE +," with an image of the king in majesty, and on the reverse was inscribed "IOHS: DVX: NORMAN-NIE: ET AQUITANNIE: COMES ANDEGAVIE +," with an image of John as knight, sword drawn and seated on a warhorse. There was a unity in the expression of rule embedded in the documents that reflected the way in which John chose to project his image to the world he occupied. It did not seem to matter to him that there might have been different practices in the different regions he governed. He had his documents written as though he provided all the unity that the lands he ruled required.

This was the fiction that John wished to sustain (it was not a fiction he invented; his brother in particular had sought to inherit his father's lands as a whole) because he was faced with a difficult political dilemma in the form of the king of France and by that king's claim to be the overlord—and therefore the ultimate political authority—over all the land that we think of today as France. That meant that Philip claimed to have suzerainty over John's continental lands and could deal with John not as a king, and an equal, but as a lord would act toward his man. In 1199, the question was whether Philip could make John acknowledge him as his overlord. If successful, then Philip would have gained a tool with which he might be able to lever John out of his duchy of Normandy. And Philip had something with which he could force John to accept his overlordship: Arthur of Brittany.

The threat that Arthur posed to John was great indeed. In the minds of some, Arthur had a better claim than John to be Richard's successor, and that made John vulnerable.[20] John, aware that his hereditary claim to the lands of his brother was open to question, was keen to stress the legitimacy of his succession. In one of the first charters of his reign, John ascribed his new role as king as having been given to him by "divine mercy . . . with the consent and favour of both the clergy and people . . . which belongs to us by hereditary right."[21] John's statement was clear: the inheritance belonged to him by right no matter what Arthur might claim. And not just in England. John was by right of inheritance the ruler of Poitou[22] and Normandy, and, although Arthur explicitly claimed otherwise, ruler of Anjou.

The fact that the Angevins chose to be buried in the monastery at Fontevraud, in Anjou and bordering Aquitaine, speaks volumes for the significance of the county to the family. John could not afford to let Anjou slip from his grasp. While it was imperative that he secure Normandy, England and Aquitaine, it was equally imperative that, once they were firmly in his grasp, he made haste to Anjou to secure his father's ancestral lands.

Immediately after his coronation, John went to the shrine of St. Thomas at Canterbury. Thomas's martyrdom in 1170 had been a direct consequence of the actions of John's father, but since then, he had been brought within the Angevin fold to become a supporter of the Angevins and a saint with special powers to reconcile the family when at war (Arthur was family, after all). John then went into East Anglia, to visit the shrine of St. Edmund at Bury St. Edmunds. Then the patron saint of England, Edmund might have been expected to bring his considerable military prowess to John's aid. From Bury, John went to Northampton, the traditional meeting place between the kings of the English and their northern subjects, and then turned southward, to Shoreham, where he met a multitude of knights and foot soldiers, who had mustered there ready to cross to the continent to provide English military might for John's ambitions in Anjou. By midsummer, he was in Normandy, at Dieppe, from where he went to the ducal capital at Rouen to meet the troops who were coming to his side from the duchy. It was at this point that John got from Philip the peace that he needed in order to secure his continental inheritance. It was set to last until 17 August.[23]

For the next two months, John traversed Normandy, shoring up its defenses against possible incursion by the French king and making sure that the duchy's nobility stayed loyal to him. He made grants to religious establishments confirming their rights and he made concessions to burgesses confirming their liberties. The Templars were also recipients of John's considerable largesse (in stark contrast to his reported miserliness at Bury St. Edmunds, where he left only a few gold coins for the saint), and it may well be that John was trying to enlist their support to maintain the peace. They had been guarantors of peace settlements between the kings of the English and French throughout the 1190s, and it looks as though John was giving them every reason to be proponents of peace again.

The two kings met again on August 17, when it became clear to John exactly what the king of France wanted. According to Roger of Howden, Philip had already made Arthur a knight in a ceremony provocatively held the day before the meeting with John. By rights John should have performed the ceremony: Arthur was his nephew and Arthur was heir to lands over which John claimed suzerainty. By knighting Arthur himself, Philip had flown in the face of convention: it was a deliberate slight to John and a deliberate statement that Philip was throwing the weight of the French monarchy behind John's rival. And in case anyone was in any doubt about Philip's intentions, after the ceremony he took Arthur's homage for Anjou, Poitou, Maine, Touraine, Brittany and Normandy. It is hardly surprising, therefore, that the three-day meeting was not a success.*[24] Philip demanded on Arthur's behalf that John give up Poitou, Anjou, Maine and Touraine, and Philip further demanded—and this was the crux of the matter—that John give up to him the whole of the Vexin.

THE VEXIN LIES BETWEEN the rivers Oise and Andelle. It was a key territory for both the kings of the French and the dukes of the Normans because it divided the two centers of their power: the cities

---

* The meeting took place near Les Andelys, between Boutavant and Le Goulet, on the Seine. It was one of the traditional meeting places of the kings of France and the dukes of the Normans, and its location marked, for the purposes of the moment, the agreed border between the lands of the duke and the lands of the king.

of Paris and Rouen. These two cities were less than 80 miles apart and they were connected by the mighty river Seine down which the Normans' ancestors, the Vikings, had travelled in the ninth century to lay siege to Paris and on which, in the tenth century, they had carved out the territory that came to carry their name: the land of the Northmen: Normandy.[25] The border between the lands controlled by the French king and by the Norman duke cut the Vexin in two. Precisely where in the Vexin this border lay depended on the political circumstances of the moment, but in general it was held to be along the river Epte. Gisors was, therefore, a key city, where the kings of the French and the dukes of the Normans often met—at an elm tree just outside the city known as L'Ormeteau-Ferré, until Philip Augustus, in the most visible demonstration that negotiations between him and Henry II were at a permanent end, had it cut down.[26]

Not surprisingly, therefore, since the Northmen had first settled in the region, French kings had focused their attention on the Vexin. It was an area of crucial strategic importance, since it was the gateway to Paris (the city had been threatened by Norman forces in 1198, for example).[27] The dukes of the Normans likewise defended their interests in the area. Just as the Vexin was the gateway to Paris for them, so, too, was the Vexin the gateway to Rouen for the kings of France (Rouen had been besieged by Philip in 1193). During the 1140s, the Norman part of the Vexin had come under French control because of the Norman dynasty's disarray after the accession of King Stephen in 1135 as successor to Henry I. Henry's grandson, Henry II, expended extraordinary amounts of energy, both military and diplomatic, in reestablishing his control of the area in the 1150s and 1160s. A series of remarkable treaties survive for the period, each of which has at its heart the Vexin and each of which allows us to see the thought that lay behind the diplomatic maneuverings that also saw, from time to time, direct war between the two rulers.

The first of those treaties concerned the union of the dynasties in the marriage of each other's eldest children: Henry's son and heir, also named Henry, would be joined in matrimony with Louis' eldest daughter,

Margaret. Flying in the face of canon law and most people's notions of decency, the two were married in 1160: he was aged five; she was two. According to the terms of the agreement that Henry and Louis had made, as soon as the two had been joined in matrimony with "the assent and consent of Holy Church," Henry was entitled to take control of the castles of the Vexin from the Templars, into whose hands they had been given for safe custody. The agreement had been made in the spring of 1160, and although there had been a leisurely three years allowed for the fulfilment of its terms, Henry moved as rapidly as he could to secure the marriage, and therefore to secure the castles of the Vexin, which were of vital strategic importance. The two were married on November 2, 1160. Within days, Henry II was demanding the execution of the terms of the marriage agreement.[28]

The issue of the Vexin, however, would not go away. By 1167, Henry and Louis were again at war, and the following year it was proposed that Richard, Henry's second son, should marry Alice, Margaret's younger sister. In return for the agreement to marry Alice (who came, most unusually, without a dowry), King Louis recognized Richard's claim to be duke of Aquitaine and count of Poitou, titles with which the young Richard was invested in May 1169. The failure of Richard to take Alice as his wife, despite their betrothal, led to further conflict over the Vexin between Henry II and Louis VII, in which Henry demanded that Louis hand over the French Vexin between Gisors and Pontoise in return for the consummation of the marriage: King Louis refused.

The death of the Young King in 1183 brought the Vexin once again into focus, and the new French king, Philip Augustus, demanded that Margaret's dowry, the Norman Vexin, should be returned with his sister. In 1186, the Norman Vexin was the focus of an agreement whereby Margaret, shortly before her marriage to the king of Hungary, gave up her interest in the territory to Henry and his sons in return for an annual payment of 2,750 Angevin pounds (equivalent, according to the agreement, to about £690 sterling per annum). The terms made it clear that should the annual amount not be paid, then Margaret would resume her claim in the Vexin and her brother, Philip, would be at liberty to attempt to enforce the terms of the contract. In March 1191, while the two kings were at Messina awaiting the arrival of Richard's intended bride, Berengaria, the Vexin was once more the focus of negotiations, with Philip giving up his rights in Gisors and Neaufle, two key citadels that sat on the border between the Norman and French Vexin, the Norman Vexin itself and Drincourt (originally named Neufchâtel-en-Bray), allowing Richard to repudiate his sister, Alice, all in return for 10,000 silver marks. The young woman was to be released from Richard's charge within one month of his return from crusade. It would not have been unreasonable if Alice had thought that her brother had sold her short.

Despite this agreement, as soon as he had returned from the Holy Land and while Richard was still pursuing the objectives of the crusade, in January 1192, King Philip demanded the return of Alice, at that time residing in the tower of Rouen castle, along with the castle of Gisors and the counties of Eu and Aumale. The seneschal of Normandy refused to acquiesce to Philip's demands. The following year, once Richard was held in captivity by the emperor, Henry VI, Philip launched himself against the walls of Gisors, which was surrendered to him, and he took the counties of Aumale and Eu, though Alice had to languish in Richard's hands until her eventual release in 1195.

The Treaty of Louviers, drawn up between January 9–13, 1196, also had Gisors, Neaufles and the Vexin at its heart. It is a treaty that shows the extent of Richard's losses at Philip's hands since, by tradition, the kings of France and the dukes of Normandy met on the border between their two lands. Louviers was almost 20 miles further into Norman territory from the traditional border between the two on the River Epte. While the diplomatic campaign was taken to the papal curia in 1198, the military campaign in 1197 and 1198 very much went Richard's way, and by the time of the Lionheart's death in April 1199, King Philip was struggling to hold onto his gains in the area. Even so, much of the Norman Vexin remained resolutely in Philip's hands. At their last meeting in January 1199, Richard stood in a boat on the river Seine between Les Andelys and Vernon while Philip sat on a horse on the bank.[29] Richard was still a long way from having regained all the lost lands of the Norman Vexin.

Richard had concerns in the south in Anjou and Aquitaine and on Normandy's other borders. The king of France had one: his border with Normandy, in other words the Vexin. While we cannot see into Philip's mind, his actions, and the fact that every treaty he made with Richard had the Vexin at its core, make it clear that the French king's consistent policy was to put pressure on what he evidently saw as a key territory. Indeed, as we now know, Philip's policy toward the Vexin went further than putting it at the heart of his treaties with Richard.[30] Philip, as king of France, was Duke Richard's overlord, and as such he offered an alternative source of power to which men could turn when they came into conflict with their duke. And this is exactly what Philip did. Whenever the opportunity arose for him to undermine Richard's ducal authority, he took it.

The border between the lands of the French king and those of the Norman duke could easily be set out in a treaty, but the greater and lesser aristocracy that inhabited the region bestrode those boundaries with their landholding and their political, social and economic alliances. The river Seine, for example, might be marcher territory as far as the king and duke were concerned, but for others it was a major economic highway between Paris, the Norman capital at Rouen and the open sea, exiting into the English Channel at Honfleur. And while Henry II and Richard appeared to have tried to maintain a tight control over the relations between those living directly under their rule, they could not stop them marrying their French neighbors or witnessing their neighbors' grants and acting as surety for one another's transactions. There was only so much authority even the most formidable of rulers could exercise. The ruler who ignored these powerful regional families was destined for trouble and the ruler who cultivated them could make great difficulties for his rival. It becomes apparent from a detailed examination of the families that wielded power in the region that, very often, the interests of these castellan families did not always ally with the interests of the dukes of Normandy.

The political dynamics of the Vexin meant that in the century and a half between 1066 and 1204 the region proved to be the lynchpin of west European politics. It was here that the Angevin continental lands would be lost. It is a testimony to Henry II that he recognized the importance of the region to the wider stability of his lands (a fact recognized by John, too). The Vexin was the focus of much of his diplomatic and military activity, and securing it was a constant thread in his life. Royal government was itinerant, with the king constantly on the move, which has enabled historians to argue that the Angevin kings, when they had a choice, spent the majority of their time within the confines of Normandy.[31] But it was a much more specific location than "Normandy" that attracted their attention. Between 1199 and 1202 (when the records allow us to see an almost daily itinerary), John spent most of his time in the Seine valley between the ducal capital of Rouen and the border of the Vexin at Les Andelys.[32] We do not have such a specific itinerary for Richard because the sources for his reign are not so detailed, but since the built landscape of this region was largely of Richard's creation in the wake of his return from captivity in 1194, we can be pretty certain that he, too, spent a great deal of time shoring up the defenses of the Vexin. And when we begin to unpick the itinerary of their father, Henry II, from 1180, when Philip Augustus came to the French throne, until his death in 1189, we can again see the focus of his activities placed firmly in the same region. In the year 1188, for example, Henry II spent five of the six months he was on the continent in the Vexin, as Philip Augustus pressed this particular border between his lands and those of the ageing Henry.[33]

In the 1180s and 1190s, King Philip was intent on redefining the political map of northern France. His acquisition of the city and county of Amiens along with some sixty-five castles from the Count of Flanders by the Treaty of Boves in July 1185 and his annexation of Artois in 1191 were crucial in establishing French royal control north of the Vexin and on the eastern border of Normandy. Then in 1195, shortly after he had regained control of her, King Philip gave his sister, Alice, in marriage to William, count of Ponthieu, who held the territories to the north of the Vexin and whose lands sat between those of the duke of Normandy and the count of Flanders.³⁴ There is no doubt at all that this was part of a wider plan to impose direct French rule over the lands of the duke of Normandy. Philip attempted to seize key positions by force when the opportunity arose. In 1193, for example, he arrived at the very gates of the city of Rouen with his soldiers and his siege engines, though he failed to take it; the following year, however, he did take Evreux. He was also willing to capture castles by subterfuge. Also in 1193, Philip took Gisors, aided by the "treachery" of Gilbert de Vascœuil. And in his diplomatic activities, too, Philip demonstrated his desire to rule parts of Normandy directly.³⁵ The January 1194 agreement by which John ceded Normandy east of the Seine all the way to the ocean with the exception of Rouen itself and its immediate environs makes this all too clear.³⁶

This, then, was the political reality that met John in 1199 as he made his bid to succeed to Richard's lands in France. Philip's policy toward the Vexin was the same whether Richard, John or Arthur ruled Normandy. Since Arthur was deep in Philip Augustus's debt, his succession to Richard's lands would play right into the hands of the French king. If Philip had to settle for John as duke of Normandy, he could still employ Arthur as leverage. Hence, Philip's demand on August 17, 1199, that John give up to him the whole of the Vexin. For the moment, John had to refuse, but how long he could hold out against the demands of Philip would depend on how well he managed to marshal his supporters.

THE GRANTING OF COMMUNE status to key cities was one of the ways in which John now mustered support within his realm. In the twelfth and thirteenth centuries, the acquisition of commune status was something to which the rulers of urban communities all aspired. The right to become a commune gave cities independence from external control and granted economically and governmentally beneficial rights to the burgesses or citizens. The urban elites took collective oaths by which they agreed to hold city property in common and to administer it for the benefit of all in the community. They organized their own militias to provide for their defense and they entered into alliances with other rulers and communities to further their ambitions. Rulers wishing to press their own advantage within towns and cities might see this independence as a threat, but on the whole, especially when a ruler held a territory that had within it many urban communities, it became advantageous to him to allow those towns and cities to become communes.[37]

In Normandy and in Poitou, John was quick to woo his town-dwellers by granting them commune status.[38] On July 8, for example, John gave the burgesses of La Rochelle the right to form a commune.[39] The same day, he also gave the same right to the men of Saint-Emilion and, a week later, the burgesses of Saint-Jean-d'Angély.[40] On July 25, John granted to the burgesses of the Atlantic island of Oléron (west of Rochefort) a similar right, confirming a grant made by his mother a few weeks earlier.[41] These communes were to play a vital part in the military organization of John's continental lands, and because the granting of rights was widespread in areas where John felt threatened, they were created in Normandy as well as in Poitou and Gascony.[42]

Throughout the summer and autumn of 1199 each side tried to win the support of neighboring princes. The first step in John's campaign was to enlist Philip, count of Flanders. In mid-August, John had received the count at the ducal capital of Rouen and taken from him his homage and the promise of soldiers to serve in John's cause when he had need, quite possibly in return for an annual payment. There had been similar agreements between the kings of England and counts of Flanders going back to the very first treaty to survive in English royal records, made in 1101. In that treaty, the then count had promised the king of England that he would support the king with a thousand knights, and if the king of France, the count's liege lord, wished to invade England, the count was to do his best to dissuade the king; if he could not dissuade him, then he would serve the king of France with the minimum number of troops. The treaty went on to stipulate that the count would provide the same number of knights in Normandy at the king of England's summons and on the same terms. Later treaties reduced the number of knights to 500, but this still represented a significant force in the English king's army.[43]

That August, too, John received the homage of Richard's adherents in France and the promise of support from his nephew, Otto of Brunswick, one of the contenders for the German throne; but things did not all go the new king's way. Philip Augustus was also building alliances,[44] and by direct action, he took a series of castles, including Conches and Ballon, and was openly making war on John. At Lavardin, where Philip had mustered his siege engines to take the town, John's forces caught up with Philip and chased him into Le Mans where, instead of making a stand, Philip undertook a tactical retreat. It was at this point, as John seemed to be gaining the upper hand, that Arthur's key supporter in Anjou, William des Roches, decided to change sides. Our contemporary witness to these events, Roger of Howden, says, intriguingly, that "by means of extreme cunning, William recovered Arthur from the hands of the king of France" and brought him to John in order to make peace between them. A day later, suspecting that John intended to place him in custody, Arthur, in the company of his mother, fled Le Mans for Angers in the dead of night.[45]

W ITH ARTHUR DISCOMFITED, JOHN could begin to think about the business of acquiring a new wife who not only befitted his elevated status, but would also help him to secure his southern territories. That bride was to be Isabella, heiress to the county of Angoulême. We cannot with certainty say when first John conceived the plan to marry Isabella, but that he had in mind to marry someone is clear, since as soon as he could after his coronation, he took steps to have his marriage to Isabella of Gloucester annulled. Her complete unimportance as a figure at court is reflected in the fact that even our most well-informed source for court politics, Roger of Howden, could not remember her name.*[46] The estrangement between John and Isabella can be traced back to around

---

* He called her Hawise, which was the name of her mother.

1196, but it was not until he was king that John had the political weight
to fulfil his wish.[47] John's determination to set aside the Gloucester heiress was perhaps because of their lack of children, though since John's
brother, Richard, had seemed unconcerned to provide an heir of his body
by his wife, Berengaria, we should not simply leap to that conclusion. All
the children of Henry II and Eleanor of Aquitaine had made marriages
into families of international standing, except John.[*48] He may have felt
that disparagement now that it came time for him to be king.

There was some suggestion in January 1200 that John might make an
alliance with the king of Portugal by marrying his daughter. The proposal came from the Portuguese king and John seems to have taken it
seriously, since he sent a return mission, led by the bishop of Lisieux, in
early February. But something happened to change John's mind, since by
April 28, and perhaps as early as late February 1200, John had decided to
marry Isabella of Angoulême.

Kings, like other mortals, had sexual needs, and John seems to have
had them in as great a quantity as had his father. He certainly sired a
number of illegitimate children, possibly as many as eight, and he was
notoriously predatory when around the wives and daughters of his barons. He took mistresses until the end of his life, though, for the most
part, these were unnamed women whose status, and therefore the status
of the resultant children, was not high. Two—of the dozen or so we
can identify—stand out: the first, the sister of Earl William de Warenne,
gave John a son, Richard of Dover and Chilham; the second, a certain
Clemency, is said to have been the mother of John's illegitimate daughter,
Joan, whom he married to Llywelyn ap Iorwerth, prince of North Wales,
in about 1205.[49]

---

* The daughters all married well: Matilda married Henry the Lion, duke of Saxony;
Eleanor married Alfonso VIII of Castile; Joanna married first William, king of Sicily, and
second Raymond, count of Toulouse; of the sons, Henry the young king married Margaret, daughter of the king of France; Richard was betrothed to Alice, Margaret's sister,
though the marriage was never solemnized, and later Berengaria of Navarre, though she
was Richard's own choice; Geoffrey married Constance, duchess of Brittany.

By John's time, only legitimate children could inherit from the father's patrimony. Kings could therefore afford to father numerous illegitimate children without raising the prospect that they might produce rival claimants to the throne. The production of these illegitimate children has given many modern historians—many still languishing under the delusion that our hang-ups about sex are the same as those held by our medieval ancestors—the opportunity to heap opprobrium on the heads of monarchs who bedded women other than their wives. And yet although the Church officially frowned on kings taking lovers, it is a well-known fact that they did, and that whatever sermons bishops preached from the pulpit about sexual continence,[50] most medieval kings felt free to enjoy many sexual partners. John was no different in this regard.

Whatever his personal feelings, to a twelfth-century king the official act of taking a high-status woman to his bed was a political gesture, and when he decided to marry, the political forces that made him marry were paramount.*[51] But the act of taking one woman above all others mattered, not only because of the political connections it brought, but also because of the potential for children who might legitimately inherit from their parents. Between 1207 (when Isabella was nineteen) and 1215, John and Isabella had five children, two boys and three girls.[52] Evidently the two were compatible in the business of producing legitimate heirs, whatever John chose to do when he was away from his queen. Whether they enjoyed the sex act or not was immaterial; what mattered was that they had children.

John chose to marry Isabella for political reasons, and those reasons had much to do with the trouble he was having in securing his hold over his inheritance and the problems he was encountering in the heartlands of his Angevin realm. The city of Angoulême was perched on a rocky spur overlooking the River Charente, which exited into the Atlantic at the port of La Rochelle, crucial for John's control of Poitou. Angoulême

---

* As Isabella of Angoulême wrote in a letter to her son, Henry III, in 1220 in which she informed him that she had married the count of La Marche, "as God knows we did this more for your advantage than for ours."

itself was a nodal point for many roads, and as such was of great tactical importance. Bringing the count of Angoulême on his side by marrying his daughter and only surviving child, and, therefore, his heir, made
good strategic sense for John, and since she came with a dowry, he stood
to gain territorially before his father-in-law died, too.[53]

   A marriage between Isabella and John also made good sense for
Count Audemar, Isabella's father. Marriage agreements were not one-
way arrangements; both sides needed to benefit from the contract. As
far as Count Audemar was concerned, Isabella's marriage to John had
very attractive political advantages. The count had been trying to press
his claim to the county of La Marche for some time. In April 1199, he
had made an agreement with Philip Augustus that he would seek justice
in the king's court concerning his claim to the county.[54] But Philip was
unable to make good on his promise because that very month, on the an-
nouncement of Richard's death, Hugh le Brun of Lusignan took the most
of the opportunity and seized the county of La Marche for himself.[55] In
1199, therefore, the only option available to Count Audemar, if he were
to press his family's claim to La Marche, was a marriage alliance between
his daughter Isabella and the newly recognized Count Hugh. This, indeed, is the option he pursued, and Hugh was happy to oblige.*

   The political landscape of this part of France was in flux, however.
Arthur claimed to be count of Anjou by right of inheritance and no doubt
saw himself by that same right as the lord of the count of La Marche. John,
too, had direct interests in the area, obviously, and, to add an extra layer
of complexity, Philip Augustus was attempting to assert his authority
here as well. Whether or not Count Audemar was content to hand over
his heir and daughter to Hugh le Brun is a moot point, but he certainly

---

   * Hugh was probably born in the late 1150s (he became lord of Lusignan in 1173), and
he sired a son, also named Hugh, in 1188. He was likely more than forty when he contracted his marriage to the eleven-year-old Isabella and he was therefore an exact contemporary of Isabella's father. It is an oddity that Hugh did not arrange the marriage between
Isabella and his son (who, indeed, in a bizarre twist of fate, Isabella was to marry in 1220),
but evidently he wanted the girl for himself, so in 1199, he betrothed himself to her.

seemed happy to renege on the agreement when it was suggested that his daughter should marry King John.

Significantly, a union between Arthur and Isabella seems never to have been proposed, which probably means that this area of the Angevin territories was thoroughly behind John. This is certainly the implication of a treaty made between John and Hugh le Brun and his brother, Ralph, count of Eu (in the duchy of Normandy). On January 28, 1200, John took oaths of fealty from them both and received their liege homage. For the purposes of contemporary political thought, therefore, these two men had agreed that their primary loyalty was to John above all other men or women and, as the agreement stated, they were to aid John "with the whole of our power against everyone and also against those of our own people."[56] At the end of January 1200, therefore, Hugh was John's ally. Perhaps he had yet to comprehend that John intended to take his hoped-for bride from him; or perhaps, as H. G. Richardson suggested, Hugh le Brun was willing to let Isabella slip from his grasp since he had what he wanted: John's recognition of his rights, newly won, in La Marche.[57] But like any thirteenth-century lord, he reserved the right to change his mind; which, in two years' time, he would.

Within weeks of his treaty with Hugh le Brun, John had determined to marry Isabella of Angoulême. She was twelve years old, so she was not in a position, yet, to provide him with heirs, but she could help John forge an alliance with her father, ensuring that a crucial area in the Angevin lands was firmly under his sway. John could now begin to think about other areas in the Angevin lands that needed bolstering, and focus on the obvious threat to his hold on Normandy from Philip Augustus and the problem that Arthur's continued freedom posed to his unchallenged rulership. With this in mind, John began to move toward making a treaty with King Philip, during which negotiations his betrothal to Isabella had to remain a secret, for reasons that are unclear but may have had something to do with the need to keep Philip from interfering with his plans.

In the context of the immediate politics of April–May 1200, the arrangements made in the treaty between John and Philip Augustus on

May 22 looked sound. John had secured the southern border to his ancestral homeland of Anjou, he had secured his position in Poitou amongst
the families of La Marche and of Angoulême, and now he sought to secure Normandy. To do so, he needed peace with Philip and, above all,
he needed Philip to abandon Arthur's cause. John and Philip met on the
border between Normandy and France at a place called Le Goulet. This
was a point still some way short of the advantageous position Richard
had enjoyed before the incursions of King Philip in 1193, but better a
peace by which John could hold on to what he had than a war that might
lose him yet more land.

The terms of the treaty began by endorsing the final agreement made
between Richard and Philip in 1196 and then went on to affirm the fact
that John was his brother's rightful heir.[58] This was an important concession, since it meant that Philip had indeed now abandoned Arthur. The
next clause defined the boundary of Normandy and the Île de France,
which was to lie in the middle of the road between the cities of Le Neubourg and Evreux. There were to be some exchanges of land (including
the county of Evreux itself, for which John promised Count Amaury sat-
isfactory compensation) to tidy up the border between the two powers*[59];
the bishopric of Evreux was divided; there was to be a complete ban on

---

* The quitclaim survives as an original, with a green wax, with ties of red silk, with
the seal of Amaury of Gloucester, count of Evreux (*sigillum Amarici comitis Ebroicensis*), in
which the count states that he has been sufficiently compensated by "*dominus meus rex Anglie mihi sufficiens escambium inde donavit,*" so therefore he is prepared to make the exchange.
The quitclaim is attested by Hubert, archbishop of Canterbury; Elias, archbishop of Bordeaux; John, archbishop of Dublin; Lambert, bishop of Meaux; Philip, bishop of Beauvais;
Herbert, bishop of Lincoln; Eustace, bishop of Ely; Hugh, bishop of Salisbury; Baldwin,
count of Flanders; Theobald, count of Champagne; Louis, count of Blois; Robert, count
of Dreux; William Marshal, earl of Pembroke; Bertrand de Royans; Made at Le Goulet,
1200, the month of May (*Layettes du Trésor des Chartes*, i, no. 588). A second copy survives
as an annex to the above letter; the wax is green, sealed sur double queue, with Amaury's
seal, which does not have the legend count of Evreux. The text expresses the count's satisfaction at the amount of the exchange and confirms his willingness to quitclaim the title
to Philip. This text is attested by William, bishop of London; Herbert of Salisbury; John,
bishop of Norwich; Geoffrey fitz Peter, earl of Essex; Robert, earl of Leicester; Ralph,
count of Clermont; Robert, count of Meulan; Robert of Thornham and others.

building new fortifications in the region; and the fortifications at Portes and Landes were to be destroyed. The issues surrounding the Vexin were solved, for the moment, in Philip's favor. John got his peace, but he had to pay for it.

On the positive side, John's claims to Anjou and Poitou were recognized, as was his overlordship of Brittany, and, importantly, Arthur was to hold the duchy as John's man and be answerable to John in John's court. Philip had cut Arthur adrift. It was as comprehensive an abandonment as John could have hoped. In return, John promised to refuse aid to his other nephew, Otto of Brunswick, who was struggling with Philip of Swabia for control of the empire.*[60] John acknowledged that the counts of Flanders and Boulogne owed homage to King Philip. This in effect took them out of the alliance that Richard had been building against Philip before he died. By these agreements, John admitted Philip's claim that, as king of France, his suzerainty extended into all his continental lands. But in doing so, he had done no more than Richard had done in December 1195 when he took off his sword and swore homage to Philip for Normandy, Anjou and Poitou. John could have argued that he at least had Philip's agreement that he was also overlord of Brittany.[61]

That the terms of the treaty had been some time in the planning is witnessed by the marriage agreement that was to cement it. Philip's first-born son, Louis, was to marry Blanche, John's niece by his sister Eleanor of Castile, and we know of this because by April 9, Eleanor of Aquitaine was in Castile to collect her granddaughter. She cannot have set out for Spain much after the beginning of February. While a rider on a fast horse could travel quickly, the aged queen and her entourage were hardly in a position to rush. It makes it likely, therefore, that the terms of the marriage agreement were first broached when John and Philip met in January 1200 and talked at length "like old friends." The marriage between Louis and Blanche completed, John handed over to Philip the

---

* Pope Innocent III wrote to John to tell him that he could not withdraw his support from Otto, as he owed his nephew the duties of support concomitant with his role as the young man's uncle.

agreed dowry, which comprised the lands of John's kinsman, Andrew de Chauvigny, who was compelled by John to give his allegiance to Philip.* As part of the treaty, John and Philip agreed to decide what would happen to the dowry lands should Blanche and Louis fail to produce any legitimate heirs. It was at this point that John revealed his own intention to marry, since he conceded to Philip that should he fail to produce any heirs, Philip would succeed to the fees of Hugh de Gournay, the count of Aumale and the count of Perche. He further promised Philip a payment of 20,000 marks (£13,333 13s 4d) as his relief for his inheritance and also for the concession of Brittany.†

For John, Le Goulet must have been a triumph: a year and a month after Richard had died, he had finally and irrevocably secured the recognition of his overlord, the king of France, for his succession to Richard's continental lands. The treaty was concluded on May 22, 1200,[62] with the nuptials of the twelve-year-old Louis and the eleven-year-old Blanche celebrated by the archbishop of Bordeaux at Ponte Audemar the following day, the same day that John received Arthur's homage for Brittany, no doubt sulkily given, but given nonetheless. The following Sunday, May 28, which was Whit Sunday, in the same chapel where Philip and his French barons had gathered to witness the marriage ceremony of Louis

---

* The mandate from John to Andrew survives in an inspeximus of Philip of Valois, February 10, 1338, "John, by the grace of God king of England, lord of Ireland, duke of Normandy, Aquitaine, count of Anjou, to our beloved Andrew de *Calvinaico* greeting. Know that, by the peace made between the lord Philip the illustrious king of France and us, the fee of *Bituresii* shall remain to the lord king of France, just as is contained in our charter which the same king of France has from us; whereof we mandate you that you make homage and fidelity to the aforesaid king of France [for it]. Teste William Marshal earl of Pembroke, at Roche Andely, 23 May [1200]" (*Layettes du Trésor des Chartes*, i, no. 579). In October 1199 (*Layettes du Trésor des Chartes*, i, no. 504) Andrew had, at the instigation of King Philip, agreed to hold his fee in Anjou of Arthur or his heir in Anjou and that, within forty days after he is made to know it, he will neither make nor permit malice by him or by his men. Made at *Aneti*.

† Numismatists work on an approximate value of 1 silver penny equalling, in modern terms, about £20. There are approximately 3.2 million silver pennies in 20,000 marks, making the payment, in today's values, about £64 million.

and Blanche, John gave thanks to God by having himself acclaimed with the coronation anthem *Christus Vincit*.[63] He must have been euphoric; he had ended his first regnal year victorious and could still look forward to a marriage to an heiress that would surely cap his triumph. As an act of piety, he established a perpetual chantry at Argentan for divine service to be sung daily for his salvation and for the souls of his father, ancestors and successors. The enormous sum of 2 Angevin shillings a day was set aside from the Exchequer of Normandy to fund the chantry.[64]

As soon as matters were thus settled, John headed south where, according to the terms of the treaty, he was to receive as his men the counts of Angoulême and Limoges "so that we may grant to them their rights." While in the south, John took the chance to meet Raymond of St. Gilles, count of Toulouse, who had been married to John's recently deceased sister, Joanna. Before her death in 1199, the couple had become estranged, though Joanna had given Raymond a son, whom the couple named after the father. The essence of the treaty was that Raymond was to do homage to John as count of Poitou for the lands he had received on his marriage to Joanna. These lands, once the younger Raymond had come of age, were to pass to the boy.[65]

John then turned northward to collect his bride. The Poitevin chronicler Bernard Itier thought that Isabella's father had to prize his daughter from Hugh le Brun's grasp "by force." Perhaps John's presence in the region added military might to Count Audemar's determination to have his daughter sprung from Hugh's clutches, but whatever the case, it is clear that by the summer of 1200, the political situation in the region was radically changed. Count Audemar was definitely John's ally while Hugh le Brun had moved into the opposition camp.

The marriage ceremony between John and Isabella took place on St. Bartholomew's Day, August 24, 1200, in the cathedral of Saint-Pierre in the city of Angoulême.[66] The archbishop of Bordeaux acted as the principal celebrant, thus emphasizing the southern focus of the marriage. Four of the other five bishops celebrating the marriage were likewise southern men: Saintes, Périgueux, Angoulême and Limoges, each the neighboring diocese to the other. There was just one northern bishop in attendance, a prelate from John's Irish kingdom: Robert, bishop of Waterford.

From Angoulême, John and Isabella went directly (though at a leisurely pace, the 350 miles taking over a month) to Barfleur to take a ship for England, not even stopping off at the Norman ducal capital, Rouen. John wanted Isabella to be received into her kingdom as soon as possible. The couple landed at Portsmouth and made directly for Westminster, where they were crowned together (Isabella receiving unction with holy oil) on Sunday October 8.*[67] John described the ceremony as his "second coronation," and after it he paid Isabella's father an unknown sum of money according to the terms of a "secret agreement" made as part of the marriage contract.[68]

T O JOHN, BOTH THE Treaty of Le Goulet and his marriage to Isabella were triumphs. In the autumn of 1200, settling into his second marriage and looking to the future, he thought that the auguries were good. The fact that not everyone agreed with him was of no concern. There are always those who are quick to criticize, and it was the hoi polloi visiting the shrine of Thomas Becket who now called John "softsword," because they thought he had conceded too much to King Philip.[69] But that was just tittle-tattle and could be dismissed as such. Their views on his marriage were equally unimportant. By his timely treaty with Philip and by his strategic marriage to Isabella, John had secured peace in his lands and his own place as the unchallenged ruler of them. Philip had been persuaded to abandon Arthur's cause, and John now had a powerful new ally in Poitou in the form of Count Audemar.

When John arrived in England, he continued in triumphal vein by forcing William, king of the Scots to come to Lincoln for a conference.

---

* John was not anointed again because anointing was seen as being like a sacrament that could be received but once: "Give from our treasure 25 shillings to Eustace the chaplain and Ambrose, our clerks, who sang the Christus Vincit at our second coronation and at the unction and coronation of Queen Isabella our wife."

The occasion was the funeral of Bishop Hugh of Lincoln, widely re-garded as a saint even in his own lifetime, at which he was to be interred on November 23. Funerals have always provided excuses for summits, and this summit, between the king of England and the king of the Scots, not only celebrated the life of Bishop Hugh (both kings played their part in the ceremony, with John carrying the bier on his shoulder from a mile outside Lincoln to the gates of the city),[70] but also established John's dominance over his neighboring king. On a hill outside the city, in front of a huge crowd and in the sight of all, King William paid homage to King John and swore fealty to him.[71] The physical act of freely handing oneself over to another man was a bold demonstration of who was in command: at Christmas 1200, it was John, both in the British Isles and in his continental lands. When John and his newly consecrated queen celebrated Christmas at Guildford and New Year at Woodstock, they must both have been feeling confident about the approach of 1201 and a long and glorious reign.

6

RETREAT TO THE CITADEL

W HEN A MAN TOOK a wife, he assigned to her dower lands to provide for her in the event of his death. She had no control over them during her husband's lifetime, but he was equally bound to leave them in good order so that his widow might be properly supported. In a charter issued on August 30, 1200, given at Chinon and in the presence of the archbishop and bishops who had officiated at their wedding, John gave Isabella the cities of Saintes and Niort in Poitou and Saumur, La Flèche, Beaufort-en-Vallée, Baugé and Château-du-Loir in Anjou.[1] These all lay close to her homeland in Angoulême and may well have been chosen so that she might return there when John died. No one, in August 1200, would have predicted that John would lose these lands; quite the contrary. The lands controlled by the Angevins had waxed and waned with the family's fortunes, but the heartlands had been under their control since the millennium, when John's ancestor Fulk Nerra had made dramatic territorial gains; there was no reason to suppose, therefore, that these lands might be susceptible to permanent loss.[2]

At the beginning of 1201, John's confidence in the future was high, and to reflect that fact, he organized yet another coronation service for himself and his queen at Canterbury, on the most auspicious day of the year, Easter Sunday itself. According to a monk of Canterbury who may, therefore, have been an eyewitness to the ritual, John and Isabella were crowned with great pomp by Archbishop Hubert Walter.[3] John liked his pomp and circumstance, often organizing ceremonial crown-wearings to satisfy his need to be acclaimed by his subjects, and we must imagine that the *Laudes Regiae* were sung again at this service as they had been at Westminster the previous October. The gathering storm of rebellion on the continent impinged on the ceremony only in as much as by Easter John must have been making plans to deal with Hugh le Brun, the man whose former fiancée John now enjoyed. For most modern writers, who in this are following near contemporary commentators, this rebellion is seen as crucial to John's downfall. The continuator of Ralph de Diceto's *Ymagines Historiarum*, for example, stated outright that John's marriage created the situation "whereby the greatest feud broke out between them."[4] And Abbot Ralph of Coggeshall, writing in around 1207, after Normandy had been lost, likewise sought to pin the blame for the king's troubles on his marriage to Isabella and the consequent fallout with Hugh le Brun.[5]

But all this is in retrospect and reads too much into Hugh's rebellion. It was not Hugh who caused John the most difficulty, it was Philip Augustus, king of France, and although Hugh played his part in the fall of John's continental lands, it was Philip Augustus who masterminded it. If Hugh had not given Philip one of the means by which he forced John to retreat to England, then someone else would have. It was Philip Augustus who brought down John because he recognized that in order to provide security for himself and his dynasty, he had to control Normandy and in particular the route down the Seine from Paris to the English Channel. One comparative example to emphasize the centrality of Normandy to Philip's ambitions is instructive. When in the fifteenth century Normandy once again fell under English control, the French monarchy moved its capital from Paris and the river Seine to the Loire Valley. Nothing else illustrates quite so clearly the centrality of the Seine to the security and prosperity of Paris. This was why Philip's policy had been consistently focused on control of the Vexin: he was determined to wrest Normandy from the control of the Angevins, and this brings us back not to the marriage of John and Isabella of Angoulême and the subsequent feud with Hugh le Brun, but to the Norman Vexin and to the Treaty of Le Goulet. Those who criticized John for conceding its terms were right in one very important regard: when he conceded that he held the Vexin from Philip he conceded too much. Hugh le Brun's rebellion gave Philip the key that would unlock John's hold on Normandy.

John must have received an indication that the rebellion was in progress before Easter (Easter Sunday fell on March 25), since on March 6 he issued orders allowing Hugh of Balliol and Thomas of St. Valéry to make war on Hugh's brother, Ralph, count of Eu, and on March 8, he issued further letters to seize Hugh's county of La Marche.[6] Shortly after the Easter festivities, John ordered his nobles to muster at Portsmouth at Whitsun, there to board ships bound for the continent: he was going to deal with the matter in person. John seems to have had a policy of permanently settling military retainers (known as bachelors) on lands in Normandy, Poitou and Gascony, and on March 29, he wrote to the seneschals to make sure that those bachelors had sworn their oaths and were ready to provide military service as required.[7] Not all of John's barons were happy to serve abroad: many had had enough of the constant burden of overseas war inflicted on them since 1193, and were suffering from exhaustion after what one contemporary called a period of "seven years of famine" caused by the relentless warfare that had only recently been brought to an end by the Treaty of Le Goulet.[8] This was the first indication that John might run into difficulties in England if he wanted to finance a continental war. Nonetheless, the army gathered at Portsmouth around May 13, whereupon John permitted some to make a payment allowing them to return home while retaining the others.[9] There was another ceremonial crown-wearing at his court during which the *Laudes Regiae* were sung,[10] and that evening, the king and queen, travelling in separate ships, along with the army that John had retained in his service, left for Normandy. Isabella arrived the following day, the 14th, though John's arrival was delayed by some unknown cause.[11]

The second hint that John might run into difficulty on the continent was communicated to him by his mother. From her sickbed in Fontevraud Abbey, Eleanor of Aquitaine had been masterminding John's affairs in the south. She called a colloquium at Fontevraud with Viscount Aimery of Thouars and there steeled the viscount in his support of John's rule. She

persuaded Aimery to write to John protesting his loyalty and assuring
the king that he had his support, which the viscount did. Eleanor urged
her son to go to "the Norman areas" and there be received by Viscount
Aimery. Alternatively, she suggested that John might invite Aimery to
visit him in England. It seems likely that John took his mother's warning
seriously, since he gave Aimery letters of safe conduct, dated April 4,
for him to come to England. At the same time, John called to his side his
father-in-law, Count Audemar, and his seneschal of Anjou, William des
Roches, and his seneschal of Poitou, Ralph de Mauléon, though there is
no evidence that they came to John in England.[12] By mid-May, however,
he, his wife and his troops (including a large contingent of crossbowmen
and Master Urric the siege engineer), accompanied by eighty dogs of the
royal hunt and their handlers (the king could hardly go without his sport
while on the continent) had landed in Normandy.[13] John meant to stay
and he meant business.

His immediate concern was to meet Philip Augustus. The two had
a secret meeting on June 9 at which only they were present,[14] and at
which John accepted an invitation from Philip to visit Paris. But before
he stepped into that arena, he made sure of his alliances. In a series of
letters issued on June 9 and 10, John ordered Geoffrey fitz Peter to make
good on the arrears of money fiefs (money granted to a warrior in order
to retain him in service) outstanding at the English Exchequer. The beneficiaries included the count of Flanders, his uncle and his chancellor,
and many magnates from northern France, including the lord of Picqui-
gny. The knots that tied the Treaty of Le Goulet were beginning to be
unbound. John, moreover, made sure to grant new money fiefs to more
allies in preparation for an impending war, and took direct action against
the Lusignans by granting out the lands of Ralph, count of Eu, Hugh of
Lusignan's brother.[15]

John's journey to Paris took place around July 1, 1201. The contemporary French commentator Rigord, writing from the royal mausoleum of
St. Denis where John was first greeted by Philip, says that John was welcomed with singing and was led into the church in a grand procession.

John then went on to Paris itself, where he was received honorably by the citizens, lodged in the royal palace and given free access to the royal cellars. Philip then gave him many gifts of extraordinary value and great beauty, including gold, silver, rich cloth and Spanish warhorses.[16] Philip and John exchanged the kiss of peace and, with Philip's license, John departed for his own lands.

The two were evidently on good terms at this stage, though John's preparations for war suggest that he was not so naive as to believe that conflict was unlikely. By late July, he was at Chinon where he seems to have spent the rest of the summer garnering support. The rolls on which we are so reliant for our detailed information about John's daily actions fail us during these months, but the chronicles make it clear that John was far from idle as he attempted to deal with the disloyalty of his Poitevin subjects.[17] One of the ways in which he did so was to establish as his seneschal of Poitou one of his most loyal and trusted men, Robert of Thornham. Robert had been with Richard on crusade and had been custodian of half the fleet that established Richard's control of Cyprus in 1191. He had remained loyal throughout Richard's reign, and when John came to power, he had been one of the first to support the count's cause, opening the treasury at Chinon for him. John clearly liked and trusted Robert. He rewarded him for his services well, and he kept him in his company throughout most of 1200 and 1201. In the summer of 1201, Robert replaced the untrustworthy Guy de Cela and was given a power-base in Poitiers with, presumably, the license to harry the Lusignans into submission.[18] John himself returned to Normandy, to spend autumn and winter in the duchy, while giving carte blanche to William des Roches to speak on his behalf in the south.[19] And, if we are to believe Roger of Howden's testimony, it must have been at this point, too, that Philip and John agreed to another peace treaty.[20]

THE ANGEVIN TERRITORIES CONSISTED of a number of independent groups of lands, one of which comprised England and its suzerainty over much of the British Isles; another Normandy and its suzerainty over Brittany; a third comprising the heartlands of Henry II's inheritance in Anjou, Maine and the Touraine; and a fourth called the duchy of Aquitaine. This last group, Aquitaine, was made up of two distinct regions: the first was Poitou and its subjected counties in the north, bordering on Anjou (with claims over the count of Anjou, seldom realized, but there nonetheless),[21] and the second was Gascony in the south, bordering on the lands of the Iberian peninsula.[22]

By 1199, the dukes of Aquitaine had had an independent existence for the best part of three hundred years, an identity completely separate from the French monarchy that emerged in the tenth century under the Capetian kings, and wholly separate from their neighbors in Anjou. The marriage, in 1152, of Eleanor of Aquitaine and Henry of Anjou appears to have done little or nothing to change that. The nobles of Poitou saw themselves as being distinct from their Angevin neighbors, and their Angevin neighbors did them the honor of treating them likewise. The charters show that the Poitevin magnates were not drawn into the orbit of the Angevin rulers; in fact the evidence shows that they were distinctly left out, only being drawn into the circle of Henry II's court when he came travelling through their regions. The duchy of Aquitaine was left largely to get on with its own business. And it seems likely that Eleanor of Aquitaine herself took the lead in this distinction of Aquitaine from the rest of the Angevin lands. When Richard was, in his turn, made count of Poitou and duke of Aquitaine in 1172, he continued the practice of giving Aquitaine (and by this we really mean the nobles of Poitou) a distinct identity from the lands of his father.[23]

Poitou was at the center of Richard's agenda for twenty years before he succeeded his father to the other Angevin lands. With varying degrees of success, he had struggled to bring under his domination the counts of Angoulême along with the counts of La Marche and Limoges, and, although he had significant moments of triumph, he never truly laid to rest the determination of these families to resist outside control.[24] The problem that confronted the count of Poitou was that he had no block of land of his own, his property being spread thinly. He enjoyed control of certain strategic castles; he had comital rights to collect revenues, especially from the lucrative trade in wine, to mint money and to enjoy the profits of justice; and he had control of the comital capital at Poitiers as well as the prestige of the title and the public authority that went with it.[25] But the four noble families who held significant tracts of land in the heartlands of Poitou—the Thouars, the Lusignans, the lords of Parthenay and the Mauléons—were the dominant political force, only cowed by their count when he turned his attention to them, and resistant to permanent suppression. The counts of Angoulême were also key players in the politics of the area, and they, too, were never permanently subdued.[26] There was a tradition of armed resistance to authority that plagued Poitevin politics long after Richard, John and Philip Augustus had passed into legend. John had to deal with the reality that Poitou, if not ungovernable, certainly presented intractable problems for its would-be ruler.

The count of Poitou had a further difficulty to overcome if he were to succeed in dominating the territory. The king of France also had an interest in the area. Kings of the French claimed to be the successors of Charles the Bald, king of the West Franks between 840 and 877. His territory had extended over the whole of the lands that we now associate with the modern nation of France, and the twelfth-century kings of the French claimed to be his successor. The reality was, however, that these French kings had little power outside their dominions, which were focused, largely, around the Paris–Orléans basin, the area which is still called the Île de France. But that did not stop them claiming what they thought was rightfully theirs. And, remarkably, many contemporaries accepted the theory of the claim and did homage for their lands to the French king even if they did not accept it in fact. In the late twelfth century, Poitou was, therefore, classic marcher territory, in which two competing superpowers battled for supremacy.

If John were to control Poitou—and it is evident that he saw it as central to his interests—he was going to need help, and that help, he hoped, would come from Count Audemar of Angoulême, which is why he had married Audemar's daughter. Audemar, it appears, threw himself into the business of supporting John's rule and was, as a consequence, handsomely rewarded. And to bolster his ambitions for Poitou, John also appointed Angevin hard men, such as Robert of Thornham and William and Peter des Roches, to key posts, so that they might act to suppress the Poitevin baronage.

It is quite likely that John's Poitevin policy was too successful, which explains why those who found themselves on the wrong side of it turned to the other power with interests in the region, the king of France. The complexity of the situation is plain to see. To begin with, when John acceded to Richard's lands in the spring of 1199, his seneschal in Poitou was Ralph de Mauléon. Ranged against John were Hugh of Lusignan and Count Audemar of Angoulême. But by early 1200, Ralph de Mauléon was dead, Hugh of Lusignan was at peace with John and Count Audemar was planning his daughter's marriage to John. The Mauléons, represented now by Ralph's brother William and Ralph's son Savaric, were in Arthur's camp. By the summer of 1201, Hugh of Lusignan and the Mauléons were against John, while Count Audemar was very firmly with his son-in-law and Poitou was under the firm control of John's new seneschal, Robert of Thornham. In this situation, those who were experiencing the firm smack of Angevin government turned to Philip Augustus.

JOHN, SECURE IN HIS right of inheritance to his continental lands bestowed by the Treaty of Le Goulet, did not realize that Philip was determined to use any means in his power to drive the Angevins from Normandy. By Easter 1202, however, John must have seen very clearly that this was indeed Philip's plan.[27] Philip was intent on placing John outside the law, and once that was achieved, he must have calculated, he could then use his military forces and his diplomatic skills to take Normandy for himself.

Philip's opportunity to act against John was provided by the Poitevins—they had appealed to him in the autumn of 1201, but Philip was not ready to move until the spring of 1202. It was then he decided to press John hard, first to answer charges of misrule over his own men—in this case the Lusignans—and then as a contumacious vassal for failing to appear at court to answer the charges levied against him. The French king took counsel with his principal barons, collected an army and attacked Normandy. At the same time, he gave to Arthur, by hereditary right, the duchy of Brittany, and further gave Arthur the authority to take for himself by force the counties of Anjou and Poitou. To help him in that enterprise, Philip gave Arthur 200 knights and a vast sum of money, and then accepted him as his liegeman,[28] making an agreement with Arthur about the conduct of the war and the way in which the spoils would be divided.

John's reaction shows that he was genuinely shocked by Philip's move and recognized it for the severe threat that it was. He wrote to his English barons protesting about what Philip had done, and also sent the archbishop of Canterbury and the bishop of Ely to England to bear witness to Philip's inexcusable behavior; but that was not going to save him.[29] Philip took his war deep into Norman territory, capturing large parts of the frontier territory until, in July 1202, he came to the gates of Gournay. There, according to the court chronicler Rigord, in a brilliant maneuver, Philip burst the walls of a large weir that lay up river and the resultant flood carried all before it, including the defensive walls; Gournay fell to the French. It was a defining moment in the campaign, and in recognition of the fact, Philip held his court at the castle and there formally took homage from Arthur for all John's continental lands, with the exception of Normandy, which Philip reserved for himself.

The document recording Arthur's submission to Philip survives. In it, Arthur describes himself as duke of Brittany and Aquitaine, count of Anjou and Le Mans, and declares that he had done homage to King Philip for the lands belonging to these titles for the moment "when, if God wills it, [Philip] or [Arthur] should acquire them."[30] Rigord also thought that Arthur was knighted at this point, perhaps for a second time.* In any event, what occurred was a clear demonstration of Philip's renewed support for Arthur and his determination to drive John from his

---

* The author of the *Histoire des Ducs de Normandie*, 92, also thought that Arthur was knighted at this point, though since we also have testimony that he was knighted in 1199 (*Chronica Magistri Rogeri de Houedene*, iv, 94–5), it suggests that there were two events that contemporaries identified as knighting ceremonies.

lands. There was to be a two-pronged attack: Philip against Normandy and Arthur against John's other lands. The text of Arthur's agreement with Philip made it clear that Arthur had renounced his claim, and therefore the claims of the Angevin family, to Normandy. "As for Normandy," the treaty stipulated, "if the lord our king of France should acquire [the duchy], he may retain it for his use for as long as it pleases him, and to his men, who for his cause lost lands, he may give them whatever he may wish of the lands of the Normans." Arthur had repeated the error that his uncle had made in 1194 when Richard was held captive in Germany and John was in alliance with Philip: he had given up Normandy to the king of the French. It amounted to family treason.

Arthur's intentions toward John's southern lands must have been helped immeasurably by news of the death of John's father-in-law, Count Audemar. He had died on June 16, 1202,[31] news of which must have reached Philip before the successful siege of Gournay. Since Count Audemar was John's greatest supporter in the region, this was a heavy blow indeed, and while it meant that John would succeed to the county in right of his wife and would, therefore, be able to use its resources in the defense of his lands, John had to face the wrath of the Lusignans and the Mauléons without the support of his principal ally. John's supporters in Poitou and Anjou, his mother, Eleanor of Aquitaine, and his seneschals, Robert of Thornham and William des Roches, were severely pressed.

Eleanor took matters into her own hands, prompted, perhaps, by news of Audemar's death, and left the comfort of Fontevraud to direct operations from Poitiers. She was enjoying the hospitality of the castellan of Mirebeau, thirty miles into her forty-five-mile journey, when the castle was suddenly besieged by her grandson, Arthur, who had decided that capturing his grandmother would speed his progress toward victory. It was a bold move on the part of the young pretender, and it almost succeeded. Eleanor's situation looked dire; it was only a matter of time before the town fell and she became her grandson's hostage. John received news of the siege on July 30. He was at Le Mans, according to his own account,[32] and, gathering his soldiers together, he dashed the ninety miles to his mother's rescue. With an overwhelming force, he caught Arthur and his allies completely by surprise. In a letter he wrote to inform his subjects of his victory, he recorded, in exhilarated terms, how he had captured Arthur and many others of his Poitevin enemies. His subjects were encouraged to "give thanks to God and to rejoice in our successes."[33]

L OOKING BACK ON THE events of John's reign from the vantage point of the 1220s, the author of the *History of William Marshal* took his narrative from John's accession to his marriage to Isabella of Angoulême and then, via a brief statement concerning the treachery of the French king toward John, to the events at Mirebeau. He compressed an action-packed three years between 1199 and 1202 into the space of a few lines, but somehow he captured the essence of the first years of John's reign: it was characterized by Philip's determination to hound John out of his lands and by John's own folly when gifted with victory. The author of the *History* devoted more than five hundred lines of his (admittedly prolix) poem to the events of Mirebeau and its aftermath. Clearly, from his vantage point, Mirebeau was decisive, but not, as it turned out, in a way that John would have wished.

The problem was that, according to our author, John not only took all the credit for the victory but also took all the spoils. The *History* records that the real hero of the hour at Mirebeau was not John but his seneschal of Anjou, William des Roches. William had shown such feats of arms and such courage that his efforts were to be marvelled at. Like any hero worthy of the name he had, by repute, three horses killed from underneath him, yet still he fought on leading his troops from the front.[34] No doubt there is some exaggeration in the telling of the tale (it is a common trope that warrior heroes have three horses cut from underneath them), but equally there is no doubt that William des Roches thought he had done enough to warrant a share not only in the profits of victory but also in the handling of the prisoners, especially Arthur, to whom he had at one stage been loyal. But John, according to the *History*, "puffed up with pride which daily grew that so blurred his vision that he could not see reason," and acted in such a high-handed manner that he "lost the affection of the barons of the land before he had crossed to England."[35] Even the most exalted of the prisoners were treated shamefully, kept in chains like common criminals.[36]

By these actions, John lost the support of all those whose allegiance was crucial if he were to hold on to his lands. In his moment of triumph, John forgot to be magnanimous to exactly the men on whom his control of Anjou and Poitou rested. For the author of the *History*, the aftermath of Mirebeau was catastrophic to John's cause in large part because it alienated William des Roches. It seems likely that he was right, because although Mirebeau robbed Philip of one vital ally, it gifted him another.

The capture of Normandy had been Philip's unwavering objective since the 1180s. If he could destabilize matters in Anjou, Touraine and Poitou sufficiently to make John take his eye off Normandy, then Philip would be able to seize the main prize. That aim was at the heart of everything that Philip undertook. The news that Arthur had fallen into John's hands was undoubtedly a blow, since he had been a key part of Philip's plan. But within a month of Arthur's capture, William des Roches had come over to the French king's camp and, in October 1202, William marched into Angers, the comital capital of John's ancestral home.[37] John had lost control of his paternal county.

John's return to Normandy with the prisoners taken at Mirebeau was trumpeted in the documents that he sent out concerning them. Hugh le Brun and his brother Geoffrey de Lusignan were confined at Caen, and their castles in Poitou were confiscated and garrisoned by the king's men; Hugh was kept fettered for a month, and then only placed in ring-chains once he had agreed to parley with John. Throughout September and October, negotiations continued, culminating in a personal meeting between John and Hugh in early November, though even then no agreement was reached and the king was at pains to keep Hugh and Geoffrey apart from the other prisoners. John spent Christmas at Caen, during which there were further talks as John tried to win Hugh over to his side. On January 17, he made the fateful decision to release Hugh on license. [38]

At Christmas 1202, John's prospects were still good. Arthur was a captive as was Hugh le Brun, and John retained the upper hand with his Poitevin subjects, even though he had lost Angers. The canonization of the Englishman Gilbert of Sempringham, which John had backed, had been confirmed, a further indication that John had the support of Pope Innocent III. In May 1202,[39] for example, the first fruits of John's diplomatic engagement at the curia over Philip's aggression began to emerge: Pope Innocent issued letters to the archbishop of Rouen authorizing him to use ecclesiastical power to suppress any revolts in Normandy.[40] (Importantly, this same authority was given to Archbishop Hubert Walter, suggesting that England was also experiencing disharmony under John's rule.)[41] And although the letter does not survive, we might surmise that the archbishop of Bordeaux, Elias, was given a similar mandate. Plans were afoot for the canonization of a second Englishman, Wulfstan of Worcester, in 1203, another cause that was close to John's heart.

Innocent III, a young and energetic pope, had declared his ambition for a fourth crusade immediately after his election in 1198. It had finally gathered in 1202 and must have been a topic of conversation that Christmas; certainly it was big news for many of the contemporary chroniclers.[42] In its ranks were some of the greatest nobles of France, a number of whom had been John's allies in his dealings with King Philip. In October 1202, the army had set out on its journey eastward, and by the end of November, the Christian city of Zara in Dalmatia had fallen to them in what was one of the most controversial events of a controversial crusade. By Christmas, not getting directly involved in a crusade that was rapidly going off course must already have seemed like a smart decision. But John was no political fool. He knew that the pope was committed to the enterprise, and so gave his support to those who had chosen to leave on the mission, giving 1,000 marks to help finance Louis of Blois' contribution to the cause. The thirty-year-old count was the son of Alice,

Eleanor's daughter by King Louis VII of France, so he was related to both John and to Philip.[43] John willingly issued letters protecting the property of those who sought to join the crusade, and he granted a for- tieth of the revenues of his own lands for the span of a year in support of the venture.[44] He also agreed to fund the establishment of a hundred knights in the Holy Land who would serve Christ at the king's expense for a year.*[45]

THE BEGINNING OF 1203 was marked by the revolt at Alençon by its holder, Count Robert of Sées (or, as he became after the revolt, Count Robert of Alençon, enjoying the title as the gift of King Philip). John was on his way to Chinon where Isabella of Angoulême was under siege. The reason she was at Chinon without her husband remains un- clear. Perhaps she had been visiting her mother, Alice de Courtenay, who may have wielded power in Angoulême on John's behalf in the months after Count Audemar's death. In any event, word had reached John that Isabella was under threat, so he marched southward to her rescue, stop- ping at Alençon on January 15 and remaining there, as the count's guest, for a week (suggesting that Isabella was not under immediate threat). On January 22, the day after John left, King Philip's troops entered Alençon, led by none other than the king's marshal, Henry Clement.

Alençon was on the border of Normandy and Maine, on the way south toward Poitou. Its loss was, therefore, a serious blow to John, who heard the news at Le Mans. Once he had been reunited with his wife, who was brought to him by Peter de Préaux, he retreated to Normandy fearing,

---

* A number of John's most important servants had clearly become carried away by the excitement of the crusade but on reflection had decided that it was better to stay at home. John tried to obtain dispensation for Geoffrey fitz Peter, Hugh Bardolf, William de Stute- ville, William Brewer, Robert of Berkeley, and Alan and Thomas Basset before Christmas 1201 (*Letters of Innocent III to England and Wales*, nos 365, 439). The constable and sene- schal of Normandy along with Count Robert of Meulan also tried to obtain licence for re- mission of their crusading vows (*Letters of Innocent III to England and Wales*, no. 356). And evidently John was aiding those who wished to renege on their crusading vows as early as September 1201 (*Letters of Innocent III to England and Wales*, nos 350, 261).

according to the author of the *History of William Marshal*, that he would be captured by his enemies at any moment. That fear did not prevent John from visiting the count's seat at Sées on January 25, enjoying the fruits of the count's lands and then redistributing them—and lands held by his followers—as punishment for the revolt.[46] But the blow to John was grave indeed, and he knew it, dating two of his documents, one on March 1 and another on April 20, 1203, by "the year in which Count Robert of Sées betrayed us at Alençon."[47] The fall of Alençon ended John's ability to intervene personally in Anjou and Poitou. It was devastating.

Equally momentous was the death of Arthur of Brittany. According to the author of the Margam annals, who may well have got his information from William de Briouze, one of the participants in the affair, John killed Arthur on the night of April 3, 1203, while drunk and possessed by demons. The corpse was then thrown into the Seine, there to be found by a fisherman; it was later buried at Bec Abbey in Normandy.[48] The story seems fanciful, especially when we begin to unpick the circumstances of Arthur's death; it appears that the decision to take his life was a coolly calculated political act. Indeed, this is exactly what another contemporary chronicler, Ralph of Coggeshall, tells us. In his account John's counsellors decided that Arthur should be put out of action (by being blinded and castrated) so that he would no longer be a rallying point for the Bretons and other rebels who were arrayed against the king.[49]

In addition to John, we know who was present when Arthur met his end.[50] William Marshal, though his biographer passes silently over it, was at Rouen when the deed was done; Peter des Roches, fast developing into one of the most trusted men in John's regime, was also there; so, too, were William Brewer and Reginald of Cornhill. Both William and Reginald were key members of John's household on whom he had placed a great deal of responsibility. William de Briouze seems to have been on the fringes of the affair, and it is quite possible that Hubert de Burgh was also at the heart of events, in the first instance preventing Arthur's mutilation, but then removing himself at the crucial moment in the drama of Arthur's death.

John may well have been thinking about making Arthur disappear as early as February 1203. At the beginning of the month he had had Arthur removed from Falaise Castle and placed in the tower at Rouen. Certainly, he was beginning to see the living Arthur as the source of his difficulties. The Bretons were clamouring for his release, and the young man was evidently a liability. He was happy to conspire in King Philip's machinations against the Angevin domain, even to the point of giving up the family's claims to the duchy of Normandy. Men must have looked askance at Arthur's behavior: he was wilfully playing into the hands of a French monarch who was no friend of his family and who, by his every action, seemed determined to drive out that family from the lands it had occupied for generations. From the perspective of John and his advisors, therefore, Arthur was acting treacherously, and so posed a severe threat to the stability of the Angevin position on the continent.

Perhaps John tried to reason with Arthur. Matthew Paris, writing a generation after the events he described, thought that John and Arthur talked just before Arthur's removal from Falaise. Matthew's informant on so much of John's reign was Hubert de Burgh, and Coggeshall has Hubert in charge of Falaise when Arthur was imprisoned there, so perhaps Matthew's story has in it a grain of truth. John is said to have pleaded with Arthur to withdraw his allegiance from Philip and to unite with his family. Arthur, we are told, haughtily refused his uncle's plea for unity, claiming that he was the rightful heir of King Richard and that he would have no peace with him, whereupon John, according to Matthew Paris, had him removed to Rouen to an uncertain fate.[51]

That fate was execution, planned by John with the advice of key counsellors, including the justiciar of England, Geoffrey fitz Peter (who can be placed at Falaise shortly before Arthur was removed to Rouen), carried out by an anonymous executioner but with the sanction of John and his most trusted counsellors. What happened to Arthur's body remains a mystery: perhaps it was placed in an unmarked grave in Rouen or, as the Margam annalist had it, in the cemetery at Bec Abbey.[52] Certainly no one outside the charmed circle of John's men knew, and no one was telling.

On April 16, John wrote letters of credence for his high-powered diplomat, Brother John de Valerant, to take to his mother, the archbishop
of Bordeaux and the seneschals of Poitou, Gascony and Perigord, and
Anjou, and to his southern deputies, including Hubert de Burgh, which
stated that Brother John would give a true account of the events that had
transpired but that they should be assured that "by God's grace . . . matters stand better for us than [Brother John] can say."[53] This was a veiled
reference to Arthur's fate. One is left to ponder Eleanor's reaction to the
news that her son had executed her grandson.

The letters show that two weeks after the event, John was still convinced that he had done the right thing. He was, however, soon to be
disabused of that notion. As it was to turn out, a dead Arthur was more of
a threat to John than a live one had been. At least when Arthur was alive
and in captivity, John could always dangle the promise of release before
his enemies. John had now done his worst and could do no more. As
soon as word got out that Arthur was missing, presumed murdered, he
became the rallying cry for John's enemies. The Bretons no longer feared
what John might do to Arthur, and Philip Augustus had something with
which he could torment his opponent. There seems little doubt that in
killing Arthur, John had miscalculated badly.

According to Matthew Paris, the French court heard of Arthur's fate
within a few days of his death; there was certainly a later Breton tradition
that John was condemned for the murder in the Breton court in spring
1203. And while Arthur's fate made no difference to Philip's determination to take Normandy, it did take from John any moral high ground
that he might have enjoyed. Men now had another reason to support the
French king in his quest to break John's hold over his continental lands.
It is impossible to gauge the significance of Arthur's death for the large
numbers of Normans who deserted John's cause after the events of Easter
1203. Philip was pressing Normandy hard, and it may be that these men
took the view that John's cause was lost and that they had better be seen
to join the winning side before that side won. But even if Arthur's death
did not cause desertion and the eventual loss of Normandy, it was part of

the picture of collapse that helped them make the decision about which
way to jump.

O N ANOTHER FRONT, JOHN was having more success, though little good it did him. Over the winter of 1202–3, John's proctors at
the papal court had been working hard to bring in the pope to mediate in
the dispute between him and Philip. John's objective was to bring about
peace, because then he would be able to focus on reestablishing his power
over the Poitevins safe in the knowledge that the borders of Normandy
were secure. But while John had got the pope's support, Philip was not in
the mood for peace: the French king wanted war because he thought that
through war he would achieve his goal. He had John on the run and he
was determined to press his advantage.

At Easter 1203, key magnates from Maine, Anjou and Poitou did
homage to Philip, and immediately afterward, at the point in the calendar
at which the campaigning season traditionally began, Philip launched an
attack. His army headed southward hoping to finally subdue Anjou, an
objective that he had achieved by the beginning of June. He then turned
northward to focus his military efforts on Normandy. Military success
followed military success, as the French king took Conches, Les Andelys
and Vaudreuil, before returning to the heartlands of his kingdom. And it
was then, according to Rigord, that Pope Innocent's representatives, the
abbots of Casamari, Trois-Fontaines and Les Dunes, appeared at court
to urge peace, proposing that a great convocation should be called between not only the kings of France and England but also between the
greatest ecclesiastics and secular magnates of both realms.[54] A copy of
Innocent's letter survives, dated around mid-May 1203, so the abbots
must have appeared at court in late June or early July.[55] Philip rejected
their peace proposal: he had no intention of letting go of his advantage.
On August 31, he collected an army and laid siege to Radepont where,
in the space of just fifteen days, he erected around it towers, and then attacked and took it, capturing twenty knights, one hundred serjeants and

thirty crossbowmen. The following month, September, he laid siege to Chateau Gaillard.[56]

Chateau Gaillard was built, provocatively, in a place that was an agreed demilitarized zone, and built at huge expense to meet the most exacting military demands of the day. Standing on a rocky outcrop lording it over the River Seine, Chateau Gaillard was to be the key to Richard's advancement into the Norman Vexin, which had fallen to Philip during Richard's captivity. In the event, Chateau Gaillard took on another guise: it was to become the key to John's defense of the duchy, physically and symbolically, in the face of King Philip's aggression. If it were to fall, so, too, would John's hopes for holding Normandy. Chateau Gaillard became the great set-piece struggle of the war and its surrender, on March 6, 1204, after a brutal siege described in great detail by Philip's court chronicler, his chaplain William the Breton, precipitated an almost total collapse of Norman resistance to King Philip.[57]

W AR WAS NOT THE only front on which Philip sustained his attack on Normandy. As duke of Normandy, John had an overlord, an overlord he had acknowledged in the Treaty of Le Goulet: the king of France. The formal process by which in 1202 Philip had dispossessed John of the duchy gave Normans a legitimate reason to support his invasion. When they sided with the French king, they could argue that he was the supreme authority in the duchy. Fighting against their duke had the force of legal authority: the authority of a king enforcing the confiscation of the lands of a vassal who had refused to obey him. It is this fact that gives the loss of Normandy its piquancy: Philip was not making an unprovoked attack against a fellow ruler, he was punishing a vassal deserving of punishment, and asserting his rule over lands that were rightfully his. As the dukes of Normandy had ruled the duchy since 911, this may seem to be an argument based on no more than semantics, but it is not. Those who experienced the wars of 1202–4 took seriously King Philip's claim to authority over Duke John's lands in Normandy.

The complexity of the situation for those who held land in Normandy is made plain by the author of the *History of William Marshal*, who tells us in quick succession two contradictory tales about his eponymous hero.

The first is that, when at Rouen, John was so hard pressed by Philip that he sent William the Marshal (known to his contemporaries as simply "the Marshal") to negotiate with the French king to beg him to make peace. The king of France was at that moment laying siege to Conches and made it plain that he had no interest in agreeing to peace terms with John. The Marshal pointed out to Philip the contradiction that he was pursuing John with the help of traitors who should, by French custom, be treated "dishonourably, burned, put to the sword, and dragged through the streets by horses." Philip is said to have replied that these men were like "toilet rags," to be "used and disposed of down the latrine when one had had one's use of them."

The second tale follows almost immediately on the first. After John had left Normandy for England, he sent another mission to the king of France led by Hubert Walter, the archbishop of Canterbury, William Marshal and Earl Robert of Leicester. They found King Philip at Bec, where they again pleaded with him on John's behalf. But Philip would hear none of it; he was determined to dispossess all those who refused to submit to him. On hearing this, the Marshal and the earl of Leicester promised to do homage to Philip for their Norman lands if John failed to retake the duchy after a year and a day. The author then spent the best part of 500 lines defending the Marshal's decision, claiming that he had John's approval for the plan.[58] The two stories reflect the fact that, for those subject to the outcome of the war, the legal situation was complex and men might argue it in whatever way it suited them, and still salve their consciences.

In the autumn of 1203, John decided to return to England. We do not know why. There has been much speculation from his own day to this about his motives for leaving Normandy while it was under such extreme threat from Philip. If Normandy were to remain under Angevin control, it needed the presence of its duke, and yet John retreated to England.

The author of the *History of William Marshal* gives us a series of set-piece conversations, and while the words themselves are surely imagined by the author, the fact that one of his principal informants was John Marshal, who was with the king in the autumn of 1203,[59] may mean that they carry some truth.

The Marshal is said to have addressed the king thus: "Sire . . . you have few friends, if you chose to strengthen your enemies, then your own power will decline; if a man strengthen his enemies, it is justifiable for men to attack him." The Marshal then laid the blame for the catastrophe that faced the regime squarely at John's door: "you paid no attention to the first sign of discontent, but it would have been better for us all if you had."[60] The Marshal had overstepped the mark (not for the only time in his career), and John reacted with fury. Speechless with rage, the king retired to the privacy of his chamber, there to contemplate his situation. The following day, he left his attendants to travel by boat upstream to do a circuit of his French lands before returning to Rouen. It was after this that John set sail for England, promising to return with all haste, though in the event he did not.

It may well be that King John felt personally threatened. Certainly an air of distrust comes through in the sources that, if they truly reflect how John felt at the time, explain why he thought that a retreat to the English citadel was crucial to his survival. The contemporary commentator Gervase of Canterbury, for example, reported that John had few friends in Normandy and the traitors in his ranks particularly damaged his cause. Since John spent Christmas 1203 at Canterbury, Gervase may well be reporting the views of the king himself, expressed at the Christmas table. The author of the *History of William Marshal*, writing long afterward, thought that John skulked back to England, though his itinerary suggests a leisurely retreat via Bonneville-sur-Touques, Caen, Le Plessis-Grimould, Domfront, Vire, Morfarville and Gonneville before embarking at Barfleur. This is not the flight of a frightened man but the dignified progress of a ruler. And yet signs that his rule was disintegrating were all around. On October 9, for example, John capitulated in the long-running dispute that he had been having over the appointment of Sylvester to the bishopric of Séez.[61] His admission of defeat in that three-and-a-half-year struggle was a further indication that his power in the duchy was waning.

John's reception at Portsmouth, where he made landfall on December 7, was rapturous and perhaps revived his flagging confidence; but there is little doubt that John's desertion of Normandy was a mistake: and a mistake that it is hard to imagine either his brother or his father would have made. Those he left behind to defend the duchy felt his absence sorely, and said as much.

7

INSIDE THE CITADEL

WHEN JOHN SET FOOT in England on December 7, 1203, he must have thought that it was a temporary arrangement and that soon he would be riding across his continental lands as he had always done, and as his brother and father had done before him.* That his stay in the British Isles, apart from expeditions to the continent in 1206 and in 1214, turned out to be permanent had a profound impact on the English kingdom and on the remainder of John's life. Indeed, it could be argued that John's departure from Normandy at the end of 1203 was the first step on the road to Runnymede and to the creation of Magna Carta.

At Archbishop Hubert's Christmas table in Canterbury, John complained bitterly of the treachery of his Norman barons and began to plan his return to the continent. But first he had to secure England, otherwise he might find himself losing that, too. Everyone expected John to make a speedy return to Normandy and it looked, in the first instance, as though that was indeed what he intended. That he never did make the journey is one of the more perplexing aspects of the loss of Normandy.

But in January and February 1204, Normandy had yet to fall, and John must have surmised that he had time to raise his forces and get them across the Channel before it was too late. Rouen was in the hands of a capable military commander, Peter de Préaux, and while Rouen held

---

* Though he must have thought he would stay for a while since the royal hunt accompanied him to England.

out, enough Norman castles remained loyal to John for him to be able to claim that he still held the duchy. And Chateau Gaillard, under the control of Roger de Lacy, hereditary constable of Chester and therefore a military man of the highest rank in English society, was holding out against Philip's attempts to seize the castle, although the garrison was suffering from extreme privation.

John sent to Normandy vast stores of money and key members of his administration, including the clerk Hugh of Wells, who was sent with a letter of credence and a secret message for the commander of Chateau Gaillard that he was to relate by word of mouth, all with the intention of preparing the way for the king's return.[1] John also met the leading magnates of the realm. And on January 2 at Oxford, the traditional place for the English political elite to meet their king, he received their backing to levy scutage (the tax on the knight's fee that the king raised when he went to war) at the rate of two-and-a-half marks on each knight's fee so that he might buy "supplies for war."[2] A month later, while at Nottingham, John wrote to the great men of Ireland, outlining his difficulties and explaining that he needed their support to raise the knights and money required to defend Normandy against Philip's unwarranted aggression. John was especially keen to point out that the French king was attempting to disinherit him despite the fact that they had made agreements, and that oaths had been sworn between them.[3] In this letter lies the message that John was promulgating to all his subjects, English as well as Irish, and, in the main, they seem to have accepted it, and in the first instance acquiesced to his demands for money.

John also tried to use diplomacy to avert disaster. In January, he sent a mission to his nephew, Otto of Brunswick, designed to enlist his aid.[4] A further mission to Otto led by the bishop of London departed from England in late March.[5] John's proctors at the papal court were also busy, and the fruits of their labor had begun to emerge just as John was decamping from Normandy at the end of 1203.[6] Innocent wrote to Philip in the strongest terms, ordering him to submit himself to papal judgment, not on the basis of feudal law, but on the basis of matters of salvation, about which the pope claimed absolute competence, and warning Philip that should he fail to obey, he would be subject to the severest action. The letter to the papal legate ordered him to bypass King Philip and directly order Philip's nobles to refrain from pursuing the war against John on pain of interdicts being placed on their households. Despite all this papal protesting, Philip continued to press his advantage. Letters sent by Innocent III in April 1204 show that the pope was still working hard to bring about peace between John and Philip. Innocent wrote to the archbishops and bishops throughout the kingdom of France again urging them to work for peace between the two rulers. Peace, of course, was what John most needed if he were to keep hold of his hereditary lands, but it was what Philip needed least if he were to take Normandy. As usual in these matters, war won over peace; even the archbishops and bishops throughout France were in favor of war, as they had told the pope in early August that year.[7]

The fall of Chateau Gaillard on March 8, 1204, came as a thunderbolt, despite indications that John had feared that it would fall, since he seems to have made provisions for that eventuality. Roger de Lacy's loyalty was unimpeachable, and his courage in defending the castle widely acknowledged even after its capitulation to King Philip's forces. No castle, not even Richard's "Saucy Castle," could hold out against a determined attacker without relief from outside. Chateau Gaillard never received that relief. Once the castle had fallen, Philip could begin the process of taking Normandy as a whole, but he moved cautiously. He received a delegation from John led by the archbishop of Canterbury, William Marshal and the bishops of Norwich and Ely, who had been instructed to sue for peace. Philip refused to agree to peace terms and declined with menace: "hand over to me the living Arthur, or his sister, Eleanor, and then you can have your peace," they were told, but of course they could not hand over a living Arthur even if they had wished it, and in any event, Philip "did not want peace."[8] That was in early April. The same month, on the 15th, John heard that Queen Eleanor, his mother and his constant source of strength, had died. When news reached him in England, he issued a general amnesty for all prisoners except incarcerated Jews and those who had been taken captive in the war with King Philip.[9] Providing succor to prisoners was one of the seven corporal works of mercy enjoined on all Christians, and kings manifested their piety by a general amnesty of crimes to take effect at the point of their death. That John used it after his mother's death reflects the strength of his feelings toward her.

Chateau Gaillard had fallen in early March and yet Philip did not enter Normandy until May 2. Presumably he was preparing the ground for his arrival: he was not intent on destruction; his purpose was to reassert French royal control of a duchy that was his by right, but that had, for almost three hundred years, belonged to another family. It seems likely, also, that Philip delayed his entry into the duchy until the completion of the Easter festivities. Philip had been consecrated and crowned king on November 1, 1179, while his father, Louis VII, still lived. It was Capetian royal practice to crown the heir in the lifetime of the reigning monarch, and in this case, the coronation was essential to maintain government, since the elderly king lay paralyzed and bedridden and was evidently declining rapidly. Philip was fourteen, and one of his first acts was to order that the Chancery (the king's writing office) should date its documents by the year of grace beginning the year at Easter. This meant that in documents issued by King Philip, Chateau Gaillard fell on March 8, 1203, though amongst his subjects and in Normandy it was March 8, 1204, where the New Year began at Christmas.

On one level, choosing Easter as the start of the year of grace was a sensible decision. Easter is the greatest feast in the Christian calendar, when it might be said that Christianity began, yet it was also a problematic starting point since in maintaining the Anno Domini system of counting the years, Philip was mixing two dates: the birth of Christ as man and the birth of Christ as resurrected man. And Easter is a moveable feast with a cycle that needs careful calculation if errors are not to be made. It is hardly surprising, therefore, that the habit did not catch on outside France. Most rulers, including the pope, dated their documents by their regnal years.

Easter marked the point of Christ's greatest sacrifice for humankind and his rebirth in human form until he would ascend into heaven to sit at the right hand of God (Ascension Day was the anniversary of King John's coronation), so in choosing Easter to mark the start of the year of grace, Philip was making a bold statement of intent about the rebirth of the French monarchy. In 1204, Easter was as late as it could be: it landed on April 25, the very last possible day in the calendar on which Easter Sunday might fall. Only six times before in seven hundred years had Easter been this late; perhaps even that fact was seen as auspicious. In any event, once Easter was completed, King Philip launched his attack on Normandy.

On May 2, he crossed the border and headed for Argentan,[10] which capitulated immediately, and then onto Falaise, where he set up his siege engines. After seven days, the citizens surrendered. From Falaise, Philip took his army to Caen, which surrendered without a fight. Meanwhile, in the west, Guy of Thouars, count of Brittany, with a large army of Bretons, laid siege to Mont-Saint-Michel, which was widely believed to be impregnable. Guy and his Bretons took it, and destroyed it by fire in revenge for the injuries caused them by the Normans. After taking Avranches, Guy was sent to take the castles on the western border of Normandy while King Philip's army went to Rouen, arriving outside the city walls by the end of May.

Looking out over the walls of the city at Philip's army, Rouen's populace, under the direction of Peter de Preaux, the archbishop of Rouen and the city's mayor must have wondered where John was and why he was not where he was needed most, defending the walls of his ducal capital. They must have wondered, too, why they should lay down their lives for a lord who had retreated to his English citadel. And when they saw Philip Augustus's army they did not see the Antichrist and his forces assembled before them determined on their destruction. What they saw was in fact Philip, king of France, and, therefore, the rightful lord of Normandy, who was justly serving on their duke the judgment of the *parlement* of Paris, which had declared that John's lands should be sequestrated. They saw, too, an army made up of Frenchmen who had taken, in relative peace, Falaise and Caen before they had arrived at the gates of Rouen. And Philip had acted magnanimously toward the men of those captured towns. At Falaise, he had confirmed the privileges of the burgesses and had given them a fair; he had also richly rewarded the mayor of Falaise for his handling of the surrender. If the men of Rouen held out for too long, they might lose out in the bonanza of land grants that were following on Philip's gradual takeover of the duchy.

The agreement that Peter de Préaux, the other knights in the city and Robert the mayor made with King Philip on June 1, 1204, made it clear that they thought that Rouen was now lost, and all that remained was to surrender it in such a way that no one lost face.[11] The agreement stipulated that if aid were not forthcoming from King John within thirty days, then the city would be surrendered. In the meantime, Philip was to have custody of certain named hostages as well as the barbican on the west of the River Seine and be allowed to strengthen it. In the meantime, those who wished to submit to Philip were to be allowed to leave Rouen immediately, with safe conducts for them and their men and protection for their property. And those who wished simply to quit Normandy were to be allowed to do so, all before the expiration of the thirty-day term. The trading privileges of the city would remain intact. But still John did not come. Instead, on June 3, Ascension Day, John was in Winchester commemorating his coronation rather than mustering his troops. It must have been a hollow celebration.

Rouen surrendered on June 24, six full days before the truce expired. Philip could now enjoy the freedom of John's ducal capital and was no doubt savoring the moment. The French chronicler Rigord could not refrain from noticing that it had, according to his calculation, been 316 years since the kings of France had held this most wealthy of cities, along with the remainder of Normandy, which had been lost to Rollo the Dane and his pagans by right of conquest.[12] It was fitting, therefore, that King Philip had now removed that stain from the pages of history: Philip Augustus had returned the duchy to its rightful place as part of the French royal demesne. The king began to make arrangements to take the war to John and prepared for an invasion of Aquitaine. It was time to eradicate John's regime on the continent. And throughout all this, John remained in England.

A MONTH EARLIER, ON MAY 5, 1204, a new agreement had been drawn up between John and his wife, Isabella, concerning her dower lands. The death of the dowager queen, Eleanor of Aquitaine, on March 31 meant that her dower lands in England and in Normandy returned to the possession of King John. He could, having already assigned dower lands to Isabella in the event that he predeceased her, have kept the lands himself, but instead he decided to reassign them to Isabella. Even though these were the traditional dower lands of the queens of England and the duchesses of Normandy, it was a generous move: John had no need to assign them in this way. The agreement had, however, a significant new clause, which had not been included in the charter of August 1200 when Isabella's dower lands were first named. The clause stated that, in the event that Isabella's dower lands in Normandy were to be lost to her as a result of the war, then she would be given an equivalent amount of land in England to compensate her for her loss.[13] John—or at least those who were looking out for Isabella's interests in this matter—clearly thought that the permanent loss of Normandy was a very real possibility. England was, increasingly, the citadel into which John retreated as the fortress of the wider Angevin lands fell.

One later commentator, writing in the 1220s, long after the events he described had followed their course to a conclusion, thought that John stayed in England while Normandy fell because he arrogantly claimed that he could easily retake what Philip had taken when it suited him, and that in the meantime he occupied himself in bed with his bride (in other words, the medieval equivalent of fiddling while Rome burned).[14] It is a view that has no contemporary basis.

The author of the *History of William Marshal*, similarly writing much later, thought that John had been extremely busy trying to raise troops to go to the relief of Normandy, but that those summoned were reluctant to go abroad, and so delayed their arrival at the muster point at Portsmouth until matters were decided in Normandy and it was too late to embark.[15] Abbot Ralph of Coggeshall had another explanation: "John gave them no help because he feared treachery from his own men" and "thus was fulfilled the prophesy of Merlin so that 'the sword was separated from the sceptre,' that is Normandy from England."[16] Like his French contemporary Rigord, Coggeshall could not resist looking back into history for a precedent, but whereas Rigord dated matters from the arrival of Rollo and his Vikings, Coggeshall dated his from the Norman Conquest of England: "Kings of England had been dukes of Normandy for one hundred and thirty-nine years, from Duke William, who had conquered England, down to King John, who had lost the duchy and many overseas lands." It did not matter that Coggeshall was ignoring the fact that King Stephen had lost Normandy, too. The power of his story lay in John's fear of treachery.

Coggeshall's explanation has a ring of truth about it. John had been received with much rejoicing in December 1203, but that had not erased the memory of his Norman subjects' treachery, which, in turn, laid the seeds of doubt in his mind about his English subjects, too. Many around him had proved unfaithful and he must have asked himself who would be next to desert him. John's priority, therefore, unsurprisingly given his state of mind, was to ensure that England was securely behind him before he launched himself against Philip's armies again. Evidently John never felt secure enough to venture away from England until after Normandy had been lost. He was not sitting idly in England between December 1203 and June 1204, he was being cautious; but in the end that caution lost him Normandy. Of course, this is retrospective judgment: had John gone to Normandy, he might well have lost England, too. All around him the edifice was crumbling.

John's actions after the fall of Rouen give us a sense of how embattled he felt. According to Gervase of Canterbury, the king made desperate preparations to defend England from possible invasion, convening, at

London, a Great Council consisting of the bishops, earls and barons of the realm, at which it was agreed that everyone throughout the kingdom would be required to swear an oath of fealty to the king. A statute for the common defense of the realm was also agreed, to which all Englishmen aged twelve or over, whether a great noble or an ordinary man, were to swear an oath to observe the statute. Even ecclesiastics were required to do so, unless they had exemption because of the obligations of their orders or had the mandate of the pope.[17] This was a huge step toward making the freemen of England subject directly to the king himself rather than having their loyalty to that king mediated through his tenants-in-chief. If John could not trust his greatest magnates, then he could appeal directly to their men and make them his men, subject to him as king of England.

Allied to this general oath to be sworn by all freemen was the creation of a system for arming the community of the realm. Constables were appointed to ensure that this militia was properly constituted and organized. The king was not going to rely solely on his barons for the defense of his kingdom. He had made that mistake in Normandy; he would not make the same mistake again. Gervase is very clear in linking these two acts to the loss of Normandy, the one at Oxford following on directly from the London meeting, and both as a result of the fall of Rouen. John was at Oxford in the first week of August 1204, so it must be then that the statute was promulgated.[18]

In the meantime, Philip's forces captured Anjou and took the city of Poitiers, where King Philip received liege homage from the men of the district. William des Roches made his peace with Philip in return for recognition of his rights as seneschal of Anjou, Maine and Touraine. At the same time, Philip made provision for the administration of Poitou under the care of another great southern magnate, Aimery, viscount of Thouars. The document recording the agreement was dated at Poitiers, "in our palace," where members of Philip's household appended their seals as witnesses to the event. King Philip had moved into John's ancestral home and was calling it his own.[19]

Queen Eleanor had been dead for just five months. Even her mortal remains, and those of her husband, son and daughter, which lay in the family mausoleum at Fontevraud, were under Philip's control. Gascony remained for John and the port of La Rochelle stayed loyal, too. For John, it was a sorry picture. But for Philip of France, 1204 marked the moment of triumph for the Capetian dynasty, the moment at which he fulfilled the hopes that had been placed in him. To the monk-chronicler Rigord, he was Philip Augustus (imbued with imperial overtones given its Roman antecedents), and to the royal chaplain, William the Breton, he was Philip Magnanimus (the great souled). He was indeed the savior of the French nation and the French monarchy.

T HE FALL OF NORMANDY brought the elite in John's administra- tion to the very point of disintegration. Some of the key men in the continental defense were suddenly under suspicion. According to a letter patent written under the king's direction on August 8 and addressed to all his faithful subjects, wherever they might be, John declared that he had received back into peace and into his service his seneschal of Poitou Robert of Thornham, Savaric de Mauléon, the chamberlain Hubert de Burgh and Gerard de Athié.[20] They had been John's key men in Anjou and Poitou, and he blamed them for the fact that Philip Augustus now occupied his palace in Poitiers. These men had spent time under severe threat from their fellow servants, who had been given license to harry them and their property. Only after his anger had cooled did John allow them back into his protection.

Another man at the heart of the regime, William Marshal, also ran into difficulties. He had played a leading part in John's rule while he was on the continent (he had been with the king almost constantly during the previous twelve months) and he had been a key player in the unsuccessful negotiations with Philip Augustus in the spring of 1204. But when Rouen fell, William Marshal came under suspicion, too. He was denounced to the king by Ralph d'Ardenne who was acting, according to one source, on the authority of none other than Hubert Walter. Hubert and William had been firm allies for many years, and yet here were these two pivotal members of John's administration resorting to squabbling. As Normandy fell, William Marshal was sent to Philip to sue for peace, but Hubert took steps to discredit the Marshal in the eyes of the French king. William's mission failed (perhaps it was always going to), and in the view of the Marshal and his supporters, Hubert had played a large part in that failure. When William Marshal returned to England, Ralph d'Ardenne further denounced him as a traitor to King John, claiming that rather than pursuing the king's interests, the Marshal had made sure that his own lands were secure by swearing liege homage to King Philip. That there was truth in the accusation is beyond doubt. William's defense was that the king knew of his plan to secure his own lands and that he had given the Marshal permission to put that plan into effect. But John claimed to have no recollection of giving the Marshal such permission[21] and thereafter looked at him with deep suspicion; again, the Marshal's partisans were in no doubt as to who had engineered his difficulties: Archbishop Hubert Walter.[22]

With Normandy lost and his regime in disarray, John sought to improve his fortunes by trying to assuage God's anger. The foundation of the Cistercian abbey of Beaulieu in 1204 (possibly intended as his own mausoleum) was his single largest act of piety. Each successive generation of English kings had deemed it necessary to found a monastic community whose raison d'être was the care of their souls. Henry I had founded Reading Abbey; King Stephen had founded Faversham Abbey; only Henry II, perhaps under the influence of Eleanor of Aquitaine, found his resting place in an already established community at Fontevraud. Richard the Lionheart, perhaps convinced that he had no need to plan for the destiny of his immortal soul—he was, after all, a crusader with all that entailed for his future salvation—did not found a monastic community. But John did.

There is some suggestion that John planned the foundation of Beaulieu Abbey before 1204. He had given the manor of Faringdon (then in Berkshire, now in Oxfordshire) to monks of the Cistercian order so that they might settle there. In early July 1203, John had found the money for them to build sheepfolds and other outhouses and he ordered Hugh de Neville, his chief justice of the forests, to provide for the monks the necessary timber. The following November, Hugh de Neville was ordered to supply more timber for what must have been an ever-growing monastic site.[23] Faringdon, however, turned out to be an unsuitable location, and when John issued its foundation charter on January 25, 1205, he gave the monks a site in the New Forest, Hampshire, with Faringdon remaining in their possession.[24] At the end of the charter, John explained why he was founding the community: it was for the "love of God and for the souls of our father, Henry, and of our brothers Henry and Richard sometime kings of England, and for Queen Eleanor our mother, and for the salvation of our soul and of [the souls] of all our ancestors and successors."

Preparations for a return to the continent went on throughout the summer months, but clearly no campaign could be launched in the autumn for that would be folly: going into a major campaign at the end of the campaigning season when the storms of winter approached was not recommended, and so John decided that his attempt to recapture Normandy must wait until the spring. In the meantime there was much to do. If he were going to make successful war on King Philip, he had to make sure that his defenses at home were secure, and that the full might of England together with its financial resources was ready to descend upon Philip. In the meantime, that October, John formally deposed from their lands those who had remained in Normandy. John then distributed these English lands to those men who had, by following him, lost their own lands in Normandy. The *terrae Normannorum* proved an important resource for maintaining the loyalty of those men who served the king.[25]

Every chronicler of the age noted that the winter of 1204 to 1205 was shockingly cold. The ground froze at Christmas time and did not thaw again until the end of March, throwing the agricultural calendar into chaos and causing widespread hardship for the remainder of the year. For the Christmas festivities, John was determined to have a most lavish celebration, not for him and his court the privations brought by a harsh winter. He was to be at Tewkesbury, so he ordered the Templars to release his coronation regalia, of which they had custody as the king made his progress around his lands. The list of items makes for extraordinary reading and demonstrates that this was to be a magnificent affair. John's crown (which had been made in London) was gold with a rich scarlet samite embroidered with sapphires, cameos and pearls around its edge to soften the touch of the crown on the king's head. The Templars also released John's coronation clothes, including a scarlet dalmatic robe with an edge worked in gold and gemstones, and a tunic of diapered white. The royal rear was to be protected against the hardness of the throne by quartered silk cloth (which must refer to its pattern), the royal feet were to be wrapped in scarlet samite socks and placed in sandals with gold bands, and a scarlet samite belt, embroidered with cameos and other stones, was to be fixed around the king's waist, a sword in a golden scabbard to be hung upon it. The king's hands were to be placed in white gloves, one decorated with sapphire and the other with amethyst. He also ordered from his coronation regalia a vast number of brooches, among them a ruby brooch and another with emeralds and rubies, which had been a gift to him from John de Gray, the bishop of Norwich. There were brooches encrusted with sapphires, a brooch with four emeralds and four other gemstones, one with nine good sapphires and another with two sapphires, two emeralds and two gemstones, while yet another had three sapphires, three emeralds and three gemstones. A further brooch had four sapphires, four emeralds and four gemstones, and a turquoise stone in a setting. Added to the list was another brooch, this time with two sapphires, two topaz stones, a large pearl and speckled with small sapphires. There was another sapphire brooch that had been given to the king by Hubert de Burgh, and another brooch with four gemstones and four emeralds. And finally there was a brooch with three emeralds, three sapphires, three gemstones, a topaz, small pearls and half rubies.[26]

This is more than a simple list of precious items; it gives us an insight into a man who evidently enjoyed the pomp and circumstance of formal occasions and wished to present himself to his court in all his magnificence. Evidently, too, one of the ways in which a servant might gain favor with the king was to commission for him a brooch. No doubt John did not weigh himself down with each of these brooches on one occasion, so we can imagine him in his private chambers surveying his riches and making a decision as to which would adorn his royal robes. Presumably at the same time he also made a decision as to which of the seven ebony staffs of office he would carry, whether it would be the one with ten large sapphires or the one with sixty emeralds, or the one with twenty-eight diamonds, or the one with seven good topaz gemstones and one gemstone of unknown type, or the one with nine topaz gemstones or the one with fourteen good sapphires in a setting. Finally, John took possession of a great gold comb encrusted with gemstones and weighing in at a huge 2 marks, 6½ lbs.[27]

The effigy that adorns John's tomb at Worcester Cathedral gives us a good idea of what John must have looked like at this Christmas feast. Although the color has now been expunged from it by the enthusiasm of its nineteenth- and early twentieth-century carers, we know what colors adorned it because of an early representation created by Charles Stothard in 1813 (see p. xvi).[28] These are the king's coronation robes, which he wore on Ascension Day 1199 and got out from storage in December 1204. John was determined to keep up appearances and, perhaps, to remind himself and others of his royal status and what that status meant. Despite (or perhaps even because of) his territorial losses, at Christmas 1204, John was going to parade himself in his full majestic coronation regalia.

Despite the dreadful weather, preparations for the campaign continued, although now there were serious questions as to whether the focus of the invasion should be Normandy. A frontal assault on the duchy might be foolish and Brittany offered few attractions, since its nobles were not well disposed to the Angevins. The focus of the king's military plans therefore settled on Poitou, where he still had the foothold of the important port of La Rochelle and where he might expect to receive support from those Poitevins who had come to see Parisian rule as less attractive than once they had. There was, moreover, a further threat to Aquitaine. The southern part of the duchy—Gascony—was claimed by Alfonso VIII of Castile as the dowry of his wife, Eleanor. But it was only Castilians who remembered that Henry II had assigned Gascony as Eleanor's dowry when he had given his daughter in marriage to Alfonso in 1170. By 1204, perhaps because Eleanor of Aquitaine was dead, but also because John's defeat at the hands of Philip gave him the opportunity to do so, Alfonso was in the mood to press his claim. In 1204, he launched a devastating campaign that only just failed to take the territory. It was a warning that John heeded: Philip might have been his enemy in northern France, but John had other enemies who were willing to take advantage of his situation. He needed to go to Aquitaine if he were not to lose the duchy to the king of Castile.

In January 1205, fifty-one galleys were requisitioned from ports of southern, western and eastern England as well as Ireland to act as additional transports for the army that was to depart for La Rochelle in Poitou that spring.[29] There was a meeting at Winchester in January 1205, at which an assize of money was agreed. The letter patent authorized the king's officers, William de Wrotham and Reginald of Cornhill, to retain and destroy false coin, stating that the measures were recommended by "the common counsel of the realm."[30] There had been a widespread outcry against coin clipping, which had caused what one chronicler called "a great disturbance in the kingdom."[31]

Money mattered enormously in the early thirteenth century, both to the king and to his subjects. There was one coin in circulation, and that was the silver penny, whose value was maintained by the quality of its silver content. Men might pay their taxes only in the coin of the realm, and when the treasury accepted coinage, it tested it as to its quality. Coin that did not come up to the correct standard was rejected, so men needed access to high-quality coin.[32] Without it, they were in default of their obligations and might find themselves subject to the full rigors of the law of the Exchequer. The king, moreover, needed coin to maintain himself and his household, and since his household was the heart of the administration of the realm and the heart of the army, coin of sufficient quantity was crucial to its operations. In losing his continental possessions, John had also lost access to vast revenues and stores of wealth. It is not possible to say with confidence exactly how much wealth John lost when he lost Normandy, Anjou and Poitou, but it was substantial; and England and Ireland now had to carry the full burden of the king's hugely costly military ambitions. John was going to need a prodigious amount of high-quality coin if he were to make his return to the continent a success. The assize of money of January 1205 was one of John's responses; it was designed to address concerns about the quality of English coin and to ensure that enough good coin was in circulation and available for collection to fund his campaign.

At the beginning of April, John again convened an assembly of his leading magnates, both ecclesiastical and secular, at Winchester; this, too, has all the hallmarks of a Great Council. The business this time (as it had been in August 1204 at Oxford) was the defense of the realm, and "by the assent of our archbishops, bishops, earls, barons, and all our faithful men of England" a provision was made whereby throughout the realm nine knights would band together to find a tenth whom they would finance with horse and arms. Letters were then sent to the sheriffs of England ordering them to ensure that the tenth knight would muster at London on May 1 ready "to go in our service where we order" and to be enjoined to remain in military service for as long as their services were required.[33]

These were the men who were to remain in England while John campaigned overseas. The knights raised in this manner were assigned to Robert fitz Roger, sheriff of Northumberland, and were responsible for the border between England and Scotland, or to Roger de Lacy, the constable of Chester and therefore responsible for the border between England and North Wales. The creation of this national army for the defense of the realm is indication enough that John recognized the dangers that his continental ambitions and the consequent dissipation of the kingdom's military strength posed to England.

At the end of April, John sent ahead to Poitou his illegitimate son Geoffrey and a dozen of his crack household troops, along with one of his most trusted military commanders, the household steward William de Cantilupe.[34] John also sent out a general summons to his English tenants-in-chief, ordering them to muster at Northampton on Sunday, May 15. Men were required to arrive with horse and arms and other necessities for travelling with the king and were to remain in the king's company for a period of no less than eighty days' service. John similarly wrote to his bishops requesting that they be at London on the same day, ready to work on his behalf and on the behalf of the community of the realm.[35] Ralph of Coggeshall records the Northampton meeting, and then says that the king went to Porchester to embark for the continent. His itinerary has him there at the beginning of June.[36]

We do not know what transpired at Northampton, but the muster at Porchester was an unmitigated disaster. The English army was gathered ready to embark, at which point the expedition was cancelled and the attack on Poitou was abandoned after much had been spent on organizing the army. According to the biographer of William Marshal, who was determined to answer the critics who laid the blame at his hero's door, John once again challenged the Marshal about his conduct the year before when he had sworn homage to the king of France, and demanded that William Marshal accompany him and his army to Poitou to fight the king of France. The Marshal baulked at the prospect of being forced to confront his liege lord on the field of battle, declaring that to do so would be wrong. Immediately John called for a judgment against the Marshal, but all refused to challenge the aged champion.[37] Even though he was a few years shy of his sixtieth birthday, the Marshal's physical presence meant that no man was prepared to risk the fight: he was an exceptionally formidable man in a world where men were trained to fight with weapons from their earliest days, and where aggression and overt acts of violent courage were celebrated. That the Marshal stood out in the company of other such men employed by the king for the purposes of intimidating his opponents gives us an insight into the capabilities of this particular royal servant. It also may have been that men feared starting a feud with someone whose retinue would make sure that anyone foolish enough to confront the Marshal would incur their lasting enmity.[38]

While the Marshal might not have wanted to go into battle against his liege lord in the kingdom of France, others might have been more prepared to fight for John. But when Archbishop Hubert Walter advised against the enterprise, claiming, amongst other things, that with an army in Poitou England would be vulnerable to attack, the campaign was abandoned in ignominy, with only a small force of knights and barons, led by the king's half-brother, William, earl of Salisbury, being sent to bolster the defenses of Poitou. The king had lost the confidence of his men. In despair, John sailed round the Isle of Wight before returning to his kingdom, having caused his subjects to fear that he had gone off to the continent on a reckless adventure without his army.[*39] Meanwhile King Philip collected a huge army and made for Loches, which was being held for John by Gerard de Athié. The city fell and Philip took captive over two hundred knights and serjeants. He then went on to Chinon, which in its turn fell into his hands. By the time Philip returned to the Île de France in mid-June, it had become clear that John's planned expedition was no longer coming.[40]

At this time, too, another crisis faced the king, this time in England. On July 13, 1205, Archbishop Hubert Walter died, and his death precipitated a drawn out and disastrous struggle to appoint his replacement. At the end of July, England was battered by hurricane-force winds and huge thunderstorms; to many, this presaged the Day of Judgment. In retrospect what it might have presaged was the titanic struggle that was about to unfold over the appointment of Hubert's replacement. At least in the replacement of Hubert as chancellor (if not as archbishop) John had little difficulty: he gave the office to Walter de Gray, nephew of John's favorite for the post at Canterbury, John de Gray, for the princely sum of 5,000 marks; evidently Walter thought that a good investment.[41]

---

* Coggeshall agrees that it was the king's two principal advisors, the stalwarts of the regime until that point, who warned John of the dangers of the enterprise.

T HE APPOINTMENT OF THE archbishop of Canterbury was always fraught with difficulty. The senior of the two primates in the kingdom, he held a special place in the affairs of the realm. An archbishop who had a good working relationship with his king could act as his deputy when he was out of the kingdom, as Hubert had for John, and he could play a senior role in the royal administration, as Hubert had, as chancellor, for John. An archbishop who had a bad working relationship with his king was a problem for everyone, as the Thomas Becket affair amply demonstrated. No one—not pope, not king, not church nor realm benefited from the struggle between Becket and Henry II. Therefore kings wanted, hardly surprisingly, to have their own man in this crucial post.

But the archbishop of Canterbury was also the leading ecclesiastic in the land and needed unimpeachable credentials as a man of religion. Since the Conquest, men of quality, mostly emanating from the monasteries, had held the post. The first exception to that rule was Thomas Becket. Hubert Walter was also an exception, though for the king a happier one. As primate, the archbishop had responsibility for the twelve suffragan bishops; and each of those bishops believed himself to have a role in the appointment of his superior.

Apart from his responsibility for the spiritual well-being of the kingdom and the leadership of his episcopal colleagues, the archbishop was also head of a monastic community at Christ Church, Canterbury. Unusually in Europe, England sported an episcopacy that was, in a significant number of cases, part of a monastic structure, and its archbishopric at Canterbury was organized in just this way. Monks, rather than canons, ran the cathedral and ministered to the religious needs of the diocese, and they, too, expected to have a say in the appointment of their superior; in fact they had a paramount right in his election, as all recognized. John's own experience during the election dispute that followed on the death of Archbishop Baldwin in 1190 and the eventual appointment of Hubert Walter in 1193 must have taught him that the monks of that community were resourceful and opinionated, and perfectly capable of following their own counsel.

The final person with a direct interest in the appointment of the arch-bishop of Canterbury was the pope. Ever since the eleventh century, popes had claimed a special competence in the cure of souls, and as such also claimed that they had the right to authorize the appointment of all archbishops. Archbishops had, since the very earliest times in the seventh century, been required to collect their pallia (the symbol of their direct authority from the pope as primate) from the pope. In theory, therefore, popes had always had the right to reject a candidate presented to them, but they seldom exercised this authority. Innocent III was made of differ-ent stuff, however, and he was not afraid to press the claims of the papacy as far as they might be pressed, and sometimes further.

John's first move, according to the monks' chronicler, Gervase of Canterbury, was to visit Christ Church shortly after Hubert's death.[42] He tried to mollify the monks by telling them that they would be able to choose someone from their own community to rule over them, but it was perhaps an error to take from them a valuable portable altar that the arch-bishop had bequeathed to the monks from his estate. John then asked for a delay in the election, to which the monks agreed, after which, according to Gervase, they sent emissaries to Rome to elicit the pope's support. In this delegation was the monks' sub-prior, Reginald, whom they had in secret elected as archbishop without the necessary royal license.

When John realized what had happened, he descended on Christ Church, arriving on December 11, 1205. The monks denied that they had elected their sub-prior and agreed, in the presence of the king, to elect John de Gray, then bishop of Norwich and one of the king's most trusted advisors. John immediately wrote to the pope informing him of the decision and asking him to ratify the election, and a further delega-tion of monks was dispatched to Rome.[43]

In 1206, therefore, Innocent III was placed in a quandary: he was faced with two rival claimants to the see, each with his own group of monks from Christ Church testifying that the election had been properly undertaken and that their candidate was, therefore, the rightful arch-bishop of Canterbury. Innocent concluded that the monks had behaved duplicitously, and said as much in a letter sent to them on March 30, 1206, admonishing them for their actions. In this letter he made it clear that he was minded to impose his own candidate on the monks for the archbishopric, and ordered a group of them to reconvene in Rome on October 1 to have their election overseen by papal authority. Innocent invited the suffragan bishops of the Canterbury archdiocese and the king to send their representatives. Meanwhile, he sent papal judges delegate to England to inquire into the way the election had been conducted.[44] It was clear that the election process was in a dreadful muddle, and Innocent now took the step of endorsing neither the monks' candidate nor the king's, but his own man. The pope was, with typical determination, minded to solve the problem himself. His decision was to persuade this group of electors to appoint Stephen Langton, a former teacher of Theology at the schools of Paris (soon to be constituted into a university, the first such organization to be created north of the Alps and the second university after Bologna), whom Innocent had earlier that year made cardinal-priest of St. Chrysogonus. It is testimony to the fact that papal claims to supremacy had become so effective that Innocent could over the course of many years impose his candidate on a reluctant community of monks and a contemptuous king. Nonetheless, it would be almost a year before Langton was formally consecrated.

The year 1205, therefore, turned out to be one of preparation for a return to the continent rather than an actual return. On November 30, John invited William, king of the Scots to come to York at the beginning of February 1206 for a parley.[45] On January 5, 1206, he wrote to the barons and knights of Poitou inviting them to return to his allegiance in exchange for a promise of clemency and a reaffirmation of grants given them by Henry II and Richard. Savaric de Mauléon was appointed seneschal of Poitou.[46] And at Easter, in early April, John invited Rögnvaldr Guðrøðarson, king of the Isles, to peace discussions with him.[47] It would be 1206, then, that would see the long-awaited return to the continent: the money was in place; the defenses of England secured; the leading magnates were either on board or, like William Marshal, effectively marginalized. John marched confidently into 1206 expecting to be received with acclamation and to begin the process of resecuring his continental lands.

THE CAMPAIGN IN POITOU had been as well planned as any. John had known he was heading for his ancestral homeland for at least eighteen months and he had been preparing the way assiduously. The ships were organized by his admiral of the fleet, William de Wrotham, who from 1205 to 1215 had control of John's navy. The logistical problems associated with transporting a large body of men not only across the English Channel but also halfway down the French coast into the notorious Bay of Biscay to La Rochelle with an enemy coast on one side and the open Atlantic on another were considerable, and were entrusted to a man of proven administrative capabilities.[48]

Also called to John's service in the month of May was a certain Eustace the Monk, a pirate whose exploits created around him legends that entered the popular imagination.[49] The letter of safe conduct issued to Eustace was dated the 25th at Portsmouth, a few days before the invasion force set sail for Poitou, and it gave Eustace, who had a base on Sark in the Channel Islands, permission to bring his ships to any port belonging to the king and to remain there until mid-June.[50] The king wanted to be sure that his ships should not fall prey to anyone as they tacked along the coast of Normandy and Brittany, before heading southward to their destination. This was a wise precaution, since piracy on both sides of the Channel was rife.

John also sent his proctors to the papal court in an attempt to make sure that he did not run foul of Pope Innocent, who was still minded to be firm with John about the appointment of a successor to Hubert Walter. These men, Amfrid of Dene and Thomas of Erdington, were given letters authorizing loans of 4,000 marks. They were also commissioned with a personal letter from John to Innocent asking him to remember the king's dignity in the matter of the appointment to Canterbury and the need for England to have a spiritual father at the country's metropolitan see.⁵¹ In addition, John organized vast amounts of money to leave England's shores for Poitou in preparation for his arrival. Everything was organized for a successful campaign, and at the beginning of June, he set sail for La Rochelle.

John's arrival at the port was the signal for furious activity, as the king was welcomed like a savior by Savaric de Mauléon and the other Poitevin barons.⁵² The king received the submission of important Poitevin magnates, and he authorized the release of some of the prisoners who had been taken at Mirebeau, including the vicomte of Fronsac, who had been languishing in an English gaol for four long years under the watchful gaze of Geoffrey de Neville's men. It took Peter des Roches a further four months to put the king's order into action.⁵³ On the other hand, the mother, wife and others who had been held captive as surety for Savaric de Mauléon's good behavior were quickly released.⁵⁴ Peter de Préaux, the commander of Rouen in 1204, was given letters of safe conduct to come to a meeting with the king. Peter had been responsible for surrendering Rouen to Philip Augustus, so a rapprochement between him and John was essential if the king were to make progress in Normandy.

The French king responded to news of John's arrival at La Rochelle by mustering his troops and taking them to Poitou. He made his headquarters at Chinon while sending his deputies to bolster the defenses of key strongholds, such as Poitiers and Mirebeau, before returning to Paris. John's priority, however, was to look southward and to attempt to undo the damage caused by Alfonso VIII. He stayed in Bordeaux for two whole months, receiving the submission of his Gascon nobles and shoring up his position in the region. Alfonso's invasion of 1204 had been thwarted in its ambition only by the resistance of the men of Bordeaux, La Réole and Bayonne. Their courage, along with the fact that Alfonso was drawn back to Castile by the threat of a Moorish invasion, prevented him taking Gascony; but Alfonso left his best soldiers led by his own seneschal in Montauban, north of Toulouse. Indeed, it seems that Alfonso did return, though he and John did not meet in battle. In mid-July, King John personally supervised the siege of Montauban, and by August 1 he had taken it. This victory marked the high point of John's Poitevin expedition: Gascony was now safe from the attentions of the king of Castile.[55]

Certain that his enemies in the south had been suppressed, in early September John turned northward to take Angers; according to the French version of the affair, he completely destroyed the city. At Clisson, on the marches of Brittany and Anjou, John called the bishop of Vannes and others to come to talk with him about the future of the duchy. The conference was to take place during Michaelmas week at the end of the month.[56] Whether or not it happened is not recorded, but that Brittany largely remained impervious to John's attempts to draw it back into his orbit is hardly surprising given his notorious treatment of Arthur. John's actions in Angers that September brought a return of the French king from Paris to Poitou.[57] He laid waste to the lands of the viscount of Thouars, who had gone over to John's side, and taunted John by bringing his army to the very gates of Thouars where, in early October, John was staying. King John refused, however, to engage openly with the French king's forces, fearing, presumably, that he did not have the military might to win against Philip in battle.[58]

No doubt it was at this moment that John realized he needed to return to England. It was evident to him and to his advisors that he had achieved all that could be achieved with the resources at his disposal. John decided to sue for peace, and on October 26 he agreed to the terms of the truce with King Philip: there was to be an exchange of prisoners and the truce was to last for two years; it would, however, be a further eight years before John could go back to France.[59] At the beginning of November, John wrote to the barons and knights of Angoulême entreating them to hold to their oath to Isabella, their "lady queen," which they had sworn in the presence of Savaric de Mauléon, John's seneschal of Poitou, that they would hold their faith to her as their liege lady against all mortals, save King John himself for as long as he lived. He then gave the son of Aimery, viscount of Thouars an annual pension at the English Exchequer until he had an ecclesiastical living assigned to him.[60] And finally, around November 7, John embarked for England, arriving in Bere Regis just over a month later.

The object of the 1206 campaign had been the security of Poitou and Gascony; in other words John wanted to make sure that having lost his father's ancestral homes in Normandy and Anjou, he did not compound that error by losing completely his mother's ancestral homes, too. He failed to secure Poitiers and his mother's palace in the city, so the campaign could not be described as a complete success, but he had, as one later writer put it, "recovered almost all of Poitou and Gascony."[61] He had also tested Philip's resolve, and had found that the king of France was well prepared to resist any incursions that John might plan into Anjou and into Normandy. It was an important discovery, and it taught him that to reacquire Normandy he needed a bigger army and perhaps, also, an alliance that would threaten the French king from two sides. Each of these would require vast amounts of cash. Raising that money would be John's priority throughout 1207 and for several years to come.

I MMEDIATELY ON HIS RETURN, John began to milk his kingdom in a way that would gain him the widespread criticism of his subjects. The chroniclers were most vociferous about the new tax that John levied: he wanted a thirteenth on all movables and revenues.[62] The king dressed up his demand as an "aid." Feudal prerogative allowed a lord to take an aid in three instances: the knighting of his first-born son; the marriage of his first-born daughter; and the ransoming of his body. John asked that the aid might now be given out of grace "for the defence of our kingdom and the recovery of our rights." He had first aired the idea to his bishops at the beginning of January 1207 and met with a negative response, so he convened a Great Council meeting at Oxford in the first week of February. According to the Waverley annalist, gathered at Oxford were a "multitude of the prelates of the church and the magnates of the realm, where the king demanded from the bishops and abbots what he had previously demanded from them." In other words, John was unwilling to take the initial no for an answer and decided to ask the question again. The response of the prelates of both metropolitan sees, Canterbury and York, was the same: the new tax was unprecedented. The king, therefore, "on the basis of more sensible counsel, relaxed his demands."

The views of the magnates gathered at Oxford at the beginning of February 1207 are not recorded. It is telling, however, that the Waverley annalist completes his account by writing that "he caused throughout the whole of the realm, that everyman of whatever fee, might reveal the value of his property, movables and non movables, and give from this a thirteenth part to the king for the recovery of his inheritance in Normandy and in his other lands," thus placing the decision to make a general tax firmly at John's feet.[63] Gervase of Canterbury goes further, calling John's actions "a statute and an order," and describing the king as "obstinate" and unwilling to listen to "entreaties."[64] And Gervase's account of the circumstances surrounding the demand for taxation is confirmed in the very language that John used in the letters patent he sent to the counties, issued from Northampton on February 17 (a week after the council had ended), declaring his intention to tax his people: the letter begins by stating that he had behind him the authority of "the counsel and assent of our council." In 1205, when he had issued the Statute of Arms, he had done so by the "assent of the archbishops, bishops, earls, barons, and all our faithful men of England."[65] In 1207, therefore, John was going out on a limb, and he had failed to take the great men of the realm with him.

The men who comprised this "council" and who in February 1207 gave the king "counsel" were those who were in constant attendance on the king: his immediate circle of friends, advisors and enforcers. High in royal favor were three bishops, John de Gray of Norwich, Peter des Roches of Winchester and Jocelin of Bath; the first two of whom were identified by Roger of Wendover as being amongst John's evil counsellors who encouraged the king to rule arbitrarily. Following these bishops were the earls: Geoffrey fitz Peter of Essex the justiciar, William de Warenne and Saher de Quency of Winchester. Then there were the hard men of the regime: Hugh de Neville, John's chief forester; William

Brewer, his man at the Exchequer; Geoffrey de Neville, the steward of the royal household; and Peter de Maulay. In addition there were the staunch loyalists: William d'Aubigny, Henry Biset, Gerard de Canville, Gilbert de Clara and Robert de Courtenay. If these were the men who made up the "council" that conceded the Thirteenth, then they were certainly not representative of the baronial or ecclesiastical elite of the kingdom.

The demand for the Thirteenth was an arbitrary act of taxation, carried out without the consent of the bishops, and the language of contemporary documents suggests that the secular magnates were also equivocal about it. After the experience of the Poitevin campaign, John had returned to England not a conciliator and a seeker of consensus amongst his ecclesiastical and secular magnates, but a man who was coming to see them as a problem getting in the way of his right to pursue his inheritance; those who opposed him were to be bullied, threatened and browbeaten into submission.

The tax itself was extraordinarily successful, realizing in excess of £57,000, twice the amount raised through mechanisms by which the king ordinarily raised revenue.[66] Some men managed to buy their way out of it, and the Hospitallers and Cistercians were exempted, but for the most part people just had to knuckle down and pay whether they liked it or not; most did not like it at all. William and Gerard of Lancaster, for example, were thrown into the Fleet prison (one of the earliest references to this notorious prison that existed on the site for almost 700 years) for crimes relating to the Thirteenth. By May 30, they had repented and were released on the direct orders of the king.[67] A letter to the townsmen of Bristol, who were also not exempt, sent on April 10, 1207, shows what impact the tax was having: "do not," the letter runs, "impede the men of Breteuil from leaving [your port] on account of the Thirteenth."[68] Irritation at the cause of the tax (the loss of Normandy, since the men of Breteuil were now subjects of the king of France) was getting the better of the men of Bristol.

It was the innovative nature of the tax that struck men hard. And given that the bishops had already proclaimed that it was unprecedented, so must others have been aware of its significance. For what it presaged was the king's attempt to open up direct taxation to a wider proportion of the population of England than had hitherto experienced the attentions of his tax gatherers. The Anglo-Saxon kingdom had levied taxes (called geld, hence Danegeld) on land that were assessed by the hide (or carucate in parts of the east and north of England or sulung in Kent). For a century after 1066, the land tax (last collected in 1161–2)[69] continued alongside a new tax based on the knight's fee, by which the lands of the king's tenants-in-chief were divided up and on which the Exchequer assessed the tax known as scutage. Scutage became the principal means by which kings raised revenue for their military campaigns, and when it was called, the king's tenants-in-chief had to pay. It did not matter to the king how his tenants-in-chief acquired the money that they were required to render.

The simple fact was that most tenants-in-chief placed on their lands sufficient tenants to whom they could turn when the scutage was levied. The king taxed his tenants-in-chief, and they in their turn taxed their tenants. The greatest in the land were thus in the position of being able to extract the taxes that they owed the king from those beneath them. It was a happy state of affairs for those at the top. But these great men could not avoid the Thirteenth because the tax was aimed directly at their movables and their revenues, no matter where they came from. Simply put, the Thirteenth was a direct attack on the pockets of the nobility, secular and ecclesiastical; no wonder they were angered by it. And it is little wonder that John, despite his blandishments, could not get their consent to it. So he turned instead to the men on whom he could rely, his most trusted counsellors, the men who made the regime work.

That John had been unable to carry his bishops with him in his attempt to levy a tax on the Church is striking. The composition of the episcopacy was, largely, of his making. Eight of the fifteen bishops in post in January 1207 had been appointed by John and the remainder, in one form or another, had been promoted from the ranks of royal servants. In the main, one did not become a bishop unless one was known to the king and had served his administration loyally. The refusal of the bishops to bow to John's demands for the Thirteenth meant that he had lost their support, which was remarkable since only a few months before they had backed his preferred candidate to the archiepiscopal see of Canterbury. It is not unreasonable to suggest, therefore, that the winter of 1206 to 1207 marks one point in John's reign during which he had lost the confidence of the good and the great of the realm, and turned ever more inward to counsel he could trust to give him the answers he sought.

John's actions during these first months of 1207 increasingly seem to be those of a man retreating into his shell. It is quite possible that—although the sources are silent on this matter—the failure of the Poitevin venture to make substantial inroads into Philip Augustus's position in Poitou and Normandy made his English magnates perceive him in a less favorable light. Certainly in the spring of 1207, he no longer held the confidence of his episcopate, although in May, with the arrival of summer and the realization that they had to live with the king that God had given them, like it or not, the mood softened. By May 26, John felt that he could write to the officials of the archbishopric of Canterbury declaring that he now had the consent of the "archbishops, bishops, abbots, priors, and magnates of the realm" for the aid that he had requested "for the defence of the realm and the recovery of our lands."⁷⁰ It had taken six months of hard negotiating for John to get to this position.

The demands for money made by John of his subjects were to have a profound effect on the economy and society of England and, in the end, it was these demands for money, ruthlessly pursued, that alienated John from his nobility. But it was more than just the demand for taxation that caused a rift between the king and his major subjects; it was also the fact that the money he collected was either transported abroad for the furtherance of the king's continental ambitions or it was tied up in a series of castle treasuries dotted around England.⁷¹

In a policy that seems to have been initiated at around the time he found himself confined to England, John set about gathering and holding a war chest of vast proportions. Quite what proportion of coin in circulation was being stored by the king and transported out of the realm is difficult to say. Economic historians have tried to imagine the amount of coin available in the early thirteenth century and have come up with an estimate of about £250,000-worth of silver pennies (with 240d to a pound, that amounts to 60 million individual coins). In 1207, of these silver pennies, between 15 and 20 per cent was under the king's direct control.

Tying up proportions of coin in an economy that needed money both as a medium of exchange and as a means of paying tax meant that England was facing strong deflationary pressures and men had difficulty getting hold of enough coin to pay their debts. Although John and his advisors did not have the economic knowledge to understand what impact they were having, it seems clear that what they were creating was a recession that, because John's plans to return to the continent remained stubbornly uppermost in his policies for the next decade, lasted for a very long time indeed.[72]

8

THE CITADEL UNDER SIEGE

A T THE BEGINNING OF June 1207, as the Thirteenth was gathered and as John and his magnates were beginning to rebuild their relationship, Pope Innocent III decided that now was the moment to force John's hand regarding the appointment of the archbishop of Canterbury. Despite months of negotiations, John had refused to accept Stephen Langton as his new primate. But, with characteristic determination, on June 17, at Viterbo, where he was making an extended stay in order to root out heresy,[1] Innocent III consecrated Stephen Langton as archbishop.[2] John's reaction was immediate: he went to the archbishop's palace at Lambeth from where he issued letters to the citizens of Canterbury and the men of the monks' estates, and all the knights and free tenants of Kent, demanding that as they "loved their honour and their bodies and all that [they held] in the kingdom" they were to obey the commands of Fulk de Cantilupe and Reginald of Cornhill, the king's men who were now in possession of the lands of the monks of Christ Church, Canterbury. The king sent his mercenary crossbowmen to Canterbury to menace the monks who, as a result of this action, took a vote on the matter and decided to go into exile, leaving behind them the elder monks and some of the younger ones who were suspected of siding with the king.[3] The archbishop's lands (separate from those of the monks) had been given over to Reginald by June 28.[4] It is also quite likely that at this point John brought further pressure to bear on his ecclesiastics by banning the sale of grain from all their estates, a ban he briefly lifted in the autumn,

149

but only until the feast of St Katherine (November 25), when it was to be reimposed.[5]

John also began the process of making sure of his defenses, so he spent the summer and autumn maneuvering his most loyal followers into key positions of trust. These included his household retainers, some knights, others men of proven administrative capacity whose special relationship with the king meant he could trust them completely. Brian de Lisle, for example, was given custody of the royal forests north of the Humber; John of Bassingbourn was given control of Corfe Castle, one of John's key fortresses; John fitz Hugh was given Surrey and Sussex; William Brewer was given custody of Hampshire, Somerset and Dorset; Robert of Ropsely took control of Warwickshire and Leicestershire; Richard de Mucegross took control of Gloucestershire; Geoffrey de Neville took Wiltshire: and in that crucial area, the Channel Islands, Philip d'Aubigny took Jersey and Guernsey, which the king evidently expected him to hold in person rather than by deputy.[6]

That autumn, John once again commissioned a review of coinage, this time ensuring that the dies from which coins were struck were brought to the Exchequer at Westminster to be checked.[7] At the same time, he called a council of his leading Irish magnates, who had that summer been involved in armed resistance against the king's justiciar, Meiler fitz Henry. The meeting took place at Woodstock in November, and Irish matters were center stage. During the next few years Ireland, along with Scotland and Wales, would feature heavily in John's life. For the moment, however, apart from these distractions, John had to manage a conflict with the pope, who at this particular moment was trying to detach the English bishops and magnates from their king.

P ART OF THE REASON that John could not persuade his bishops to stay with him in the matter of the Canterbury election was that Innocent III not only pressed ahead with the consecration of Stephen Langton despite John's objections, but he also enlisted the English bishops in the process of persuading John to allow Langton to take up residence in England. It was a clever move on the pope's part because it made it impossible for the bishops so chosen to sit on the fence. Innocent was forcing them to decide either to support him or their king. On August 27, Innocent wrote to the bishops of London, Ely and Worcester, instructing them to go to John and convince him to take the sensible course of action and defer to the decision of the pope; if he were to remain obdurate, then they were authorized to place the kingdom of England under an interdict by which all ecclesiastical offices would be suspended except "the baptism of infants and the confession of the dying."[8] All three bishops were king's men to the core; in choosing them, Innocent was adroitly attempting to separate John from these key allies.*[9]

The same day, Innocent also wrote to the bishop of Rochester ordering him to enact a sentence of excommunication on Fulk de Cantilupe and Reginald of Cornhill, and any others who had followed the king's orders and despoiled the property of the monks of Christ Church.[10] Kings had long forbidden their bishops to excommunicate their officials without royal license. Four key bishops were, therefore, drawn into the fray on the pope's side, be it willingly or, more likely, unwillingly. On November 19, Innocent wrote generally to the bishops exhorting them to promote the cause of Stephen Langton, warning them that Adam had been ejected from paradise for disobedience and that his fate awaited them should they continue to support John; Innocent had yet to fully detach the senior clergy from their king. He also wrote to the three bishops whom he had charged with the duty of imposing the interdict, and it clearly reveals that none of them had yet had the nerve to implement the sentence in the face of their king's intransigence. [11]

The magnates, too, by separate letter, were encouraged to counsel John to accept Langton. In this letter Innocent likened John to Rehoboam, the

---

* The bishops of Ely and Worcester were also required to censure John about his failure to settle the dower of Berengaria, Richard I's widow.

Biblical tyrant of Israel who, in the face of rebellion, lost the majority of the lands over which he ruled and ended his days as monarch of the much-reduced kingdom of Judah.[12] While it is difficult to see how this message was promulgated, given the vigilance with which the ports of England were watched,*[13] if it did get through, the comparison of John's current predicament with the life and rule of Rehoboam would have been lost on no one; the fact that Rehoboam was Solomon's son made the analogy all the more poignant. The Margam annalist states his case simply: "there was a discord between Pope Innocent and John the tyrant of England, [but] almost all of the laity and clergy favoured [the king]."[14]

Innocent, despite his best efforts, had yet to impose Stephen Langton on Canterbury and England. And that autumn there was further good news for John: on October 1 at Winchester, Queen Isabella gave birth to a son, whom the couple called Henry.†[15] Aged almost forty-one, John had produced his first legitimate child and, importantly, that child was a boy. There would be more children, but given the centrality of males to the inheritance of land, the fact that John now had a male heir must have eased his worries a little about the future. He quickly set about producing more children, and another boy, to be named Richard, was to follow in early January 1209.

John's resistance to the pope's demands centered on his resolve to maintain his rights, as he saw them, the most significant of which was to play a part in determining who would be archbishop of Canterbury. From the neutral observer's perspective, John had a point. While it was undoubtedly true that the monks of Christ Church, Canterbury traditionally elected the archbishop, tradition also dictated that the king had a crucial role in deciding the identity of his principal ecclesiastic. As John stated outright in a letter addressed to the bishops of London, Ely and

---

* Innocent complained about his proctors being detained at Dover.

† Isabella was given rich cloths for herself and her maids as she approached the six-week period before the birth when she was expected to withdraw from the world to the comfort of her birthing apartments.

Worcester, the pope's proctors in this matter, he accepted the pope's ultimate authority in the appointment to Canterbury, but he still expected Innocent III to acknowledge, recognize and not to disregard the dignity, rights and liberties that belonged to him and his heirs.*[16] But Innocent was not going to move on the matter and was determined to proceed with the interdict if John continued to refuse to bow to his will.

IN THE LEAD UP to the interdict, John assembled his maritime defenses, ordering, on March 17, 1208, a muster of a fleet at London which was to follow the orders given by the admiral of the fleet, William de Wrotham.[17] Further letters of safe conduct were sent early in April to Eustace the Monk to come to England, and other English shipmen were recalled to England with the threat of dire consequences if they refused his summons.[18] There is no mention of the use to which these ships were to be put. Further orders were issued regarding the security of the coast in May. On the 26th of the month, orders were given for the seizure of all foreign ships in ports throughout England and Wales, "except those of Denmark and Norway and its dependencies who are not against us."[19] The implication of those words is that John believed that everyone else was against him. Perhaps the ships that were mustered at London at Easter were, therefore, for defense against the possibility of invasion rather than in the hope that another campaign to the continent might be launched.

As the interdict was declared, John ordered books to be sent from Reading Abbey, which were delivered by the hand of the abbey's sacrist.[20] John did not explain why he chose this moment to catch up on his reading, but it is worth considering what he wanted to have with him at

---

* Issued on January 21, 1208, and witnessed, significantly at Lambeth, by the king's senior secular supporters Geoffrey fitz Peter, earl of Essex, Ranulf, earl of Chester, William d'Aubigny, earl of Arundel, William, earl of Salisbury, Richard de Clare, Saher de Quency, earl of Winchester, Aubrey de Vere, earl of Oxford, Robert fitz Roger, Roger constable of Chester, William Brewer.

a moment of extreme crisis for himself and for the kingdom. There were
six volumes containing the whole of the Old Testament. This was a particular favorite of medieval kings since they liked to model themselves
on the bellicose David in particular. The sacrist also brought Hugh of
St. Victor's *On the Sacraments of the Faith*, the greatest work of one of the
greatest minds of the twelfth century; since the pope was withdrawing
the sacraments from John and from his people, it is not surprising that
Hugh's book was on John's reading list. There were also more esoteric
works, including the Letter of Candidus to Marius Victorinus. Marius was
an early Christian theologian who adapted Stoicism for Christian purposes: John would have to be stoical in the face of the pope's onslaught,
so this text was a good place in which to find inspiration. Another text
that John had brought to him from Reading Abbey was Valerius Maxi-
mus's *Memorable Deeds and Sayings*. Written in about AD 31 to provide
moral guidance to his Roman readers, Valerius's work covered such topics as Courage, Endurance, Determination and Self-Confidence, crucial
for the coming struggle, along with some that John might have wished
to pass over, such as Loyalty to Parents and to Brothers. The more standard works in the collection of books delivered to John included Peter
Lombard's Sentences (*Quatuor libri Sententiarum*), perhaps the leading
theological work of the age, with the fourth book devoted to the seven
sacraments and to the subjects of death, judgment, hell and heaven. John
also received Origen's treatise on the Old Testament, in which the author
uses allegory to explain the text. In the minds of modern theologians,
Origen's methodology amounts to no more than reading into the text
what one wishes to read into it, not quite making it up as one goes along,
but not far short; the fact that John chose to read Origen perhaps gives us
a further, unflattering insight into the king's mind at this point in his life.
The final selection was from the work Augustine of Hippo, including his
City of God, a treatise that, amongst other things, notices that "all men
desire to be happy" and then goes on to question what happiness might
be. None of this is light reading and all of it suggests that there was some

serious discussion under way in the close circles around the king concerning the impact of the interdict. John was applying his mind as well as his might to the problem.

On the whole, interdicts on kingdoms did not last very long; and Innocent expected the interdict on England to swiftly make King John obedient. That is the only possible reading of a further interdict that Innocent ordered to be laid on the province of York should John fail to restore the property of Archbishop Geoffrey of York, issued on May 27, 1208 (Geoffrey had been in dispute with John since 1204).[21] In another letter, issued on June 14, sent to the bishops of London, Ely and Worcester, he expressed the hope that the interdict would soon be lifted, but acknowledged that, in the meantime, its existence caused problems. One that he noted was the fact that the chrism, a year's supply of which was traditionally made every Maundy Thursday, was not made in 1208. This made it difficult to baptize infants (the one rite still permitted under the terms of the interdict). The hand of a bishop or priest should mix more oil, Innocent directed, with the remaining chrism left over from that made on Maundy Thursday 1207. Furthermore, he declared, while it might seem essential that the dying should receive the viaticum of the communion, they were to be sacrificed to the greater cause of bringing the king to order. However, as long as the services were conducted in hushed tones behind closed doors and without the clamor of church bells or the company of those excommunicated or those under sentence of interdict, monks were allowed to conduct the normal religious services, as were conventional churches, which were allowed to celebrate the mass once a week.[22]

Not everyone followed the diktats of the pope concerning the interdict. In one of his letters, Innocent III singled out the English Cistercians as being blatantly guilty of continuing to celebrate communion and the solemnities of the mass in defiance of his mandate. They thought that they were exempt, but Innocent was keen to disabuse them of that view, though his repeated blandishments suggest that the Cistercians were not listening to him.*[23] And perhaps as they did so they had the greater good at heart. The lack of religious guidance was enough to encourage the growth of heretical leaders, such as Simon of Atherfield from the Isle of Wight, who was murdered by his wife in 1211 and who appears to have been a religious leader of sorts whose cult, after his death, Peter des Roches did his best to suppress.[24] At least some English men and women had, therefore, when cut adrift by the papacy, sought out spiritual consolation from unauthorized preachers.

Perhaps counterintuitively, Innocent expected some church business to be maintained. He was willing, for example, to continue to hear cases in the curia and to make judgments concerning disputes between litigants. He persisted in appointing papal judges delegate to investigate specific cases. He expected appointments to ecclesiastical offices to go ahead. So, for example, he instructed the chapter at Exeter to appoint a new bishop, despite the interdict, and in his letter authorizing the election, he criticized John for holding the see vacant for too long (three months was deemed the maximum acceptable, according to the Second Lateran Council of 1179). On the same day, Innocent wrote to the deans and chapters of Lincoln, Coventry, Durham and Chichester, instructing them in like manner and complaining again about John's failure to allow the appointment of successors. At the same time, Innocent III wrote directly to John expressing these precise concerns. The king must have wondered if he was being sent mixed messages.[25] But John evidently took the pope at his word: by April 12, 1209, for example, he had installed his clerk Hugh of Wells as bishop of Lincoln.

In the curia at Anagni on May 27, 1208, the day's business focused on affairs in England. Not only did Innocent address a letter concerning the conflict between John and Archbishop Geoffrey of York, he addressed a further four letters to various recipients concerning the main interdict

---

* A privilege extended to Stephen Langton and the bishops of London, Ely and Worcester along with members of their respective households should they visit England during the Interdict.

itself. These letters seem to suggest that Innocent thought that John was coming round to the idea that he might accept Langton as his archbishop and that he would allow the monks to return to their monastery.[26] In July, John issued letters of safe conduct for Simon Langton (Stephen Langton's brother and the chief negotiator for the papal party), two monks of Christ Church, Canterbury and the bishops of London, Ely and Worcester to come to him in order to conduct further negotiations concerning the appointment to Canterbury. The safe conducts were to remain valid until September 8. On September 9, they were renewed for a further term, from the end of September for a period of three weeks, suggesting that Simon had not been in England that summer.[27]

T HE MULCTING OF CHURCH property began on March 17, when the king issued letters declaring that the negotiations that had been taking place at Winchester had broken down and, as a result, the possessions of named bishoprics were to be placed in the hands of the king's men. The king himself witnessed the letters announcing the decision: John was taking personal charge of the situation.[28] Instructions were issued to confiscate the property of any of the clergy who, from March 24 onward, refused to celebrate divine services.

The enthusiasm with which the king's officers launched into the business of taking Church lands is witnessed by a plethora of writs that had to be issued within weeks of the initial orders for sequestration, protecting the property of those churchmen in the king's favor. The men whose job it had been to take over Church land seem to have done so without fear or favor. Even the highest in John's regime were affected by the actions of the king's officers. The lands of Richard Marsh, for example, a clerk of the king's chamber and therefore one of the principal members of the royal household who held an office that involved daily contact with the king, got sucked into the general offensive on Church lands. He held properties in Kent, Surrey, Westmorland, Northumberland, Lancashire and in the bailiwick of the chief forester, Hugh de Neville, all of which needed writs ordering their protection from the overenthusiasm of the men on the ground putting the king's wishes into operation. Even that stalwart of John's regime, the admiral of the fleet William de Wrotham, who was also archdeacon of Taunton and, therefore, an ecclesiastic by the definitions of the day, required letters of protection to defend his property from the actions of another senior member of John's regime, the household knight Robert of Burgate.[29] The two men must have been known to each other and they were supposed to be on the same team; the zeal with which the king's officers undertook their duty to sequestrate Church lands resulted in a rapid, and sometimes even arbitrary, seizure of property.

Of course, not all Church property found itself in the king's hands, though the monastic chroniclers, outraged by the king's behavior, would have us believe that it did; and it seems likely, too, that as time went by, John relaxed his attack on ecclesiastical property. The lands of those bishops and abbots who decided to remain with the king, for example, stayed safe. The temporalities of the bishop of Norwich were protected by special royal mandate; the lands of the bishopric of Bath remained firmly in the bishop's hands by order of the king. Peter des Roches, occupant of the richest see in England, Winchester, continued to enjoy the revenues of his bishopric and took into his protection the property of the cathedral priory and of other communities in his fee.[30] Henry, abbot of the Cistercian foundation of Bindon, Dorset, continued to serve in John's household after the interdict was declared and played his part in the administration of the king's business, eventually receiving his reward by promotion to the see of Emly, Ireland, in 1212.[31] The key negotiator on the king's side, Hugh, abbot of Beaulieu, a man noted more for his eloquence than his character, acted as John's proctor throughout in the negotiations with Rome.[32]

If we are to take seriously the wording of the royal letters sequestrating the lands of ecclesiastics who refused to perform divine service during the interdict, then we should assume that communities that received

letters of protection were delivering their contractual duty of minister-
ing to their parishioners. The author of the Worcester annals, at least,
gives that impression when he writes that John made "restitution to the
religious" of their lands. There are many of these letters of restitution,
such as to the abbots of Reading and Abingdon, to the priors of Merton
and Newark, and to the abbesses of Godstow and Wilton, which provide
positive evidence that the Church did not maintain a united front against
the king in the early months of the interdict.* Letters of protection were
also issued for individual ecclesiastics such as William, priest of Brad-
well, William of Necton and two canons of Hereford Cathedral, William
Folet and John Clement. Indeed, the wider evidence would suggest that
very many individual churchmen continued to control their property and
so, presumably, continued celebrating divine service throughout the period of the interdict.[33] Taken at this level, the effects of the interdict seem
less than united, an indication, therefore, that the clergy's strike was not
as universal as either the pope would have wanted or as the monastic
chroniclers would have us believe. John was not entirely without friends
in the kingdom, and many religious men and women saw the strength
of the king's case against the pope. And there is some indication that
although his first reaction to the interdict was to issue sweeping orders
sequestrating ecclesiastical lands, John rapidly came to modify his view.
The temporalities of his principal belligerents remained in royal hands,
as did the lands of those bishoprics and abbeys whose occupants died or
abjured the land, but that still meant that after the initial vehemence of
his response, much Church property remained in Church hands.

The administrative burden of organizing the sequestration of Church
property was great indeed, and it involved not only the king's own
officers (the men of the household as well as sheriffs and other local

---

* Beneficiaries of these letters included the abbots of Reading, Abingdon, Hide,
Langlay, Ramsey, the cathedral priory of Worcester, canons of Exeter cathedral, and St.
Frideswide, Oxford; the priors of Fromton, Coges, Esson, Daventry (Cluniac), Coventry,
Merton, Newark; the abbesses of Wilton, Godstow, Wherwell, Amesbury, Shaftesbury.

custodians), but also the very lynchpin of Angevin administration: the law-worthy men of the English shires who acted as the jurors in hundred and county courts. On April 6, orders were issued to grant a pittance to the regular and secular clergy, "namely two courses for a meal," on the witness of four law-worthy men from each parish. On April 13, Reginald of Cornhill was ordered to pay pittances to the canons lodged at Upchurch, Kent.[34] Equally, the monks of Battle Abbey were not to starve: Reginald de Cornhill was ordered to find for them their pittance "just as it is ordered for other religious men."[35] The Church had withdrawn its labor, and so he withdrew the support that the Church enjoyed for that labor. The jurors were asked to adjudicate on what was a fair pittance; what they decided, we do not know, and we are left to guess at how generous they were to their ecclesiastical neighbors.

We should imagine that the ecclesiastics who had control over their own temporalities as de facto officers of the king were kinder to their brethren than were the four law-worthy men from each parish; at least that is the implication of the comment by Peter of Blois concerning the wickedness of the men who guarded the clergy's barns.[36] The abbot of Bury St Edmunds received permission to account for the revenues of the abbey and to determine the pittance due to the monks, as did the dean of Lincoln for the cathedral community and canons therein. The master of the Gilbertine Order, Master Gilbert II of Sempringham, was to enjoy the right to account to the king for all the possessions of the order, amounting to some fifteen houses of monks and nuns.[37] Similarly the prior of Lenton, the abbot of St. Peter's, Gloucester, the prior of Llanthony Secunda, Gloucestershire, the abbot of Cirencester, the abbot of Winchcombe, the abbot of Tewkesbury, the abbot of St. Augustine, Bristol, and the prior of Beckford all enjoyed the right to administer their own lands and revenues for the king.[38] According to one contemporary commentator, John demanded 1,000 marks from each religious house for the privilege of doing so, and another observer, Adam of Eynsham, thought that Raymond, archdeacon of Leicester, was "almost the only one who of his own free will chose a long exile" rather than to "pay money for the redemption of" his possessions,[39] but the evidence, problematic though it is, does not substantiate sweeping statements about what John did to the Church; what occurred was much more complex than the outraged monastic commentators wanted us to believe.[40]

There is little doubt, however, that much Church property did find its way into the king's hands, and the king made a very great profit from it. We do not know the value of all the land and revenues paid to the king because so few transactions made it into the official records, but we get a sense of the scale of John's gains from the discussions about appropriate reparation made at the end of the dispute. The damages agreed in 1214 amounted to some 100,000 marks, two-thirds of a king's ransom (Richard's ransom in 1194 had been set at 150,000 marks), which were not deemed sufficient to fully recompense the clergy for their monetary losses. The thirteenth-century compilation known as the Red Book of the Exchequer provides us with a figure of £100,000 (a mark was an accounting measure equalling two-thirds of a pound—13s 4d, where 20s is equal to a pound), a full king's ransom, but this is also likely to underestimate the total profit that John received from Church lands during the interdict.[41]

One example of how the king used the revenue of the Church will suffice to demonstrate its huge potential, not only for diverting revenue into the king's hands, but also offsetting the expensive business of getting the king's household through each financial year. In the Michaelmas Term of 1212, John fitz Hugh accounted at the Exchequer for some of the revenues of the Christ Church, Canterbury estates that had been diverted to pay for the king's expenses: £82 11s 1d was spent on supporting the king's pack of hounds, his huntsmen and their horses; £128 0s 18d was used to buy lavish clothing for the king, his former wife, the countess of Gloucester, and other select members of the royal household; a further £957 5s 5d was expended on cloth that would be made up to clothe the wider royal household; 60s was spent on the rent for a house in which to store the 7,500 ells of cloth that the monks' money had bought; £383 18s 9d was paid out to cover the cost of the lodging and upkeep of the king's horses; more than £50 was used to buy various spices for the king's table, including pepper (262lb), saffron (2lb), cumin (25lb), nutmeg (1lb), cinnamon (3lb), cardamom (2lb) and ginger (3lb); 230 marks were spent on the gold and jewels used to decorate one of the king's many crowns; and £485 was paid directly into the king's chamber for sundry expenses. Most provokingly, perhaps, if the monks had known how their resources were being used, the revenues of Christ Church were diverted to acquire large quantities of military equipment, including 2,000 crossbow bolts, 4,000 doublets and 140 pairs of gilded spurs. Shields, mail tunics and various pieces of armor were also bought with the monks' money. The king's tents were repaired at the monks' expense, as were several of his own houses. The monks even had to pay for the patterned coats that were worn by the king's lion and its tamer. In short, there was nothing to which the king would not apply the monks' revenues, spending in total £2,223 7s 6d during the year.[42]

John clearly thought that he could use Church property as if it were his own and spend the revenues as he saw fit because twelfth-century English kings believed that all property belonged to the king and was held on sufferance by his tenants; John applied the same principle to lands held by the Church. Thus when a bishop died, until the appointment of his successor, the temporalities of the see returned to the king, who proceeded to enjoy the revenues of the bishopric, sometimes for a very considerable time. Bishops, moreover, like other crown tenants, held their lands in return for service. In the case of bishops, that service was not only secular, it was also spiritual, and their tenure of the temporalities belonging to the see depended upon their continued service in both spheres. By withdrawing their spiritual labor, they had, in the king's mind, forfeited their right to the property that pertained to those services, so when Pope Innocent III proclaimed the interdict across King John's lands, those bishops who complied with the pope's order lost their lands. The same went for abbots and their monks along with other ecclesiastics who withdrew their labor.

O NE OF THE KING'S reactions to the dangers posed by the interdict was to put the kingdom on a defensive footing. The ships that had been mustered in the spring of 1208 were recalled by a further summons to the fleet in July, ordering them to meet at Portsmouth on September 21. In letters of September 16 John ordered those who had come from the Cinque Ports to follow the instructions of the admiral of the fleet, William de Wrotham. William's duty was to distribute the sailors with their ships to various ports around the country, leaving some behind in Portsmouth to await the arrival of the king.[43] And, according to Roger of Wendover, John also ordered the taking of hostages from leading magnates whose loyalty was suspect:

> King John . . . was afraid that, after the interdict, our lord pope would excommunicate him or absolve the nobles of England from allegiance to him. He therefore sent an armed force to all men of rank . . . and demanded hostages of them . . . many acquiesced in the king's demands . . . but when at length they came to William de Briouze, a man of noble blood . . . Matilda, wife of the said William . . . said "I will not deliver up my sons to your lord, King John, because he basely murdered his nephew, Arthur, whom he ought to have taken care of honourably." . . . On hearing a report of Matilda's words, John determined to seize William and his family but William, being forewarned by his friends, fled with his wife, children, and relatives into Ireland.[44]

In this one statement, Roger of Wendover vividly captures King John's venality, putting the attack on William de Briouze in the context of both John's conflict with Innocent III and his murder of Arthur of Brittany, and then adding the extra dimension of Ireland. The problem is that not a single other author from the time links these events with the fall of William de Briouze.* And when we begin to examine the tale in detail, it turns out that Roger was being economical with the truth.

There is no doubt that John undertook a sustained attack on William de Briouze and his family, and the events surrounding that attack have been a cause célèbre since the early thirteenth century. For Roger of Wendover writing in the 1220s, and for Matthew Paris, Roger's continuator, it was the single defining act of John's brutal rule and it has characterized our view of the king ever since. It is not, however, a straightforward story.

---

* The Barnwell Chronicler (*Walter of Coventry*, ii, 202) does not mention the events of 1208 but, under 1210, places John's journey to Ireland in the context of Hugh de Lacy's rebellion and his alliance with William de Briouze who attacked the frontiers of England. John, Barnwell wrote, wanted to bring about "peace and stability to the land," but in the face of William de Briouze's military exploits, John was forced to confront him militarily; even though his wife and son were starved to death, William was forced to flee (rather than avenge them) because of the fury of the king's army. *Ralph of Coggeshall*, 164, does not mention the events of 1208 and wrote of 1210 that John went to Ireland with his army and expelled Hugh de Lacy and all of Ireland surrendered to him, that William de Briouze fled from England and that his wife and son "died at Windsor castle." The author of the *Histoire des Ducs de Normandie*, 112, 114, under the year 1210, recorded the death of Matilda de St. Valéry, William's wife, and their son, William, and described the pathetic state in which Matilda was found, having died in her son's embrace, at Corfe Castle, where they were incarcerated. The author of the "Annals of Margan" (*Annales Monastici*, i, 29–30), under the year 1208, wrote that "King John sent William de Briouze into exile with his wife and children and the whole of his clan and occupied his lands." He followed this with the annal for 1210 stating "in the month of June, John crossed to Ireland." The annalist then immediately started to recount John's oppression of the Cistercians before returning to the matter of Ireland where the author noticed the flight of Hugh de Lacy from Ulster, the capture of William de Briouze the younger, with his wife and multitude of children ("*pluribus filiis*"), and his mother. They were taken to Bristol and then Windsor where they were required to pay 50,000 marks for their redemption. William senior fled to France, whereupon his wife and son were starved to death. The author of the "Annals of Waverley" (*Annales Monastici*, ii, 261–2) in a full account of 1208, wrote that William and Matilda were exiled in that year and their lands were occupied by John and then, in 1209, the king invaded Wales "after the ejection of William and his wife." The death of Matilda and her son was recorded under 1210 and placed at Windsor where they were "starved" (*Annales Monastici*, ii, 265). This is the fullest account of William's fall, and though it shares much with Margam, it has added subtlety. The author of the *History of William Marshal* (lines 14179–14232) has William arriving with his wife and children and being sheltered by the Marshal until it is pointed out to him that he was giving sanctuary to a traitor, but does not mention the fate of Matilda and William the younger.

William de Briouze was a hard man of the Angevin regime, who had served Richard and John loyally and had been richly rewarded for his efforts on their behalf. He had started his career as sheriff of Hereford-shire, a post that he held for a decade, during which time he regularly made war on his Welsh neighbors. He can be found on the continent in Richard's armies, and, by one account, he played an important role in helping Count John to succeed to his brother's lands in 1199, after which William was in almost constant attendance on King John. The family did well out of royal service. In 1200, for example, William's second son, Giles de Briouze, then aged about thirty, was promoted to the bishopric of Hereford, and in the same year, William was given permission to wage personal war on the Welsh in order to extend the territory he controlled as part of his barony of Radnor. William continued to prosper from royal largesse, expanding his landed interests into Ireland where he acquired the honor of Limerick in northern Munster, for which he offered King John 5,000 marks. His fall from grace—given the heights to which he had risen—was, therefore, spectacular and, for many, became symptomatic of what was rotten at the heart of John's regime.

The seeds of William's fall had been sown long before March 1208. They can, indeed, be traced back to 1206, when John first began to undermine William. In that year, John gave permission for another of his servants, Peter fitz Herbert, to pursue a suit for a third of the lordship of Brecon against William. This is a remarkable event. John was assiduous in protecting his men from litigation in his courts and we regularly find cases brought to a standstill in the Curia Regis with the simple phrase "because the king wills it." At Easter 1206, the king willed that William de Briouze be put under pressure, and he did so while he in person presided over the court's proceedings. William must have understood that he was being deprived of royal favor.[45]

If William were in any doubt about his position, John then allowed another case to be brought against him, though this particular sitting was presided over by the justices of the Bench and not the king. By the standards of the great cases of the day, this was a relatively minor suit, concerning advowson (the right to receive the revenues of a church and to appoint its vicar) of the church of Ewhurst in Surrey, brought by Walter, prior of Merton. Merton was a community of Augustinian canons that, although well respected in the upper echelons of English society, could not be described as being of the first importance in terms of its wealth and power. To take on William de Briouze, therefore, the prior needed the king's support, and quite clearly he had it.[46] Both the speed and the ease with which Prior Walter won his case were designed to send to William de Briouze a clear and unambiguous message. The relationship between the king and William had, therefore, obviously been going wrong at least two years before the declaration of the interdict; by the autumn of 1207, there was an open rift.[47] But the destruction of William de Briouze was not, in fact, wrapped up with John's problems with the pope and Langton's appointment to the see of Canterbury but with John's policy in Ireland.

Just as he had in England, in the wake of the loss of Normandy, John applied financial pressure to Ireland to help build the war chest that would take him back to the continent. He began by introducing English administrative structures through which he might raise revenue from Ireland.[48] A castle had been built in Dublin, and by 1204 the area around the city had already been constituted into a shire. It was from Dublin Castle that the administration of Ireland would be directed. John introduced the shires of Waterford and Cork, which were administered as one unit from 1207–8, and he was, by 1206, making preparation for introducing a shire of Meath, though it does not seem to have been formally constituted until 1211–12. The lands in Meath were, however, to be carved out of lands held by William de Briouze as part of his honor of Limerick.

The instrument of John's policies in Ireland, both financial and judicial, was Meiler fitz Henry. The author of the *History of William Marshal* had few good things to say of Meiler, but that was because William Marshal was one of the Irish barons who stood to lose from the policies Meiler was pursuing at John's behest. Meiler pursued his master's interests (and perhaps his own also) with the sort of enthusiasm that won him no friends amongst the English elite in Ireland. In the winter of 1206–7, Meiler launched an offensive against Limerick and thus against Walter de Lacy, William de Briouze's son-in-law, who at that time had custody of the honor of Limerick on William's behalf. The Irish barons were under sustained attack from John and were finding it uncomfortable; in 1207, they protested to John about Meiler, but to no avail. The king was determined to support his justiciar, who was implementing the policies that he himself had authorized.

John was resolute in his attempts to increase his royal prerogative in Ireland even if it meant doing so at the expense of his baronial elite, and even if the members of that elite had served him with the utmost loyalty, as William de Briouze and William Marshal had done. William de Briouze was a belligerent man who had made his mark in the world by being as violent and as aggressive as they came. He reacted to John's policies, therefore, with violence and pugnacious determination to resist; in the end, Briouze was broken because no lone man could resist the king.

It was the colonial aristocracy at whose expense John's expansion of royal rule in Ireland was being made, and it was the colonial aristocracy who presented John with his major problem in the Irish kingdom. William de Briouze's son-in-law, Walter de Lacy, was recalled to England in April 1207, though he seems to have been given leave to remain in Ireland until July, as were William Marshal and William de Briouze. And in November 1207, William de Briouze and King John definitively fell out.[49]

In Ireland, Meiler fitz Henry continued to push through the king's policies, and John issued letters that ordered the complete break-up of William de Briouze's Irish estates. John also planned a major expedition to Ireland for the spring of 1208, but it had to be postponed because of the emergency triggered by the interdict. The postponement of the expedition created a temporary setback, especially after word arrived that Meiler fitz Henry had been captured. John was forced to make concessions to his colonial baronage, but that did not mark the end of his campaign to bring Ireland firmly within his administrative orbit.

The destruction of William de Briouze, therefore, was a result of the political situation in Ireland not the conflict with the papacy. Our later authority on William's fall is entirely wrong as to its causes. He is also wrong about the flavor of the persecution. We are led to believe that William's wife, Matilda de St. Valéry, and their son, also William, were helpless victims in the face of John's unwarranted aggression, but Matilda was a fearsome lord in her own right, and her son, William, far from being a weak and vulnerable child, was a man in his forties who was quite capable of being an equally formidable aristocrat. There is, moreover, an important corrective to the chroniclers' view of the fall of the Briouze clan. In an unprecedented move, in August 1210, John issued a *querimonium* or complaint against William de Briouze, explaining why he had proceeded against him. This complaint survives in two thirteenth-century manuscript copies, both semi-official compilations. One, The Little Black Book of the Exchequer, was compiled during John's reign; the other, Liber A, is a miscellaneous collection of Exchequer documents dating to the 1280s.[50] This, then, is the official version of the affair.

In John's version of events, the king was reason incarnate. William de Briouze had promised 5,000 marks for the Munster lordship and additional money for the city of Limerick, and yet after five years and repeated deadlines, he had failed to settle his debts with the king. It was with great regret, therefore, that John applied the "customs of England and the law of the Exchequer" to seize William's possessions for nonpayment. But worse was to come, for although John sought by legal means to compel William to pay his debts, William hid his movables, making it impossible for John's officers to take what rightly belonged to their master. More significantly still, William responded to the legitimate actions of the king and his men with violence: he laid siege to castles that had been sequestrated, he destroyed the property of the Church, he killed some of the king's men, and when confronted by the forces of Gerard de Athée, John's representative in the region, William retreated to Ireland to be sheltered by William Marshal and the Lacy family.

In utter despair at the actions of not just William de Briouze but also those barons who sheltered him, John, according to his own account, summoned an army to embark for Ireland. Even at this juncture, according to the complaint, William de Briouze made promises to pay the king, meeting him through intermediaries at Pembroke just before the army set sail, promising to pay the king 40,000 marks for the return of his property and the king's good will. John, however, stated that he knew that this was a ridiculous promise, one which William could not keep, and that William's wife, Matilda de St. Valéry, was much more likely to be able to pay. John suggested, therefore, that William accompany him to Ireland to take counsel with his wife. William refused the offer and when John was in Ireland, William attacked and destroyed yet more royal property. According to John's complaint, Matilda was complicit in her husband's failure to pay. She, too, promised John 40,000 marks and an additional 10,000 marks for the king's goodwill, none of which was forthcoming. And when William de Briouze gave John the slip and fled to the French court, Matilda continued to be obdurate in the face of demands for the fine to be paid. The king, as he retold the events, had no choice but to retain her, her son and her "people" in royal custody. Although John's letter does not say so, it was in prison that Matilda and her son William died.

It is obvious, therefore, that what was actually at stake was the expansion of royal rule in Ireland, which John's colonial barons were seeking to limit. William de Briouze was the most famous victim of John's determination to strengthen his grip on Ireland because of the height of his former glory and the grisly end of his wife and son. Other men played their hands more wisely and did not suffer William's fate.[51] John used the fact that William owed him money for Limerick to press him to acquiesce in his plans for the colony, and when William refused to do as he was bid, John followed through on his threat to call in the debt. We have enough evidence to show that John regularly quit men of their debts at the Exchequer when it suited his purpose, and it is a good assumption that men who were close to the king expected that he would indeed do so. When William de Briouze proffered 5,000 marks (a tonne and a half of silver pennies) for Limerick, it is likely that he did not expect that the debt would have to be paid. William, because of his obduracy in the face of royal policy, was called to account, an account he could not (or would not) make. As a consequence, he and his "people" suffered the ultimate penalty. John appears to have felt the need to justify his actions against William and his clan because John's treatment of them became a symbol of how men came to see John and his rule. The issuing of the *querimonium* by John in the late summer of 1210 shows that he had enough sensitivity to know that many were uneasy about the fate of the Briouze clan.*[52] To his subjects, John now appeared to be a king who was prepared to pursue his ambitions ruthlessly even to the destruction of those closest to him. It was a chilling prospect.

---

  * *Histoire des Ducs de Normandie*, 114, claims Matilda died after eleven days, lying between the legs of her son. At the end of his life, John showed some remorse for what he had had done to the Briouze family when he gave three carucates of forest at Aconbury in Herefordshire for the foundation of a female community of the order of the Hospital of St. John (later turned into a community of Augustinian canonesses) in the memory of William, Matilda and their son William.

9

LORD OF THE BRITISH ISLES

O N JANUARY 12, 1209, Innocent wrote to John to express grow-
ing exasperation at the king's obduracy. The pope threatened that,
should John fail to accept the decision to appoint Stephen Langton within
three months, he would be subject to a sentence of personal excommunication. This would be "solemnly repeated on successive Sundays and
feast days, with tolling of bells and candles lit, until adequate satisfaction
[was] made."[1] Innocent also hinted darkly that he would "proceed against
[the king] in still other ways" if John did not swiftly correct his error, and
reminded him that "once wounded by the arrow" of excommunication,
he might never fully recover. Innocent had already passed a sentence of
excommunication on Fulk de Cantilupe and Reginald of Cornhill, the
two men who had enacted John's orders in Canterbury.[2] Innocent also
raised the matter of Queen Berengaria's dowry that January, and threatened excommunication for John's failure to deliver its terms.*[3] But still
Innocent held out hope that John would repent, expressing that view as
late as March 6, 1209.[4]

For John, however, it was not papal threats that dominated the political
agenda at the beginning of 1209; it was the issue of Scotland that needed
his personal attention. In January, the king sent orders to William, king

---

* Eighteen months later, on May 14, 1210, Innocent wrote to Gilbert, bishop of Rochester, and Herbert, bishop of Salisbury, ordering them to publish the sentence of interdict
on England and to enforce it fully (*Letters of Innocent III to England and Wales*, no. 868).
One is left to wonder what the impact of a second interdict was supposed to have on John.

of the Scots demanding that he meet him at Newcastle-upon-Tyne. The meeting had to be postponed because of the aged king's illness (he was sixty-eight), and when John heard of his recovery, he wrote to William in the kindest of terms expressing his pleasure at hearing of the king's revival, while sending a high-powered delegation to conduct the king to the agreed meeting place at Newcastle. The conference lasted two days, and then, on April 26, William fell ill again and John solicitously urged him to return home to recover.[5] All seemed to be well, and certainly the two sets of households thought that peace had been made.

But it had not. Evidently John had put a proposal to King William (we do not know what it was) that the king conveyed to his barons at Stirling on May 24. They, in turn, refused John's scheme, at which point John, according to Gervase of Canterbury, flew into a rage and mustered his army for war. He demanded that William give him three castles (unnamed in our sources) and his son Alexander as hostage. John then took his army northward to menace the Scots, an army that comprised almost all of his tenants-in-chief. In Herefordshire and Lancashire, for example, every knight who was directly due to render service to the king either did so or sent his representative in his place. John pursued a deliberate policy of incentivizing all English knights to service on the Scottish campaign, presumably both as a means of demonstrating the overwhelming might of the English war machine, and also as a means of gathering around him the leading men of the realm. There was nothing quite like a successful campaign for binding a nation to its king, and given the circumstances in which John found himself, binding his military tenants to his cause was a primary concern.

John and his army arrived at Newcastle-upon-Tyne by the end of July, at Tweedmouth by August 3 and then at Alnwick on August 7, where he received an oath of fealty from King William's son and heir, the twelve-year-old Alexander, who performed, according to a later source, homage for Scotland. The Treaty of Norham returned Scotland to the subservient status that it had endured since 1174 and had emerged from by the quitclaim of King Richard on December 5, 1189. John then took into his custody William's two daughters, Margaret and Isabella.

Many suggestions have been made about the cause of John's anger against King William, but the most convincing one is that John discovered that William had made an alliance with Philip of France (probably on May 28, though that does not explain the earlier negotiations between John and William). One much later source suggests that Philip offered himself as a possible bridegroom for one of William's daughters. An alliance with the king of France might have given William the opportunity to press once again his claim for the earldom of Northumberland. He had held the earldom for a brief time between 1153, when he had been invested with it by his grandfather, and 1157, when his brother had surrendered it to Henry II. Ever since then, William had tried repeatedly and unsuccessfully to reestablish his claim to the territory. It may well have been that he saw an alliance with Philip as providing a final opportunity for him to realize this ambition before he died. If he did, he was very much mistaken. John brought the full military might of the English kingdom to bear on his northern neighbor to bring the matter to a comprehensive conclusion. The boot of the English king was once again firmly on the neck of the king of the Scots.

One might also ask what Philip hoped to get out of the agreement. An alliance with a king of the Scots who had landed ambitions in the north of England might certainly have appealed to Philip, who wanted to keep John from returning to the continent. He cannot have been unaware of the potential for an alliance between John and his nephew, Otto of Brunswick, now the undisputed dominant force in the German empire after the death of his rival for the throne, Philip of Swabia, in 1208. John's relations with Otto had been unhappy for a considerable time and he had had to be reminded of his family duty toward Otto by none other than Pope Innocent, who had backed Otto for the imperial throne. By 1208, however, John's relations with his nephew had warmed. An alliance between the two against the king of France was not out of the question and would, in fact, materialize later in the reign. Philip Augustus was an astute diplomat; the possibility of an alliance forming against him could not have passed his notice. Meddling in John's affairs in the island of Britain was one way in which Philip might hope to keep John from the continent.

A S JOHN TURNED SOUTHWARD at the head of an army that had not even had to fight in order to crush its enemy, word came of the collapse of the negotiations at Dover between John's representatives and those of the pope. According to Gervase of Canterbury, the king was represented by his most senior servants, including his justiciar, Geoffrey fitz Peter, and his principal bishops, including Peter des Roches of Winchester, to negotiate with the papal representatives, the bishops of London, Ely and Worcester. There the pope's terms for peace were presented: the demand was that John must allow Langton to take up his seat at Canterbury; the monks of Christ Church were to be allowed to return to their monastery; and restitution was to be made to the Church for its financial losses. John sought to delay matters, but the papal envoys distrusted his intentions and demanded that he accept the terms of the peace by September 23 or they would proclaim against him a sentence of personal excommunication. In this context, John turned to the subjects of his realm, reaching beyond the immediate body of his tenants-in-chief to secure the allegiance of the wider political community, as he had done in early 1204 after his return from Normandy. In a dramatic move, he called a series of assemblies at which all freemen above the age of fifteen (or twelve, depending on which source one reads) were required to swear fealty to the king and to perform homage.

It is likely that there was more than one assembly where these ceremonies took place (Nottingham and Woodstock are both named as meeting points, and both were on the king's route from the north), since the mass act of obeisance must have involved somewhere between a quarter and half a million men.*[6] The culmination of this act of loyalty was held at Marlborough on September 30, at which the king received in person the oaths of thousands of his subjects. These subjects also performed the act of homage to him, whereby they kneeled before him as they spoke the

---

* The population of England in 1200 might have been 3 million. Estimates of what proportion of that population was free suggest about two-fifths, which would make 1.2 million people. Women were excluded from the oath swearing, as were those under fifteen (or twelve).

words of the oath. There, too, these men swore an oath and performed homage to John's son, Henry, then aged two, "as the king's heir."[7] It was a moment of high drama: the king stood before the freemen of the realm in his glorious majesty and they could see their king in person. At the end of the ceremony, John proffered a kiss of peace to his subjects that, since it was presumably not given in person to each individual, represents one of the earliest air kisses to be recorded in English history. The widespread compliance in this public act of loyalty to John and his heir are attested to by the few, but draconian, fines that are recorded as having been paid for non-attendance, the burgesses of Norwich, for example, being fined the huge sum of 500 marks, as was the unfortunate Hubert Broc, another East Anglian.[8]

John needed to take the sentence of excommunication seriously. The Church taught that those no longer in communion with Holy Church were to be shunned by all her faithful coreligionists. This, by extension, meant that John would, after being excommunicated, be unwelcome anywhere in Christendom, including his own kingdom. In the past—and John was a keen student of history so he would have known this—popes who had excommunicated rulers who proved obdurate then had them declared deposed and authorized the faithful to make war on them. The distant past offered one very famous example: in 1076, Pope Gregory VII had excommunicated and declared deposed Emperor Henry IV.

Indeed, Gregory had gone further and promoted the election of an anti-king, Rudolf of Swabia. Stephen Langton certainly knew of this precedent and made reference to it, and John knew that there was a potential anti-king waiting in the wings. Louis, son of Philip Augustus, had a claim to the throne of England through his marriage to John's niece, Blanche of Castile; Louis would later use this as one of the key arguments in favor of his pursuit of the Crown.[9] Worse still, the pope might declare a crusade, a Christian Holy War, against John, for which participants would receive absolution of their sins. Innocent III was the first pope to use this weapon against heretics, calling for a crusade against the Albigensians in the Languedoc in 1208; and he was the first to use this weapon against a lay ruler, calling for a crusade against Markward of Anweiler in the kingdom of Sicily in 1199.[10]

If Louis, Philip's son, did invade, therefore, he might do so under a papal banner as the leader of a crusading army (in 1213, Innocent invited Philip Augustus to invade England under just such terms). Gervase of Canterbury imagined that the soldiers who went northward to Scotland in the summer of 1209 worried that they were "like pagans, without the protection of God." If Gervase were correct, those soldiers would have feared being led by an excommunicate king. Securing the fealty of the freemen of England for himself and for his heir was an important act that helped to ensure John's security, and demanding from them an act of homage was an unprecedented move that strengthened the connection between the king and all his free-born subjects, who might then be expected to fight for him no matter what sentence the Church had placed on him. On October 16, at Woodstock, John received the homage of the Welsh princes. On November 9, 1209, the archbishop of Reims and his suffragans solemnly declared John excommunicate.[11] The king was now in the gravest spiritual danger, which could easily transform into physical danger, but if it did, he had done his utmost to bind his subjects to him.

JOHN HAD INTENDED TO go to Ireland in 1208, but circumstances had meant that his plan to add his personal weight to the business of imposing English administrative and legal practice there had to wait. It was now imperative, though, that John make the journey to his other kingdom, to bring royal power to bear on the Irish magnates who had stood in the way of the expansion of his administration, making the kingdom more capable of providing much-needed revenue for John's military needs.

John mustered his troops at Cross-on-Sea, Pembroke, at the beginning of June 1210. The sixty-three day campaign that John waged in Ireland that summer shows us the power that the English king had at his disposal. At a simple numerical level, the figures are impressive enough. There were something like seven hundred ships employed to take the king and his army across the Irish Sea, an army that included several thousand foot soldiers and crossbowmen and the full company of miners, carpenters, stonemasons and ditchers who were all required for the business of laying siege to castles. In addition, accompanying John were more than eight hundred knights, many of them described as "knights of Flanders" (a shorthand in the English governmental records for "mercenary"), each of whom received payments to sustain them on campaign were individually entered on a household account roll, known as the *prestita* roll, so-called because it recalled the imprests, or loans, made out of the king's purse from the household treasure. This roll gives us the first ever full account of how an Angevin king financed and organized a military campaign.[12] As with the Scottish campaign, John ensured as full a turnout of his tenants-in-chief as he could muster. He levied a scutage on those who preferred not to serve of 3 marks on the fee, an unprecedented demand and one that would not be made again until the king went to Poitou in 1214. This rate was clearly designed to encourage personal service rather than payment in lieu of service, and it was a policy that met with success. Men who had served together in Scotland in 1209 could reacquaint themselves with each other in Ireland, in what the king hoped would be an equally successful and morale-boosting campaign.

John arrived at Crooke near Waterford on the morning of June 20. He then lodged at William Marshal's house in New Ross from where he left to make his progress to Dublin, arriving a week later, according to the author of the *Histoire des Ducs de Normandie* (a possible eyewitness to the Irish campaign in the entourage of Baldwin de Béthune, count of Aumale), to a rapturous welcome.[13] At Dublin, John set about organizing administrative reforms and receiving the submission of many of the native Irish rulers, including the king of Connacht, Cathal Crobderg Ó Conchobair, who, with his military forces, joined John's army, which was making its progress from Dublin to the stronghold of Carrickfergus, north of what is now the city of Belfast. According to the account in the *Histoire*, King Cathal was delighted when John gave him a fine warhorse with its tack. He proceeded to remove the warhorse's saddle and stirrups, and mount the beast on its bare back, much, apparently, to the amusement of the English king.

John claimed political suzerainty over the entire island and all its inhabitants, whether native or incomer, but that suzerainty depended very much on his ability to impose his authority. King Cathal might be willing to perform homage to John while he was in Ireland, for example, but what he did when John was no longer present was another matter. What was true of the native Irish was equally true of the incomers, who all publicly acknowledged John's authority, but how they conducted their affairs depended on the possibilities for gain that might be open to them. If he wished to rule Ireland effectively (and, to John, that meant the kingdom would provide the financial support he needed to help him return to the continent), John needed to balance the competing powers within Ireland, but he had no compunction in moving ruthlessly against those who stood in his way.

Earlier in the reign John had also been complicit in allowing one Anglo-Irish lord, Hugh de Lacy, to remove from power another Anglo-Irish lord, John de Courcy, lord of Ulster, for much the same reasons, though without the dire consequences for the individual involved. In 1203, Hugh de Lacy had attacked and defeated John de Courcy at the Battle of Downpatrick (the latter fled the field of battle). King John took advantage of de Courcy's problems by summoning him to court and giving the Lacy brothers, Hugh and Walter, along with the Irish justiciar, Meiler fitz Henry, license to make war on him. At the Battle of Dundrum, County Down, in 1204, John de Courcy was captured, and Ulster fell into the hands of Hugh de Lacy who, the following year, was given the title earl of Ulster. By the time John came to Ireland in 1210, Ulster was, therefore, the stronghold of Hugh de Lacy, and since John was in dispute with Hugh (whom he suspected of plotting against him) and with his father-in-law, William de Briouze, it was to Ulster he headed, and especially to Carrickfergus, where William's wife and son were taking refuge with Hugh.[14]

Perhaps because of the fear of treachery, a team of ten knightly body-guards of the royal household now attended John constantly. As far as we can tell, this is the first time that the king resorted to such a measure. King John had no intention of falling victim to an attempt on his life nor of falling into the hands of the Anglo-Irish conspirators. At Carrickfergus, another Irish ruler, Áed Méith Ó Néill, came and did homage to John. The two met on foot, their respective armies encamped in separate locations, and John offered to acknowledge Ó Néill's right to his land if he would agree to pay John an annual tribute. In the end, the agreement foundered on the issue of hostages: John wanted Ó Néill to hand over sureties for his side of the agreement, and Ó Néill refused. The two parted in anger, with Ó Néill taking plunder and retreating to the mountains, and inviting John to come and get tribute if he could. At that point, too, King Cathal withdrew from John's service and refused to hand over his son as a hostage. John's dealings with these Irish rulers were, at this stage, unsuccessful, though he would later have his revenge on both King Cathal and King Áed Méith Ó Néill.

However, what seems to have mattered most to John is that his arrival in Ulster forced Hugh de Lacy to flee (eventually to France, where he remained in exile for more than a decade, only reacquiring the earldom in 1227) and created the circumstances where Matilda de St. Valéry with her son William de Briouze the younger could be captured. Ulster was now firmly in the hands of the king, as were Meath and Munster. In other words, John's personal intervention in the island had brought about a rapid establishment of English administrative organization in the settler-dominated parts of Ireland. A policy that had been in train since 1203 or 1204 was thus firmly established, and all the great Irish magnates except William Marshal had been removed from the scene. The Marshal survived because he knew when to submit to the king, and in the end John could find no reason to remove him from his lands. At Carrickfergus, John also began the redistribution of the lands of those who had stood against him, before returning to Dublin, and, at the end of August, setting sail for England, arriving at Fishguard on July 26. The Irish expedition had been a success.[15]

Cash was still the order of the day. Ireland was now fully contributing to the king's regular revenue and, after his return from Ireland, John also imposed severe taxation on the Jews. According to the account of the Waverley annalist, the Jews were forced to pay 66,000 marks (£44,000), the tax being levied on November 1, according to an entry in the pipe rolls.[16] The Jews enjoyed special protection under the king since they existed outside the normal bounds of the structure of English society. This status came at a price, however, and kings frequently used special taxation of the Jews in order to enhance the royal treasury. Monastic houses, too, were taxed in late 1210, with the king raising huge amounts of money from all the religious houses, including the Cistercians, who had traditionally enjoyed exemption from taxation. The pipe rolls also show a large number of men making payments to the king "for his good will," which suggests that John was using financial penalties to further boost income. The court at Westminster had been closed in 1209 and a greater and greater proportion of court cases were brought directly before the king's court, with the king often presiding in person. And for John, one of the beneficial consequences of his direct control of judicial business was an increase in revenue.

In the business of the forest, too, John initiated a series of forest eyres aimed at increasing revenue from this particular economic resource. In medieval England, when land was placed under forest law it became directly subject to the king and his justices. The law that pertained in the forest was exactly the same law as everywhere else in the land: the common law of England. But in addition, forest law added a series of burdens designed to protect the trees and the beasts of the forest, and the vert (the green vegetation that provides cover for the deer) and the venison (the flesh of the deer, boar, hare, rabbit or other game animal killed in the forest). On first glance, it looks as though the king was merely protecting his hunting rights so that he and his court might enjoy the pleasures of the chase. In fact, for those living under forest law it was much worse than that because it restricted the economic potential of the land afforested. The king was reserving to himself economic rights that made the land in the forest if not worthless then certainly worth a great deal less than it would have been outside the forest.[17]

People who lived in the forest could, for example, neither hunt nor forage for wood, either as firewood or for building materials. Neither could those living in the royal forest build or make ditches or create enclosures. Dogs had to be leashed; bows could not be carried; land could not be cleared for cultivation. The massive expansion of royal forest by William the Conqueror in the wake of the conquest of 1066 and its further extension by Henry II, Richard I and John had a severe economic impact on rich and poor alike. It stopped them from using the resources of the land and so had an impact not only on their ability to live, but also on the value of their property. Having one's land excluded from the royal forest was a huge economic benefit, boosting its value considerably. And infringing forest law (if caught) brought significant financial consequences.

Between 1207 and 1210 there was a series of forest eyres designed to raise revenue. Contemporary commentators remarked on the severity of these eyres and the pipe rolls suggest that large amounts of money were raised during this period, perhaps as much as £8,500–£9,000. It is noteworthy that the heaviest fines were levied on Northumberland and Yorkshire, both of which counties were to provide the greatest number of rebels in the last years of John's reign.[18] It is also worth noting that the forest proved to be such an extraordinary bone of contention that by 1217 it had its own Charter of Liberties, to match that of Magna Carta.

The final source of taxation to pay for John's plans came from towns and cities. The tallage levied on them in 1210 returned over £10,000 to the Exchequer, which, with the exception of London which waited until 2011 to render its 2,000 marks, was paid in full. John was running his kingdom at maximum as he continued to gather funds. The financial strain on those who carried the burden of taxation was becoming ever greater.

I N 1210, JOHN CELEBRATED Christmas at York, where he wore his most magnificent robes that had been brought to him from Bristol especially for the occasion. He was there with a vast array of soldiers and crossbowmen, many of whom had been with the king in Ireland.[19] Perhaps they were looking forward to the new year, for plans were afoot to bring the full weight of the king's army down on the head of the Welsh ruler, Llywelyn ap Iorwerth, prince of Gwynedd and John's son-in-law (he had married John's illegitimate daughter Joan in 1205). Whilst John had been in Ireland, perhaps encouraged by William de Briouze who was himself making war on John in Wales, Llywelyn went into rebellion. John's response had been to send in the earl of Chester and then, in November 1210, to restore Gwenwyneyn, Llywelyn's great rival in north Wales, to his lands. Calling a meeting of other Welsh princes at Chester, John determined to isolate Llywelyn and move against him.

But Llywelyn was not his only focus. Wales and Ireland were inextricably linked, not only because of the connections across the Irish Sea between the native Irish and the native Welsh, but also because, in significant part, the Anglo-Irish settlers were descended from men who enjoyed landed connections in Wales. The great Irish magnate and survivor of John's 1210 campaign, William Marshal, was earl of Pembroke in right of his wife. The defeated William de Briouze had extensive Welsh interests as lord of Monmouth and later lord of Radnor.[20] The exiled Walter de Lacy and his brother Hugh were major landholders in Herefordshire, and evidently also had extensive interests in Wales proper. In other words, the leading Anglo-Irish magnates were also amongst the leading Anglo-Welsh magnates. It was perhaps not surprising, therefore, that after routing Walter de Lacy and William de Briouze and subduing William Marshal, John's mind should turn to Wales. He had made an impressive march through southern Wales on his return from Ireland, taking in the Marshal's Welsh town of Pembroke. In early March 1211, John was again on the Welsh Marches, lodging his hunt at Hereford while he and his army went to Abergavenny, part of the lordship of William de Briouze, to make sure that the tenants of their exiled lord knew how things stood.[21]

Matters settled here, John could turn his attention directly to Llywelyn. Mustering his troops at Chester in mid-May 1211, John launched an attack against the heartlands of Llywelyn's principality in Snowdonia. The first sortie into north Wales was countered by the traditional north Welsh retreat into the mountains and, sure enough, John's troops ran out of food and the king was forced to retreat. A second assault was more successful, however, resulting in the burning of Bangor and the seizing of its bishop. It was a devastating campaign and came within a hair's breadth of destroying Llywelyn, who resorted to sending his wife, Joan, to negotiate the terms of the settlement with her father. On August 12, 1211, Llywelyn was forced to cede Perfeddwlad (the land between the Conway and the Dee) and to give hostages from the chief men of his territory, including his son, Gruffydd, as well as a promise to pay John tribute in cattle and horses. At the end of the campaign, John set about building castles to pin down the newly conquered territories.[22] He was intent upon bringing Wales—as he had Ireland—under his direct control. There was, as the Barnwell chronicler put it, "now no one in Ireland, Scotland or Wales who did not bow to his nod, a situation which, as is well known, none of his predecessors had achieved."[23]

10

The Enemy at the Gate

T HE SUMMER OF 1212 was a turning point in John's life. There
was an atmosphere of panic in the royal household as well as in the
wider country. England labored under the interdict and the king was still
an excommunicate; there was, moreover, a rumor that he would soon
be deposed. According to the Barnwell chronicler, that year, a certain
man of Wakefield called Peter, "a simple uneducated fellow who lived off
bread and water," was seen as a prophet by the people in the locality in
which he lived. "He foretold that King John would not reign beyond the
next Ascension Day [May 23, 1213], since it had been revealed to him that
the king would not rule for more than fourteen years." Apparently Peter
made enough of a nuisance of himself that the king's men, concerned
by the public unease the rumor had caused, seized him and placed him
in jail. When the Ascension Day concerned came around, John spent
the day in public feasting so, it was said, that men could see that he was
still alive, and when it was apparent that Peter's prophecy had not been
fulfilled, the wretched man was dragged from Corfe Castle in Dorset the
four miles to Wareham, where he and his son were hanged.[1]

In the summer of 1212, Peter was not the only man predicting the
demise of King John. In Cornwall, two of the king's household knights,
Alan de Dunstanville and Henry de la Pomeroy, claimed that they had a
special commission as "knights of the king's private household" to report
directly to the king anyone spreading rumors of the king's death. Two of
their men, Ranulf of Denbury and Gilbert de Germanvile, had accused

a neighbor, Baldwin Tyrel, of having declared that the king had been murdered by his enemies in north Wales. Baldwin denied the charge, and the case then seemed to hang in the balance with the sheriff of Cornwall determined to deal harshly with anyone declaring that John was dead. Either Baldwin or his accusers, Ranulf and Gilbert, were doomed, since the words had been spoken by someone and that was enough to condemn the miscreant. The case was removed to the king's court at Westminster, where it remained only to determine who had spoken the forbidden words.[2] Men were beginning to think the unthinkable: that it might now be the time to unseat their anointed king.

At the start of 1212, John had again been planning to return to Poitou to complete the recovery of his continental lands. He had put the king of the Scots in his place, he had quelled the situation in Ireland and he had extinguished the fire of rebellion in north Wales, as well as bringing the Anglo-Welsh lordships fully under his sway. At the Christmas festivities of 1211 at Windsor, John no doubt believed that his citadel was now secure and that he might return to the business of claiming back his lost inheritance. The matter of John's own mortal soul and the spiritual health of the kingdom had still to be resolved. John's decision to launch himself at Poitou was therefore a bold one; he was still an excommunicate king and men were supposed to avoid any contact with him. There was a suggestion, moreover, that in 1211, Innocent III had declared John's deposition. But John had evidently decided that the peril in which his soul stood was not going to prevent him from achieving his ambitions.

At the beginning of John's fourteenth regnal year, which began on May 3, 1212, the series of Chancery rolls begins again.[3] In these documents we can see the detail of John's preparations for war, and it is evident that we are entering the story midway through the arrangements. John's diplomatic plans were well advanced. Negotiations were being conducted at the very highest levels between John and his nephew, Emperor Otto IV. On the very opening day of the new regnal year, the viscount of Thouars and the count of Boulogne were received in England on the emperor's business, and the king's chancellor, Walter de Gray, his

steward, William de Cantilupe, his household official, Robert de Tres-
goz, and one of his most trusted earls, Saher de Quency, were dispatched
to the imperial court to conduct further negotiations. When John eventually did return to the continent, he did so in alliance with the emperor;
perhaps the plans were laid at this point for what would happen when the
two came to confront Philip Augustus.

The count of Boulogne did homage to John and promised to serve
him against the king of France and his son, Louis, while John in his turn
promised not to make peace with Philip or Louis without the count.
Other notable lords from the Low Countries came to John's service, including the duke of Limburg and the count of Flanders,[4] and a series
of military commanders from the same general region were employed.
Adam de Wallingcourt, for example, was castellan of Ypres and of Bail-
leul, and although we do not know how many men he brought with him
in 1212, we do know that in 1215, when John employed similarly large
numbers of Flemish knights to harry his enemies, Adam was at the head
of a group of twenty-five knights.[5] Hugh de Boves also came to John's
service in 1212, a notorious mercenary captain who commanded many
knights. By the middle of May 1212, the forces that were primed to destroy King Philip Augustus were gathering for the final push.

From the king of France's perspective, things must have looked desperate. His enemies were forming a significant alliance, and it was plain
for him to see that the members of this coalition intended to bring the war
directly to Philip's door (as indeed they would in 1214). John hoped to
witness Philip's downfall in 1212; but the French king had a plan to stop
John's Poitevin adventure in its tracks. Philip had been working hard at
his own diplomacy, in particular with Llywelyn ap Iorwerth. In what
was a remarkable diplomatic coup, Philip now managed to goad Llywelyn into rebellion. At Easter 1212 (which that year fell on March 25), Llywelyn had been in John's company. All seemed well between them. But
after Llywelyn left the king's company matters turned badly for John.
Philip negotiated a treaty with Llywelyn, which we know of because
Llywelyn's rather ingratiating (and we may suspect ill-judged) response

survives in the French royal archives; in it the two, apparently, agreed to work together against John.[6] It has been suggested that the reason that John suddenly changed his plans to bring the full weight of his military might down on Llywelyn and to postpone his campaign in Poitou was that he heard rumors of the alliance.[7] This seems a plausible suggestion. It certainly became clear to John that he had to deal with Llywelyn and do so decisively if he were to move forward in Poitou. Perhaps Philip was merely using Llywelyn, letting John know (by surreptitious means) that north Wales was a problem that needed to be solved before he launched his attack on Poitou. But that is to speculate. What is not in doubt, however, is that Philip Augustus was a complex character who would not have relied on only one course of action to keep John from the shores of France. And he was certainly happy to receive dissidents from England whenever the opportunity arose.

As late as June 15, 1212, when John issued a letter at Westminster summoning men with horse and arms "to be well prepared for a crossing with us in our service,"[8] it looks as though the Poitevin campaign was still going ahead. But by July 10, the focus was suddenly switched. On that day John issued multiple letters ordering his sheriffs and other custodians of lands to gather honest axemen who were brave and vigorous, as well as carpenters and ditchers. All were to muster at Chester, there to serve the king for forty days, and their names were to be made known to the king in writing. The date of the muster was set as Sunday, August 19, and all the evidence suggests that it was to be a major campaign. As well as knights, serjeants and engineers, there was a large contingent of Flemish mercenaries (over twenty cohorts), and the king also summoned from Ireland William Marshal and John de Gray, bishop of Norwich, with their troops.[9] Llywelyn was to be the recipient of an attack that had been intended for the king of France.

But then, just as suddenly, John called off his planned campaign. He had learned that there was a plot against his life. According to the Barnwell chronicler, the English barons planned to replace him with another king, and Roger of Wendover gives a principal place to John's illegitimate daughter, Joan, Llywelyn's wife, as the source of the alarming news. The Dunstable annalist, writing in the early years of Henry III, imagined that the barons had a candidate in mind: Simon de Montfort, the leader of the Albigensian crusade[10]; Louis of France had yet to emerge as the barons' preferred candidate for the throne. But however John was informed, his reaction was immediate. His first thought was to cancel the Welsh campaign, and on August 16, he disbanded the army and ordered men to return to their own territories. For the next week he remained at Nottingham refusing, according to the Barnwell chronicler, to go about unarmed or without a bodyguard. But he was not idle. He began the business of rooting out his enemies. The chroniclers noted the flight of two men in particular, Robert fitz Walter and Eustace de Vescy, Robert to France and Eustace to Scotland. In the king's eyes, therefore, both had declared themselves guilty.[11]

Members of John's own administration also came under suspicion, among them four Exchequer clerks, William of Cornhill, William of Necton, Stephen Ridel and Geoffrey of Norwich. The first bought his freedom, the second and third fled to France and the fourth died in prison. The brother of the king of the Scots, Earl David of Huntingdon, was ordered to provide his son as hostage to act as guarantor of his loyalty and to relinquish his custody of Fotheringhay Castle, the principal seat of his earldom,[12] to Hugh de Neville, Simon of Pateshull and Walter of Preston.[13] John was willing to use the threat of force should Earl David prove reluctant to do as he was bid, calling out the military might of the town of Northampton to menace the earl at the very gates of his castle.[14]

The northern baron and friend of Eustace de Vescy, Richard of Umfraville, gave up his four sons and his castle of Prudhoe in Northumberland as surety. The king suspected him of being in contact with those who plotted the rebellion. Two of the younger boys, Odinel and Robert, were sent to the queen's household, where they were to serve at table when Isabella took her lunch, and each night the boys were "to lie in the hall and be held in honourable custody."[15] It was not going to be an arduous confinement, but they would be kept to guarantee their father's good behavior. John, though taking hostage Richard's boys, obviously did not expect Richard or his tenants to starve that winter, since he gave him license to move a shipload of wheat from St. Botulph's to Newcastle-upon-Tyne.[16] This was a purge of potential traitors, but not one that saw widespread executions.

Having disbanded the army that was to have conquered north Wales, John called to his side the mercenaries he had obtained from Flanders and Hainault and made sure, too, that they had been paid; an unpaid mercenary captain is the very opposite of an asset.[17] Northumbria was given to three of the king's staunchest men, William de Warenne, Aimeric, archdeacon of Durham and Philip of Oldcoates, while William Marshal's son, William the younger, was placed in their custody. Philip captured Eustace de Vescy's castle at Alnwick. John also ordered the building of two siege engines.[18]

John thought that the problems came from the north and so, once he had settled his nerves, he made haste there. But it was not an unplanned visit. Accompanying him were his army, three hundred dogs of the royal hunt and "the Great Crown and all the coronation regalia that pertained to it." John was going to impress the northerners with his might and with his majesty. Undoubtedly he planned to have a crown-wearing ceremony, and since he was in York on August 30 and 31, it is likely that this is where it took place. York was the capital of the north and the place where John's predecessors had performed the same ceremony when the need arose to demonstrate that there was only one king of England. John then moved on to Durham, which was as far north as he was to go on this campaign: at Durham he organized the fortification of its castle and many others before turning southward in early September. By the 20th of that month he was back in London, at the Tower. It had been a lightning strike and one that quelled any overt rebellion. Meanwhile, in London, John had ordered the destruction of Baynard Castle, held by Robert fitz Walter. The Welsh were not entirely off the hook, either. Falkes de Bréauté continued the campaign against them, and a fleet of twenty-eight galleys was placed under the command of Geoffrey de Lucy, who was ordered to sail around the coast of Llywelyn's lands to destroy enemy shipping. Suspicion had also fallen on William Marshal, and Geoffrey was to keep a lookout for any ships from the Marshal's lands in Ireland.[19]

B ESIDES DEMONSTRATING HIS MILITARY might in the region that he felt was most likely to become openly hostile to him, John also began to relax his administrative stranglehold. It seems that even he had begun to realize that his constant demands for cash and service were weighing heavily on Englishmen. The Barnwell chronicler talks of John mitigating the force of the forest eyre that he had launched earlier in the year. He also thought that John made efforts to restrain "those who had imposed new exactions and those who had, under pretext of guarding the ports, molested citizens, travellers and merchants, and he repealed the new exactions, so that he would be said to be merciful and concerned to keep to the terms of the peace."[20] On August 18, two days after he had learned of the plot on his life, John wrote to the sheriffs ordering them to summon all those with debts to the Jews, "except counts and barons, to come to our court on All Saints Day because we wish, by the grace of God, to relax their debts." By royal prerogative, debts owed to Jewish moneylenders on the death of the moneylender were transferred to the Crown. It was a lucrative business for the king, but a painful one for those who found themselves answerable to the full might of Exchequer law for the money that they owed. On the same day, John also ordered his sheriffs to summon six law-worthy and discreet knights of the shire to come with the sheriffs to the king's court at the feast of All Saints there "to hear what we have to say to them."[21] John had been startled into appealing once again directly to his subjects.

Sometime in late October or early November, too, John wrote to William Marshal thanking him profusely for his efforts on the king's behalf in assisting the justiciar in the security of the kingdom. William had offered to come to England to help the king, but on this occasion John chose to keep the Marshal in Ireland.[22] And on October 30 the Marshal was instructed to make a profession of fidelity to John's son, Henry,

saving what he owed to John himself.[23] The Marshal would not be permitted to leave Ireland until May 1213 when John had need of his services
in England. The Marshal was one of a number of barons who were beginning to enjoy more favorable relations with the king. It was as if John
had woken up to the fact that he needed friends amongst the magnates;
up until this point, he had seen them only as a source of revenue and of
irritation. Now, at last, he seemed to understand that he needed them on
his side.

I T WAS ALSO AT this juncture that John decided that he also needed
the Church. Being an excommunicate left him vulnerable, friendless
in a world in which the friendless man was potential prey to his enemies.
If men wanted to rebel, they had a perfect justification for doing so, and if
they rebelled, they would have the support of the king of France who, it
was rumored, had plans afoot for an invasion; it was time for the king to
remove that possible excuse and reconcile himself to the pope.[24] On November 11, John sent Thomas of Erdington, Philip of Worcester and the
abbot of Beaulieu to Rome with instructions to accept the pope's terms
for peace.[25] It was a remarkable volte-face, and testimony to the shock
that had struck at the very core of John's regime by the plot of 1212. Now
all the king had to do was to await the pope's decision. He was hardly in
a position to negotiate the terms of his surrender; they would be whatever the pope determined. But John's diplomats now went to the papal
curia with a letter of support for the king from the barons of England and
Ireland, in the hope that Innocent would see that the king had a strong
hand.

As a sign of his goodwill, John began to treat the Church in England
with greater leniency. Early in the New Year, a plethora of vacancies to
ecclesiastical benefices were suddenly filled.[26] The signals of good intent went both ways. The pope agreed that the dying might receive the
viaticum of the last communion,[27] and he agreed to meet John's representatives. Despite negotiating hard, however, they could not persuade
Innocent to move forward from the terms of the 1211 proposal, which

John had at that time vehemently rejected. Innocent now stipulated that John should submit to the terms of the agreement by June 1, 1213. In April, the king's messengers returned to England to communicate the pope's demands, at precisely the point that Philip Augustus was making preparations for the conquest of England. For the pope, it was a propitious moment (one that he had engineered by encouraging Philip in his invasion plans); John had little hesitation in capitulating. There was still some hard negotiating to be done, but, in essence, after five long years of chastisement, John, having repented his foolish behavior, like the prodigal son would be received back into the fold.

T HE START OF 1213 had also seen the continuing relaxation of the iron grip of royal rule. On February 25, the king responded to the "frequent complaints from many people" that the sheriffs of Lincolnshire and of Yorkshire had been abusing their powers and were guilty of extortion against the men of the counties concerned. He removed from their offices the sheriffs Gilbert fitz Reinfrey in Yorkshire and Hubert de Burgh in Lincolnshire (Robert Aguillun acting as Hubert's deputy) and put in their place local men. Robert de Percy was appointed to Yorkshire while Alexander de Pointon was appointed to Lincolnshire. The king then ordered a high-powered inquiry into the complaints led by Robert de Ros, William d'Aubigny, Simon of Kyme and Thomas of Moulton.[28] Simon and Thomas were Lincolnshire men, and Robert and William had Yorkshire connections. All four ended up on the opposition side in 1215 and were, therefore, chosen in 1213 precisely because they were no friends of the king. It seems likely, too, that John had not yet abandoned his plans to go to the continent, which had been postponed from 1212. On March 23, John closed the ports to all shipping, from whatever nation, in preparation for using them for a crossing, and on March 25, he summoned to Portsmouth all ships capable of carrying six horses or more.[29] The crisis of the possibility of a French invasion meant that these plans had to be delayed once again. At Soissons, on April 8, 1213, prompted in part by the pope, Philip had declared to the assembled chief men of his realm that he intended to invade England, and he asked them to follow him in his venture. Only the count of Flanders refused because of the agreement he had with John.[30] Philip intended that his son Louis would take the crown of England should fortune smile on their plans.*

Quite when John realized what Philip had in store for him is difficult to say. Perhaps a writ issued on April 12 to Engelard de Cygogné ordering him to muster all the knights of Gloucestershire and the Welshmen in his service to bring them to Winchester marks the point at which he heard of the invasion plan.[31] Whatever the case, it cannot have been long afterward that John knew an army was being prepared against him because a general muster to Dover, Faversham and Ipswich was called for April 21. Meanwhile, the fleet that would carry Philip's army had arrived at its assembly point at Boulogne by May 10.

From Boulogne, the French fleet moved along the coast to Gravelines, near Dunkirk. The army that the ships were to carry consisted of the men of Brittany, Normandy and Burgundy, as well as Aquitaine and the heartlands of the kingdom of France. It was an invasion force that would have rivalled in size that which had accompanied Duke William of Normandy to England in 1066. But first Philip had business to attend to in Flanders. In punishment for the fact that its count had refused to join his expedition, he marched his army through the county, making it as far as Bruges where he was to meet the fleet, which anchored itself at Damme, a few miles from the city, there to prepare for the crossing to England. Unable to resist the opportunity to hammer the Flemings further, Philip first laid siege to the city of Ghent, leaving his ships lightly guarded.

In England, as Philip's plans for the invasion of England gathered momentum, frantic preparations were made to resist it. The Barnwell chronicler suggests that John even proposed that he would free those tied to the

---

* *Foedera*, I, i, 104, where the document is dated April 1212, but given the dating system in Philip's Chancery, which started the New Year at Easter, April 8, 1212, refers to two dates, the one in 1212 (Easter fell on March 25) and the other in 1213 (Easter fell on April 14). Given that the preparations for the invasion were underway in 1213, the agreement is likely to have been made in the latter year rather than in the former year.

land in serfdom so that they might take up arms in defense of the realm. The Waverley annalist talks of John's terror at the approaching army.[32] The king needed to conclude his negotiations with the pope as soon as possible, and thus remove any shred of legitimacy from Philip's cause. On May 13, the papal nuncio, Pandulph, sailed from Wissant to Dover and, on that very day, the letters patent in which John agreed to the terms of the peace between himself and the pope were drawn up. Two days later, on May 15, John resigned his kingdoms of England and Ireland into the hands of the pope, from whom he would now hold them in fief. The interdict itself would not be lifted for another year, while the payment for reparations for Church losses were negotiated, but John was at least safe in the knowledge that he was reconciled to Holy Church and would soon be in communion with it again.[33]

John spent Ascension Day, May 23, 1213, in public feasting. It was an auspicious day: he was reconciled with the pope, and it was becoming clear that he had ridden out the difficulties of the previous twelve months and had the support of his kingdom. Peter the Hermit's prophecy that John would not rule beyond Ascension Day 1213 had not come to pass (not literally, anyway, though some did note that in having handed his kingdom to the pope, John had, technically, lost it). He was alive and well, ready to meet the challenge presented by King Philip's invasion force.

And then, as if as a signal of God's pleasure at John's return to the fold, an incredible victory was delivered. On May 30, while King Philip was laying siege to Ghent, the English fleet, under the command of the king's half-brother, William, earl of Salisbury, Reginald, count of Boulogne and Hugh de Boves, caught the French fleet at anchor and captured or destroyed the better part of it. William the Breton, who as Philip's chancellor was on the expedition and saw much of the action for himself, describes in detail the ships' capture and the aftermath, which involved an engagement on land between the English and French forces from which the English only just escaped. The biographer of William Marshal (who was now returned from Ireland and at the king's side) gloated that the

English "towed away many of the ships containing wheat, sides of bacon, and wine . . . and never before booty on such a scale came from France to England, since the time that King Arthur conquered it."[34] The author went on to depict King Philip's anger at his loss, burning the remaining ships of his fleet in a fit of pique. More realistically, William the Breton has the French king taking his revenge on the people of Flanders, before returning home loaded down with hostages and money from the men of Ghent, Ypres and Bruges, who paid heavily for the king's peace.

T HE SUMMER OF 1213 was spent in reestablishing normal religious service. On May 24 and 27, safe conducts were issued for the return of the exiles, including Eustace de Vescy and Robert fitz Walter, who had been at the heart of the 1212 conspiracy and whose return to England was part of the peace agreement. On July 21, their stewards received compensation for damages caused to their masters' properties.[35] Throughout June, orders were issued for the restitution of church lands, and on June 3, a truce was declared with the Welsh, having been negotiated by the papal legate, Pandulph.[36] Stephen Langton arrived in England on July 9, and at Winchester on July 20 he formally relieved John of the stigma of excommunication. John now entered a new relationship with the Church, by which he was to be the pope's favored vassal. Innocent took seriously this new-found status for John and so quickly became his staunchest supporter. In the words of the modern scholar who knew more about England and the papacy than any other, "hereafter, Innocent's attitude to King John was uniformly indulgent and favourable."[37] The barons were urged to support their king, Stephen Langton was admonished to "do all you believe helpful to the salvation and peace of the kingdom" and John was assured that the pope would "always do what will result in your advantage and glory."

The financial consequences for the Church of the interdict and John's reaction to it were profound, and a key part of the agreement was that full restitution should be made. How much that amounted to was a matter for intense negotiation at the papal curia, with John's representatives arguing his case. But while this took place, the fact was—for ordinary men and women—that England still labored under the interdict. The archbishop of Canterbury, in a sermon preached at St. Paul's Cathedral in London on August 25, stung by widespread criticism, explained why it was essential that the interdict should continue. England, he argued, was like a sick patient who, though on the road to recovery, was not yet strong enough to be "fed on beef-steak or fat goose." These must have sounded like hollow words to those who heard them, as the archbishop himself conceded. "Do not," he said, "blame or abuse us . . . we act not out of greed but for the honour of mother Church."[38] Stephen Langton had become sensitive to the charge that the Church was being unnecessarily harsh on its flock.

P OITOU WAS NEVER FAR from the agenda, and in the summer of 1213, the king made strenuous efforts to mobilize his resources to make yet another bid to return to the continent. Buoyed up by his reconciliation with the Church and victory against the French, John was determined to press ahead despite widespread disquiet. In June, he sent a high-powered delegation, including the hero of Damme, William, earl of Salisbury, to Flanders to begin negotiations for a joint campaign against King Philip. William took with him 10,000 marks as an incentive for the count.[39] In July, the earl, John de Gray and William Brewer were sent on a legation to Emperor Otto IV, and throughout the summer and autumn months a succession of delegations were sent to Flanders and to Peter, king of Aragon.

But the expedition was again postponed. According to the Barnwell chronicler men were not best pleased at the thought of undertaking the long and arduous journey to Poitou when their purses were empty; he stated that John was persuaded by the bishops and archbishops, who were newly returned from exile, to delay his departure.[40] That decision had been made by August 17, when the king wrote to his allies, Raymond, count of Toulouse, and Guy, count of Auvergne, promising support and succor, but apologizing that "a great storm" had delayed his plans and

that he would come with his army as soon as he could.[41] He was being dis-
ingenuous (or perhaps metaphorical): resistance to the intended Poitevin
campaign had risen to such levels that he had no choice but to abandon,
for the moment, his plans. But that did not mean he could not plot for the
future. On August 21, 1213, John ordered that a naval force consisting of
ships of the Cinque Ports and of the ships of Bristol, Wales and Ireland
was to be ready to depart overseas by the feast of the Purification of the
Blessed Virgin Mary (February 2, 1214). The date of departure was set.
In the meantime there was much to be done. On August 22, 1213, he
issued a letter to Savaric de Mauléon notifying him that he was sending Geoffrey de Neville, the royal chamberlain, and Philip d'Aubigny to
Poitou to plan with Savaric the forthcoming campaign. Geoffrey was to
become John's principal representative in the region as seneschal of Gascony. At the same time, the king issued letters of safe conduct for Savaric
to come to England to discuss matters with him directly. The seneschal
of Poitou, Ivo de Jallia, was also directed to come to John in England.[42]

JUST BECAUSE JOHN NOW enjoyed the pope's favor and the end of the
interdict was in sight, it did not mean that there was an end to vocal
criticism of his rule. As yet there was no concerted opposition to him, but
there was undoubtedly a general reluctance to be drawn into agreeing
to go abroad on campaign, whether it be from financial exhaustion, a
reluctance to follow a king who had, until July 20, been excommunicate,
or a firmly held belief that service overseas was not part of the contract
by which the tenants-in-chief held their lands of the king of England.
If John were to go to Poitou, he needed to win the hearts and minds of
his baronial elite, especially those in the north who seemed especially
keen to bring their king to the negotiating table before they would consent to serve in his army.[43] And it was this task that would dominate the
late summer and autumn of 1213. The Barnwell chronicler mentions the
fact that John began to "eliminate evil customs from the kingdom" by
the advice of the bishops and "to restrain the activities of his sheriffs."[44]
Roger of Wendover (perhaps with a hint of hindsight) thought that John
promised to restore the good laws of King Edward (by which he meant

Edward the Confessor). John was making promises to grant general reform rather than yielding specific concessions to meet particular grievances. But doing so made men think that it was possible that the king might be forced to make concessions on matters of principle.

I N NOVEMBER 1213, THE sheriffs of England were ordered to send four knights from each of their counties to assemble at Oxford on the feast of All Saints (November 1) "to speak with us concerning the affairs of the realm." Once again the king was seeking to bring into national government representatives from the counties of England, and it marks the very first time that a meeting of a national assembly comprised the knights of the shire. It is therefore part of the prehistory of parliament.[45] By the time that the knights summoned were ready to make the journey, John had stipulated that he wanted them to attend with their weapons of war. Presumably he wanted to know that he could count on their military backing should the need arise. At home all was now in place for the planned expedition, while abroad the diplomatic campaign continued apace. One notable victory for John was the formal renouncement by Guy, viscount of Limoges of his homage to King Philip as he declared himself for his "natural lord, John king of England" to whom he had "sworn fidelity and liege homage against all mortal men."[46] On December 22, 1213, at Windsor where John was celebrating Christmas, the Great Seal of England was handed over to Ralph de Neville to hold it under the supervision of Peter des Roches, bishop of Winchester.[47] The justiciar, Geoffrey fitz Peter, had died on October 14 and John needed an utterly reliable man to be in charge in England while he was away. The formal appointment to the post of justiciar was issued on February 1, 1214, but that Peter was to be the ruler of England while the king was in Poitou had been decided weeks before.[48] And John needed a trusted servant with a proven capacity to rule to remain in England, for as the approach of the day of departure came closer, it became more and more evident that the north had not been brought fully into line. As a precaution, John reversed the decision he had made in 1212 to place local men of influence in charge of Lincolnshire and Yorkshire. These counties were placed in the hands of king's men: John Marshal (also custodian of the Welsh Marches) was installed in Lincolnshire and Peter fitz Herbert was appointed to the sheriff's post in Yorkshire. The king's northern castles were made ready for any eventuality.[49]

J OHN WAS TO BE away from England for the next nine months with a large army that was organized and disciplined through the royal household. Everyone in the army was subject to one of the king's marshals, each of whom was appointed for a particular region of John's lands. These men undertook the responsibility for keeping the peace of the Church and maintaining the discipline of the army. Reporting to the marshals were the barons, constables of the household and knights, as well as the chief serjeants of the marshal's household, who had a duty to identify miscreants and bring them to justice. All swore not to requisition produce for the army except by the payment of a reasonable price.[50] John was going to Poitou not as an invader to pillage the land but as a long-absent lord returning to his grateful people. He did not want the men of Poitou to see him as a predator.

On February 15, John arrived at La Rochelle there to be received by the mayor and its citizens, and to begin what has been described as the greatest gamble of his life.[51] Since 1212, John had faced real criticism of his rule, from within his baronial elite, from the Church and more generally from his English subjects. There was a palpable sense of disquiet, largely as a result of John's conviction that it was his destiny to return to his continental inheritance. Since 1204, his every action had been in some way designed (or at least justified as being designed) to bring John closer to the reconquest of lands that he believed were his by right of inheritance.

His kingdoms of England and Ireland had been squeezed of resources to provide the coin stored in barrels in his castle treasuries. One scholar has estimated that John had tied up almost half the coinage then in circulation, which, if correct, would have created a desperate need for scarce cash.[52] The goodwill of his secular and ecclesiastical elites had been stretched to the very limit. In the secular realm, John had come to see his baronage as a resource rather than a partner in rulership; for him, they were part of the problem rather than part of the solution. Likewise, John's ecclesiastical elite had been forced to face persecution on an unprecedented scale as king and pope went to war. His people had also been forced to pay, and they, too, had faced the spiritual privation brought about by the interdict. In short, all hardship, all misery, all sacrifice had been focused on this one moment: John's return to the continent. Were it anything but triumphant, the opposition, much of which waited at home in the north of England, would be out in force.

O N MARCH 8, JOHN wrote home from La Rochelle to inform his subjects of his safe arrival and the immediate successes of his mission. He reported that, "to the joy of his friends and the confusion of his enemies," many people had returned to his side, that he had successfully laid siege to the castle of Mille-Ecus (lying a few miles outside La Rochelle, it was captured on March 4), after which a number of senior members of the Poitevin baronage came to his side, including Savaric de Mauléon, whom he received into his peace. This was an auspicious beginning, especially as John was also able to convey the longed-for news that the terms of the interdict were to be relaxed.[53] The next day, March 9, John began his progress to his wife's land of Angoulême, where he might expect to be received well. By March 21, John was at Aixe-sur-Vienne where, in a lightning attack, he took the castle. He then went on to Limoges to be welcomed by its citizens. In response to John's arrival, according to Bernard Itier, the historian of Limoges and eyewitness to the events, the people of the city prepared to resist King Philip.[54] On April 3, John was at Limoges, where he stayed for just a day before turning his attention to the Lusignans.

By the end of May, John had brought the Lusignan family to their knees, and he again sent a triumphant letter back to England. In it, he recalls how, on May 16, he had taken his army to Mervent, a castle of Geoffrey de Lusignan, and within a day captured it. Taking advantage of the speed with which Mervent had fallen, John moved rapidly to another of Geoffrey's castles, Vouvant, a few miles away. Geoffrey and his sons were besieged in the castle, and just before John was about to breach its walls, a peace was negotiated between John and all the Lusignans. Its terms were drawn up as a final concord on May 25 at Parthenay.[55] This was the high point of John's Poitevin adventure, after which the campaign took a turn for the worse, which even the capture of King Philip's first cousin, Robert, son of Robert of Dreux, at Nantes did little to alleviate.[56]

Between June 19 and July 2, 1214, John laid siege to Roche-au-Moine on the Loire. As he sat outside the gates of the stronghold, he heard that the French king's son, Louis, was approaching with an army. When he understood that Louis' army was smaller than his, John planned to meet it in open battle, but soon began to suspect that he could not rely on his Poitevin allies: John was forced to retreat to Saint-Maixent in some disarray. Louis, according to one account, also turned tail, fearing that John might have the power to engage him in the open. He need not have worried.[57] On July 15, John wrote from La Rochelle, pleading for those who had not come to Poitou with him now to come to his aid.[58] It was a plea that was ignored.

JOHN'S FUTURE WAS DETERMINED not in Poitou but in Flanders. It was the most significant moment of his life and he was not there. The arrival of Louis and his army had sent John into the south, first to La Rochelle, and then to Cognac, Niort, Saint-Jean-d'Andély and, on July 27, a Sunday, to Buteville, 400 miles from the center of action. In the sense that John had created a grand coalition against Philip, the Battle of Bouvines was a brilliant moment. The most powerful ruler in western Christendom, Emperor Otto of Brunswick, had been enlisted in John's plans and had brought himself and his army to the field of battle. There, too, was Ferrand, count of Flanders, William "the Hairy," count of Holland, Reginald Dammartin, count of Boulogne (though no longer commanding his county), Henry of Louvain, duke of Brabant, the mercenary captain Hugh de Boves, and finally, appointed as marshal of the English troops who had been mustered, John's half-brother, William Longspee, earl of Salisbury. Such a coalition would make anyone quake at its approach, even Philip Augustus, king of France. Gathering up his nobles and knights as well as the citizen militias of his towns, Philip prepared to face the most significant moment in his own life.

John would not have been the first ruler (nor would he be the last) to use another power in the pursuance of his objectives. Getting someone else to make a sacrifice in order to reach one's goal is always wiser than having to make it oneself. It was the execution of the plan, however, that brought catastrophe. On that hot Sunday in July, at around noon, the respective armies of the coalition first engaged with King Philip. Philip was at the heart of the French army, and before him was held aloft the Oriflamme, the symbolic pennant of the patron saint of France, St. Denis, blood red (legend had it) from having been dipped in the saint's decapitated body, and which had been brought out to great success ninety years before, in 1124, the last time that a German emperor had invaded France.

Reports of the battle, one of the few from this period for which we have detailed descriptions, give testimony to the importance that was placed on its outcome.[59] Battles on this scale were rare because the quickest and surest way to win was to neutralize the leader of the opposing army, so each leader was the focus of rather more attention than was welcome. At Bouvines, Emperor Otto was determined to press his attack unswervingly against the spot in which King Philip was directing his army. The emperor's soldiers succeeded in dragging the French king off his horse to the ground, and only his armor saved him from death. Rescued by his troops, Philip recovered his horse and mounted it to lead his troops once again. Otto, too, survived an attack by lucky chance, but his horse was so startled that it bolted, and the emperor had the ignominy of showing his back to the enemy. It was a pivotal moment in the battle. With the retreat of Otto, and his abandonment of the imperial standard, the struggle swung in favor of the French, and it was not long before they were in possession of the field of slaughter.

The consequences of the Battle of Bouvines were profound for all who were associated with it. As the victor, King Philip, of course, emerged from the day with more prestige and in an unassailable position. It cemented his conquest of Angevin lands, especially of Normandy, and it ensured his lasting legacy as the savior of France while also immeasurably boosting his personal wealth. The impact on Ferrand of Flanders was catastrophic. Philip had long sought to make real his claim to the overlordship of Flanders, and he now held its count in his prison. At the Treaty of Paris on October 24, 1214, Countess Joanna was forced into conceding humiliating terms that resulted in the destruction or surrender of a number of key fortresses and the effective rule of Flanders from Paris. Philip even demanded that she annul her marriage to her husband and marry Peter Mauclerc, duke of Brittany, though this never actually happened. Ferrand was to be held captive for a decade, before he was eventually released in 1226 after the payment of 50,000 *livres* Parisian. The consequences for the emperor were even more ruinous. While he had escaped with his life and his freedom, his defeat gave impetus to his rival for the kingdom of Germany and the imperial throne, King Frederick of Sicily, Philip's ally. Within a few weeks of Bouvines, the princes of Lower Lorraine, their confidence in Otto shattered by his defeat, submitted to Frederick, and one by one the other German provinces also fell to him; within a few months of Bouvines, Otto was restricted to Cologne, and by July 24, 1215 (when John was facing his own political crisis), Frederick was crowned king of the Germans at Aachen. Otto was to live out the remainder of his life in retirement at Brunswick.[60]

It is not hard to imagine John's demeanor when news of Philip's victory was delivered to him.*[61] His plans were in tatters and he must have understood, too, that matters at home might prove difficult. On August 16, he sent back to England two of his most trusted diplomats, Thomas of Erdington and Henry de Ver, "to report to you that which we do not wish to commit to writing . . . and concerning the safety of our castles and our person."[62] The two had been in Rome on John's behalf and were now heading to England to report on that business, and, presumably, to prepare for what would undoubtedly be an awkward homecoming for

---

* Though I am unconvinced that we have to believe Roger of Wendover's imaginative reconstruction that John bewailed the fact that his misfortunes had occurred since reconciling himself with the Church.

the king. All that was left for John to do was to secure in what way he could the lands that remained to him and to make a lasting truce with King Philip. On September 6, he obtained the release of his half-brother, captured at Bouvines, in exchange for Robert, son of Robert, count of Dreux,[63] and then, on September 18, he agreed to a truce to last five-and-a-half years, until Easter 1220. In the court of the papal legate and in the company of five counts, two abbots and twenty-nine of the most senior members of his court, John swore to uphold the truce. The original document, sealed in white wax with John's great seal, is still in the French royal archives.[64]

It has been suggested that in failing to bring his forces directly to bear against King Philip, John was making a grave mistake, since Philip's destruction was the primary objective of this Poitevin campaign. When a king loses a campaign, there is no doubt that he has made a mistake, and John lost the Poitevin campaign, but in order to understand what John was attempting to do, it is worth considering the situation from his perspective. Since the beginning of his period of rule, John's policy in Poitou had remained unchanged: to secure the county, he needed to bring the major families of the region under his control. With hindsight, it seems clear that Normandy was the lynchpin of the empire, and that control of Normandy, and especially the Vexin, was crucial to the maintenance of Angevin rule. But for John, Poitou was the key to victory. This is the only possible explanation for the years that he devoted to securing the loyalty of the Poitevin aristocracy or suppressing those families whose loyalty he could not procure, and the only thing that can explain John's unwillingness to go to Normandy both in 1206 and in 1214 to confront Philip directly. That he was profoundly wrong in his assessment is proved by events but that does not vitiate the fact that this was his judgment on the matter at the time he faced the decision about where to launch his own troops.

BY OCTOBER 18, 1214, John was at Corfe. In exactly two years' time he would be dead, his barons would be in revolt, a foreign prince would be stalking his land and his kingdom would be in ruins.

All this was a consequence of his ambition to reestablish his rule on the continent. John's single-minded determination had brought the realm of England to the very brink of disaster. Had his allies won at Bouvines, his return to England would have been met with rejoicing; as it was, John's return was met with outright rebellion. On November 15, 1214, Pope Innocent III wrote directly to Eustace de Vescy, ordering him "to place no obstacles in the way of King John's justices and officials on the pretext of former conspiracies against the king."[65] Innocent had evidently heard that there was a movement emerging against John.[66]

In fact, so deep-seated were John's problems that his officials could not (or would not) render their accounts at the Exchequer, which were due at Michaelmas 1214 (September 29). The accounts for the shires of Yorkshire, Lancashire, and Norfolk and Suffolk were not even drawn up in that year, and although the accounts for Essex and Hertfordshire were entered on the Exchequer record, the pipe roll, they remained unpaid. The account for Worcestershire has no payment made by the sheriff, the account for the city of Lincoln was left outstanding, and the account for Nottinghamshire and Derbyshire was only partially completed. Before the Michaelmas Term pipe roll was drawn up, it was decided to further relax some of John's financial policies, but even after this concession, there was still widespread resistance to the payment of taxes, especially to the payment for the scutage of Poitou, levied at the enormous sum of 3 marks for each knight's fee, as well as to the tallage on towns.[67] Not since the reign of King Stephen sixty years before had there been a widespread refusal to account for the revenues of individual shires. It was a startling moment in the history of the Exchequer, and it is the greatest witness to the fact that in summer 1214 there was serious and sustained resistance to the machinery of John's government.[68]

The Garrison Turns on Its Leader

ABOUT THE TIME THAT John was making his way back from Poitou, "the earls and barons of England" gathered at the monastery of Bury St. Edmunds, supposedly for prayer, "but secretly for another reason." The feast of St. Edmund, king and martyr, fell on November 20, and this seems to be the likeliest date for the meeting. The barons had before them a copy of Henry I's coronation charter, provided for them by Stephen Langton, and, on the high altar of St. Edmund's, each man present swore that if John refused to confirm the liberties contained therein, they would go into open rebellion against their king. The first confrontation was set for January 1215.[*1]

---

* The leading modern historian on Magna Carta, J. C. Holt, was unwilling to believe the events as described by Roger of Wendover, despite having the opportunity to state and, later, reiterate his views (J. C. Holt, *Magna Carta*, 1st edn (Cambridge, 1965), 138; Holt, *Magna Carta*, 2nd edn (Cambridge, 1992), 406–11). But there is sufficient evidence to show that the meeting took place. The author of the *Histoire des Ducs de Normandie*, who was in England in 1215, thought that the barons met shortly after John returned to England "from the defeat of Bouvines" and he names the participants. Robert fitz Walter, Saher de Quency, Gilbert, son of Gilbert de Clare, Geoffrey de Mandeville "and many other barons assembled to talk." In addition, the author names men he calls the Northerners ("Norois"), so called "because they have their lands in the north." Amongst these were Robert de Ros, Eustace de Vescy, Richard de Percy, William de Mowbray and Roger de Montbegon. Gathering in what the author calls a "parlement," these men demanded that John grant them the rights that were contained in the coronation charter of Henry I (*Histoire des Ducs de Normandie*, 145). The Barnwell chronicler, too, talks of the centrality of the coronation charter of Henry I to the barons' cause, which he places under the year 1214, saying that "this was postponed for another year" (*Walter of Coventry*, ii, 218).

Henry I's charter had a central part to play in the creation of Magna Carta. Granted on the day of his coronation on August 5, 1100, the concessions outlined in this, above all other charters issued by twelfth-century kings on their coronation days, came to have a totemic value. In 1100, it had been issued to all shires of England, and a copy had been kept at Winchester for general reference. Sometime in the buildup to the events of 1215, one of those copies came into the possession of Stephen Langton, who used it to compile a dossier of key texts that would guide the baronial negotiators in the early stages of their discussions with the king.[*2]

The text of the charter of 1100 began by bemoaning the heavy exactions that had been laid on the kingdom, which must have had a particular resonance for those reading its terms in 1214. It went on to talk about the abolition of "evil customs by which the kingdom of England has been unjustly oppressed." That, too, must have struck a chord. Other key points conceded by Henry I included the agreement that men might enter their inheritances by the payment of a "just and lawful relief," and that women would not be married without the consent of their families or without their consent if they were widows. These clauses (much expanded to fit the specific details of the time) were to form the basis of the key terms of Magna Carta.

In the second week of January 1215, John met a delegation of discontented barons who demanded that he confirm Henry I's charter. According to the Barnwell chronicler, they thought that it "stood for the liberty of the Church and of the kingdom" and that it should indeed form the basis of the commitment John made to them. John played for time and agreed that he would give his final answer by April 26, the first Sunday after Easter, Low Sunday.[3]

John was forty-eight, and an adept political strategist who knew the value of stalling for time before eventually making astute concessions

---

* The coronation charters of kings Stephen and Henry II were included in the dossier, and all were translated into French so that they might be more easily understood by the barons.

that would, ultimately, be to his advantage. John's contemporaries understood this, and tried to counter his tactics in whatever way they could. But John was intent upon outmaneuvering his critics on multiple fronts; most significantly, John seems to have been set on managing his opponents into a position in which they stood outside the law.

It is a fundamental aspect of the politics of 1215 that each of the parties was attempting to pursue its objectives through legal means. Neither side wished to be seen to be acting illegally and, as a result, both acted cautiously. Since England was now a papal fief and its king subject to the pope, Rome was an obvious source of legal appeal for both King John and the rebels. But if the rebels thought that the pope might listen carefully to their complaints, they were to be sadly mistaken. Innocent's default position was to support his penitent sinner against all his opponents, including those within the English Church, and it was a stance that John shrewdly encouraged.

On January 15, 1215, John had conceded free election to episcopal sees (a confirmation of a grant made on November 21, 1214), which was confirmed by the pope on March 30, 1215 in a letter to the bishops and abbots of England.[4] On purely tactical grounds, John's concession was masterful, since free election of prelates was at the heart of the dispute over the appointment of Stephen Langton and had been at the heart of papal policy since the eleventh century. John knew that in surrendering this important concession, he was giving Innocent yet another sign of his good intentions.

If Innocent was delighted by John's concession, he was evidently ecstatic when he heard that John had agreed to join his planned crusade to the Holy Land. Taking the cross was a brilliant move on John's part. At the outset of his pontificate in 1198, Innocent had been the moving force behind the fourth crusade, which, by an unfortunate set of circumstances, had ended up conquering Constantinople and attacking the Ayyubid Sultanate of Egypt. The failure of that expedition to reach Jerusalem was a cause of deep regret to Innocent, and as he approached the culmination of his life's work, his mind turned once again to the liberation of the

Holy Land. In April 1213, he issued two crucial bulls, the first calling a Great Council of the whole Church, the fourth Lateran Council, and the second launching the fifth crusade. John's promise to join this second enterprise virtually guaranteed him Innocent's unconditional support. Innocent's letter to John of March 4, 1215, says it all.[5]

> We rejoice that the right hand of the most high has wrought this change in you because now . . . you have not only restored your liberty and peace to the English Church, but have freely and gladly subjected your kingdoms to the lordship of the Apostolic See; and further you have denied yourself and taken up the cross for Christ . . . Come, therefore, glorious king! Equip yourself mightily to win the crown which the lord laid up for you . . . and He in whose hand are kings and kingdoms in reward for your devotion will on earth secure and confirm the throne of the kingdom [of England] to you and your heirs.

The sheer distance between Rome and England meant that, if he were to play a role in the drama that was unfolding in his newest fiefdom, the pope had to take a principled stance and maintain it in all circumstances.[6] And as if to emphasize his support for John, Innocent dictated a letter to England on April 1 that specifically addressed the problem of the Poitevin scutage. Refusal to pay this scutage was the weapon with which the barons hoped to bring King John to the negotiating table. Innocent removed it from them.

The second means by which John planned to undermine the barons who stood against him was to appeal once again to the wider public. According to the Barnwell chronicler, John decided that his people should "swear to him that they stood with him against all men and against this charter, in addition to the usual oath."[7] This may be reflected in the instructions that John sent to the shire courts on February 10, asking that they receive certain named individuals who would explain what was going on. John asked those attending the shire courts to "listen sympathetically to what they have to say on our behalf."[8] Certainly, as he had done before, John was prepared to go beyond his tenants-in-chief to talk directly to the community of the realm.

John also prepared for the eventuality of war. The troops he had brought back with him from Poitou were to form the core of his military force, and they were to be organized and paid for by Falkes de Bréauté, by this time steward of the royal household. Castles were restocked and their garrisons strengthened, with key strongholds, such as Knaresborough and Nottingham, being used for storing the siege engines that were being constructed. In February and March, troops were sent to England from Poitou, and John again began to recruit mercenaries from the Low Countries. If the negotiations went wrong, John wanted to be able to crush his opponents.[9]

ON FEBRUARY 19, JOHN issued letters of safe conduct for the barons from the north (known to contemporaries and to us as the Northerners) to meet Stephen Langton, his fellow bishops and William Marshal at Oxford three days later.[10] The Barnwell chronicler believed Oxford to be one of the key locations of negotiations between the Northerners and the king, though whether the king was actually at Oxford on the 22nd is unclear. What is apparent is that the opposition to John was becoming frustrated by his actions. The letters representing Innocent III's first foray into English politics in 1215 were issued on March 19; if they had been dispatched immediately, they would have been received by their recipients around Easter time (in 1215, Easter Sunday fell on April 19). The first letter was to the magnates and barons of England, ordering them to desist from threatening to use arms against their king and ordering them to disband all sworn conspiracies against him. At this point the barons must have known that they could not rely on Innocent's help.

The second letter was addressed to Stephen Langton and his bishops, ordering them to work toward a peaceful settlement between the two parties. The tone of Innocent's letter to Stephen is full of irritation at his archbishop: "we are forced to express surprise and annoyance . . . that, when peace has been happily restored between you and John . . . wilfully shutting your eyes and not troubling to mediate for the settlement . . . you are suspected by some of giving help and favour to [the king's] opponents." The letter goes on to condemn those who create "leagues or conspiracies against [King John] and [have] presumed arrogantly and disloyally by force of arms to make claims which, if necessary, they ought to have made in humility and loyal devotion." Stephen was instructed, with the full force of the papal majesty, to bring about peace. The third letter of March 19 was written to John, asking him to graciously receive the petition of the barons and to grant them safe conducts so that they might attend the talks.[11]

The arrival of these papal letters in England might well have been the catalyst for the next stage in the revolt. In mid-April, at Brackley in Northamptonshire, the representatives of the king met those of the barons, but despite John's promises, it was at this point that a significant portion of the barons (identified in the chronicles as "the Northerners") lost faith in the king, and so they began to make preparations for war.[12] Innocent III's letters had turned John's critics into rebels by comprehensively placing them and their sworn association outside the bounds of the law, and they no longer trusted the king to act honorably toward them. They therefore had only two choices: to capitulate or to fight. They chose to fight. After the Brackley conference had broken up in disarray, the rebel barons, "by their intermediaries, formally renounced their homage to the king." The author of the Southwark annals dates that act of repudiation to May 5.*[13]

MATTERS BETWEEN THE TWO parties had deteriorated in part because of the support that Innocent gave the king, but also in

---

* The Latin "*regem diffiduciantes per internuncios*" means much more than "sending defiant messages." It smacks of the formal process of "*diffidatio*," by which a man who considered that he had been treated unjustly might legally defy his lord. The Southwark annalist uses exactly that phrase, "*hunc etiam regem diffidere fecerunt*," adding the detail that it was undertaken by certain black canons at Reading.

part because, by April, the barons were no longer content to win from John merely his confirmation of Henry I's coronation charter. It was not only that they no longer trusted the king, it was also that their ambition had extended to the desire to extract further concessions. The momentum was for major reform: their intention was to force John to grant an unprecedented series of concessions that would be recorded in a Great Charter appended with the king's seal. But Magna Carta did not spring into the minds of the barons in finished form, and we can see something of the development of their ideas in two documents that predate the issue of Magna Carta in June 1215.

The first is the Unknown Charter, given that name by its first English editor in 1893.[14] The date of the document undoubtedly lies somewhere in the lead-up to the concession of the terms enshrined in Magna Carta and it represents a stage in the negotiating process as reported to the French king's court (it is preserved in the French royal archives). The text begins with an imperfect transcription of Henry I's coronation charter, which is then followed by twelve further clauses outlining the additional demands of the barons.[15] The first clause is in the third person singular: "King John concedes that he will not take a man without judgment, nor accept anything for doing justice and will not do injustice."* The second clause then turns into the wholly anachronistic first person singular (John would have used the first person plural—the royal "we"): "And if my baron or my man should happen to die and his heir is of age, I ought to give him his land at a just relief without taking more."[16] This makes it a very informal document indeed, which further strengthens the argument that it had no official status but was rather the work of a witness to the negotiations between the representatives of the king and of the rebel barons.

Two clauses in the Unknown Charter have attracted particular attention from historians. The first, clause 7, refers to service overseas, and

---

* This clause finds its way into Magna Carta 1215, in clauses 39 and 40.

the second, clause 8, talks of the amount of scutage that the king could levy in times of war:

> [7] In addition, I grant to my men that they shall not serve in the army outside England save in Normandy and Brittany, and this properly, because if anyone owes me the service of ten knights it shall be alleviated by the counsel of my barons.
>
> [8] And if a scutage takes place in the land, one mark of silver will be taken on the knight's fee, and if the burden of an army occurs, more may be taken by the counsel of the barons of the kingdom.[17]

Neither clause found its way into Magna Carta and nor did they appear in the second of its precursors, the Articles of the Barons. Both clauses dealt with issues that were, however, of deep concern since they addressed what was at the heart of the barons' dispute with John before his departure to Poitou. Both clauses were absolutely of the moment after the arrival of Pope Innocent's letters concerning the scutage of Poitou in April 1215. Here, we see John the negotiator at work. At some point (perhaps at Brackley), he had conceded the argument on service in Poitou and that concession was preserved in the Unknown Charter. Later, John would retract it, hence the absence of the two clauses in the final agreement reached in June.

Two documents that John issued on May 9 and 10, 1215, give us an insight into what the king was attempting to do. The first was a charter addressed generally "to all those in the faith of Christ," announcing that he had proposed that the barons' case should be brought before the pope who would act as arbiter between them and the king. Given that Innocent III had already stated his position, that concession was hardly going to mollify John's critics. More importantly, however, John also conceded by letter patent, addressed generally, that he would not move against the barons with force while discussions were ongoing, and that he would only proceed against them "by the law of our realm or by the judgment of your peers in our court."[18] This was a repetition of the first clause of the Unknown Charter and therefore a formal step in attempting to bring about a settlement.

And a settlement, not war, seems to have been central to what John was trying to achieve at this time. When he wrote to Pope Innocent at the end of May on the eve of the events at Runnymede, where the final set-piece negotiations between the parties would take place, John assured the pontiff that he had done all in his power to bring about a reconciliation, but that it was the intransigence of the barons that was at the root of the conflict. He had offered to abolish the evil customs that had arisen not only in his own reign, but also in the reign of his brother, and said that he would willingly submit himself to the advice of his faithful men to determine what had been the good customs of the realm in the time of his father, and to take advice on how they might be reinstituted. This, he told the pontiff, they had refused, and so he had asked Stephen Langton and his suffragan bishops to excommunicate the barons as disturbers of the peace; but the archbishop had declined to do so. After all this, John said, he had offered his barons arbitration, but that, too, they had rejected. This letter to Pope Innocent is of vital importance in recording King John's own version of events before the end of May.[19]

To be sure, this was John's own spin on proceedings, but from his perspective, it must have looked as though the barons were determined to drive the situation into all-out conflict. And John, too, while speaking words of peace and reconciliation, was simultaneously attempting to root out opposition. He had attempted to discover the names of rebels in the wider country by ordering his sheriffs to make their identities known to him and to proceed against their property. This letter was issued on May 12.[20] There were clearly suspicions that the barons leading the revolt might have widespread support in the shires, and John was attempting to undermine it as a further means of placing pressure on them. The rebels responded by marching into the city of London, where they were admitted by its citizens, on Sunday, May 17. There they made a sworn association that neither the barons nor the Londoners would make peace with John without the agreement of the other party.[21] By the time that John wrote his letter to Innocent, therefore, he was no longer in control of his capital city.

T HE SECOND KEY DOCUMENT on the path toward the creation of Magna Carta was the Articles of the Barons. It is a unique text in both content and form. It is headed "these are the articles (*capitula*) for which the barons petition and which the lord king concedes," and was written in the hand of one of the king's Chancery scribes and sealed with the king's Great Seal. Unlike the Unknown Charter, therefore, the Articles of the Barons was an official document bearing the king's seal, meaning that he had authorized its content.[22]

It has been supposed that the Articles of the Barons formed one of the penultimate stages of the peace process before the meeting between the representatives of the king and the barons at Runnymede on June 15. There must have been some to-ing and fro-ing between the parties as they moved towards agreement, and these are probably represented by the letters of safe conduct that were issued to Stephen Langton, on May 27, and Saher de Quency, on May 25, who were "to come to us at Staines for drawing up a peace between us and our barons."[23] On June 8, the safe conducts were extended beyond Langton and Quency to include a wider group of negotiators who were "to come to Staines [to speak on behalf] of the barons on [June 9] . . . for making and confirming the peace between us and our barons." The safe conduct was to last until June 11. However, on June 10 an agreement was reached, and the king issued a letter to his chief supporters telling them that there was to be a "truce lasting from 11 June until the morning of the Monday after Trinity Sunday (15 June)."[24]

The Articles of the Barons represent in all likelihood, therefore, matters as they stood on June 10, and the document itself might well be the very parchment that the envoys took to London. They had negotiated hard and had delivered, in writing at least, a set of terms that seemed to deliver reforms that the barons could support. That has to be the presumption behind the fact that the final terms of the peace, which are those enshrined in Magna Carta itself, are almost wholly present in the Articles.

For the next five days, the barons were no doubt exhilarated. By standing on principle and by using the threat of violence, they had forced John to yield to their demands, which could be simply summarized as the requirement that he rule according to their principles. These principles were clearly set out in the Articles, to which John had affixed his seal, demonstrating to all that he was willing to abide by its terms. Between June 10 and 15, further amendments were made, some by the barons, some by the king, and in the process the final wording of Magna Carta began to emerge. It is likely that John, for example, inserted clause 1:

> We have first of all granted to God, and by this our present charter confirmed, for ourselves and our heirs in perpetuity, that the English Church is to be free, and to have its full rights and its liberties intact, and we wish this to be observed accordingly, as may appear from our having of our true and unconstrained volition, before discord arose between us and our barons, granted, and by our charter confirmed, the freedom of elections which is deemed to be the English Church's very greatest want, and obtained its confirmation by the lord pope Innocent III; which we will ourselves observe and wish to be observed by our heirs in good faith in perpetuity. And we have also granted to all the free men of our kingdom, for ourselves and our heirs in perpetuity, all the following liberties, for them and their heirs to have and to hold of us and our heirs.

This clause, as John himself was at pains to point out, repeated the concessions he had already given to Pope Innocent and so reemphasized the fact that he was a true penitent son of the Church. Should the text of Magna Carta come before the pope, therefore, Innocent would be assured of John's continued support for one of the principal tenets of papal teaching.

But the barons also made addition to the terms as outlined in the articles. Magna Carta clause 14 in particular has all the hallmarks of having
been first presented by the barons, since it goes to the heart of one of
the key issues—the ways in which the king had levied taxation for his
war effort. It was then amended by John's negotiators, who added the
stipulation that although consent was needed, not all those summoned
had to be present for consent to be given.* There were other minor additions, too: clause 21, which dealt with the financial penalties that might
be imposed on earls and barons, clause 53, which focused on forests,† and
clause 54, on the right of women to bring murder cases to court.‡ The last
two clauses, traditionally numbered 62 and 63, set out the essential terms
that would put the agreement into effect: that John agreed to pardon anyone who had stood against him, promising that he would not hold any
grudges against them; and the fact that oaths had been sworn between
the parties concerning the terms of the peace. The text of Magna Carta
finished with the witness and dating clause:

> Witness the above mentioned and many others. Given under
> our hand in the meadow which is called Runnymede between

---

* [14] And in order to have the common counsel of the kingdom for the levying of
an aid, other than in the three instances aforesaid, or for the levying of scutage, we are
to cause the archbishops, bishops, abbots, earls and greater barons to be summoned individually by our letters; and moreover we are to have a general summons made, through
our sheriffs and bailiffs, of all who hold in chief of us; for a fixed day, at least forty days
thence, and at a fixed place. And in all the letters of summons we are to set out its cause.
And after the summons has thus been made the business is to go forward on the appointed
day according to the counsel of those present, even if not all those summoned have come.

† [53] We will have the same respite, and in the same fashion, for doing justice concerning
the disafforestation or retention of forests which Henry our father or Richard our brother afforested, and concerning wardships of lands which are part of another fee, wardships which
up till now we have had by reason of a fee which someone held of us by knight tenure, and
concerning abbeys which were founded on a fee other than our own, in which the lord of the
fee has claimed his right. And when we have returned, or if we stay at home without going on
our crusade, we will at once do full justice to those complaining of these things.

‡ [54] No man is to be arrested or imprisoned on account of a woman's appeal for the
death of anyone other than her own husband.

Windsor and Staines on the fifteenth day of June in the seventeenth year of our reign.

M AGNA CARTA, IN THE form we have it now, was not, however, created on June 15. Although the words of the king's charter suggest that it was, in fact there is compelling evidence that authenticated copies of Magna Carta did not exist until at least June 19.[25] The explanation for this can be found in the events of that day.

The truce that John had issued on June 10 was due to expire on June 15, when the representatives of both the king's and barons' parties were scheduled to meet to finalize the agreement. On the morning of June 15, the delegates first met at Windsor, there to finish up the final details of the peace agreement.*[26] Then in the afternoon, they moved to the field of Runnymede between Staines and Windsor. Lying on the edge of Windsor Forest, it was symbolically significant, a liminal space where no one party enjoyed supremacy and where events could be witnessed by large numbers of people. Neither John nor the rebel barons conducted the business in person; rather it was undertaken by their proxies: as the words of Magna Carta make clear, these proxies swore on behalf of their parties to uphold the terms of the agreement.† On June 15, 1215, neither king nor rebel barons swore oaths in person.[27]

It is also likely that on June 15 neither king nor barons were actually at Runnymede, but were represented by their proxies on the negotiating field. The final dating clause of Magna Carta, June 15, which was preceded by the phrase "Given by our hand in the meadow called Runnymede," might suggest that John was, but the phrase merely means that the text, as it is presented, was authorized by the king, not that he was actually on the field of Runnymede on June 15.[28]

---

* This version was dated at Windsor and the security clause is in the future tense, not the present tense, and clause 55 matches word-for-word clause 37 of the Articles of the Barons. Roger of Wendover's *Chronicle* also has a draft version.

† "This has been sworn to both on our behalf and on that of the barons."

At the end of the day's proceedings, each party returned to their lodgings, the king's delegates to Windsor to meet John, and the barons' delegates to London to meet their masters. But although the parties had agreed terms, the important process of reconciliation had still to be effected. When the barons' delegates arrived in London to declare their victory, some in their party voiced scepticism. The Barnwell chronicler, for example, thought that some of the barons (he identifies them as Northerners) did not like the agreed terms. A surviving copy of Magna Carta, dated June 16, which has the relief for a baron set at 100 marks (£66 13s 4d) rather than £100,*[29] may represent an attempt to reopen negotiations with John, though if it does, the king demurred. The terms as agreed on June 15 were his final offer. Equally, what John needed from the barons, above all, was their personal oaths of fealty and their public homage, which he had yet to receive. No peace could be declared until king and barons were formally reconciled.

Discussions in London must have rumbled on, but on June 18 John heard that the barons had agreed to accept his terms for the peace.†[30] The next day the king met the rebel barons in person, again at Runnymede, where they performed the physical act of homage to the king and swore fealty to him and to his heirs.‡[31] This marked the moment at which peace between the king and his subjects was declared and the terms agreed could take effect—but only with those barons who had performed their personal homages and given their oaths of loyalty. Those who were absent on the day, Earl David of Huntingdon, for example, could not benefit

---

* The view amongst some that the relief on a barony should be 100 marks continued throughout the thirteenth century until it was finally accepted in the reissue of 1297.

† On that day he issued a letter patent addressed to Stephen Harengod. "Know," Stephen was told, "that a firm peace is made (*facta est*) by the Grace of God between us and our barons from the Friday closest after the feast of the Holy Trinity (19 June) at Runnymede-next-Staines." Stephen was John's man in Essex, controlling Colchester Castle as well as the borough, and he was the principal jailer of rebels for the region. The letter to him in which the peace was announced ordered him not to do harm to the barons and to release those men he held captive.

‡ The Dunstable annalist places a meeting at Runnymede on June 19.

from the peace terms until they had performed their homage in person.*[32] There followed a great banquet at which food and drink were shared, while the Chancery scribes began the process of writing up copies of the peace terms, which were to be expressed in the form of a charter.

This last point is crucial because it brings into sharp relief the nature of the agreement as it was to be promulgated to the wider public. The barons might have forced John to make concessions about how he would rule, but no king could allow himself to be seen to capitulate to his subjects; he was, after all, set over them by God. So while it was acceptable for rulers to create peace treaties between themselves in which the agreement was expressed in terms of equal parties (the Latin term applied was *conventum*), it was not acceptable for them to do likewise with their subjects. The terms of Magna Carta were, therefore, couched in the form of a grant from a benevolent king to his faithful subjects (his *fideles*): the terms would never apply to rebels.†[33]

That evening, the king wrote to all his "sheriffs, foresters, warreners, custodians of rivers, and all his bailiffs," informing them that "a firm peace is restored between us and our barons and the free men of our kingdom just as you are able to hear and to see by our charter which we have made." This writ makes it clear that the text of the agreement was

---

* He gave homage to John on June 21, after which he received letters patent returning to him Fotheringhay Castle.

† When they had lost the argument but retained power, kings gave charters conceding terms in precisely the language that John used to concede the provisions enshrined in Magna Carta. In November 1153, for example, King Stephen issued a charter in which he acknowledged that he had made the future Henry II his heir. This agreement was forced on Stephen by his barons who had refused to maintain his war against his rival for the throne and was in all but name a peace treaty, but for the sake of appearances, the document that emerged from that peace was not an agreement or a treaty but a charter given by Stephen conceding that he had "established Henry, duke of Normandy, as my successor in the kingdom of England, and [had] recognised him as my heir by hereditary right." In return for recognizing Henry as his heir, Stephen got Henry's acceptance that he was the legitimate king and that he would succeed to England through Stephen's rights and not through those of his mother, the Empress Matilda. Both sides, therefore, made important concessions, but the language of the text is about King Stephen's magnanimous treatment of his inferior, Henry.

now being turned into the text that would come to have the title Magna Carta.*[34] The four engrossments that survive to us are four of at least thirteen that were made and distributed.[35]

It was in this writ, too, that John gave permission for juries to be set up in the counties to investigate the extent of the "evil customs" that had arisen and that were to be quashed (Clause 48). And it was in this writ that we hear the most radical of Magna Carta's clauses, Clause 61, had been put into operation.[36] Clause 61 was the security clause, the solution to the problem of what to do about a king so adept at sidestepping his obligations. John had a reputation for being a wily character, difficult to pin down and proficient in using all the political tricks of the trade to outmaneuver his opponents. Those who wished to prevent the king from circumventing the terms of the agreement needed to ensure that the peace was maintained. Oaths, of course, were taken, and promises made, but oaths and promises could be broken, or at the very least bent so far that they became unrecognizable. Those who drove the program of reform came up with the far-reaching idea that there would be a body of men who would provide a check on the king's actions. It was a remarkable leap of the imagination to think that a king might be controlled in this way:

> We grant that the barons shall choose any twenty-five barons of anyone in the realm they wish, who with all their might are to observe, maintain and cause to be observed the peace and liberties which we have granted and confirmed by this our present charter . . . and anyone within the realm who wishes may take an oath to obey the orders of the twenty-five barons in the execution of the aforesaid matters.

The twenty-five were to be chosen from amongst the ranks of the barons, and they were to be the final arbiters of whether or not the king was

---

* Copies of the writ of June 19 authorizing the peace, for example, were being distributed as late as July 22.

ruling according to the terms of the agreement. If it appeared that John or his subordinates were in breach of it and were failing to make amends, then the remedy would be war, led by the twenty-five barons, who would bring with them a force of knights capable of meeting the king in armed conflict. That number, according to one list, would amount to almost 1,200 knights.[37] In a world where 500 knights made up a substantial army, this was a huge force to put into the field.[38] On June 19, John gave authorization for oaths to be sworn to the twenty-five barons, meaning that not only now were their identities known but also that the mechanism for curtailing royal power was in place.[39] This was to be the strength of the peace-making process, the promise of coercion if John failed to keep to his oaths; it was also, however, to be its fatal flaw. When Pope Innocent III came to understand the terms that John had conceded, it was the security clause that caused him to condemn the agreement outright—and, by his letters of August 24, to nullify the charter.[40]

M AGNA CARTA REPRESENTED A recording of John's concessions to his faithful subjects. As a text, therefore, it represents one stage in a peacemaking process that went on long after mid-June 1215. But the very act of writing down the terms agreed, and then distributing copies to be widely circulated and (evidently) translated into the French spoken by the elite of early thirteenth-century England so that it might be more commonly understood,[41] turned an event into a text. Almost immediately after the events of June 1215, men rapidly began to refer not to the agreement of the 15th, but to the actual charter itself, as though it granted the rights and liberties that it recorded.[42] Magna Carta became a yardstick—albeit a generalized and imprecise one—by which the king's performance could be measured. It did not take long for people to begin to argue that the king was not honoring its terms.

What struck contemporary commentators about the events of June and then July 1215 was how short the period of peace was. The Dunstable annalist wrote that it "lasted only for a little time," while the Barnwell chronicler noted the speed with which matters deteriorated.[43] The

Northerners, he tells us, "renewed hostilities to create discord and sought opportunities for terminating the friendship which had been initiated." He had to admit, however, that the distrust went both ways: "the king did not believe them himself and they, in their turn, refused to come near him."[44] At some point in June or early July (probably earlier rather than later), John asked the barons if they would now grant him the security that he needed to assure himself of their goodwill. He wanted from them a charter recording their promise to support him and his heirs "in life and limb and preserving his honour against all men who are able to live and to die": in other words, John wanted the barons to issue a companion text to Magna Carta.[45] The barons declined to put such a promise in writing.

The king must have begun to wonder if they had his eventual overthrow in mind. In a letter of July 7, Innocent III voiced his fears regarding John's fate: "those men [the rebel barons] are undoubtedly worse than Saracens, for they are trying to depose a king who, it was particularly hoped, would succour the Holy Land."[46] It would have been no surprise if John had shared his overlord's concern. And, in the peace treaty between the king and barons, the identification of Robert fitz Walter, the leader of the baronial party, as "Marshal of the Army of God and of Holy Church in England," must have given John pause. The treaty stated that London was to remain in the hands of the barons and that Stephen Langton would retain the Tower of London until August 15 as security for the terms of the agreement. By that date, too, oaths were to have been sworn to the twenty-five, and the restorations promised by the terms of the Charter were to be made.

The agreement settled at Runnymede on June 15, 1215, whatever the political reality, was founded on the legal nicety that the king, out of "reverence for God and for the salvation of our soul and those of our ancestors and heirs, for the honour of God and the exaltation of holy church, for the reform of our realm, on the advice of [named]" had freely "granted to all free men of our kingdom, for ourselves and our heirs for ever, all the liberties written below." The concessions, therefore, were still governed by the age-old principle that the kingdom was the king's and it was from him that liberties were given. The barons may have constituted twenty-five of their number to uphold the terms of the agreement, and they may have held London and the Tower as hostages to the king's performance of his promises, but legally, the terms were only ever concessions given by John to his faithful men. Those who were unfaithful or who remained in rebellion were not to benefit from the terms of the peace.

Moreover, while on June 15 the barons had wrung from John the concession that he would "appeal to no-one to revoke or diminish the concession" given (Clause 61), the kingdom was no longer John's to dispose of. He held it in fief and was answerable to the pope for his actions. Happily for John, the pope took the view that the barons' attempt to restrain the king was an illegal act, and he further took the view that the barons' acts of rebellion had delayed the king's participation in the fifth crusade. Neither was acceptable. And it cannot have escaped the barons' notice that if the king had the pope on his side, then it was unlikely that they would achieve their aims by negotiation.

The Articles of the Barons had expressly stipulated that John was not to appeal to the pope, though the relevant clause was watered down in the text of Magna Carta to "appeal to anyone." Those who drew up the Articles knew that the pope was John's trump card. And by the middle of July at the latest, John had decided to play that card, for on August 24, Innocent wrote a letter to the "barons of England" lambasting them for their "recklessness" in turning "against their lord" and "against the apostolic mandate." They were to desist in their activities immediately and to "make amends to the king and his people."[47] In the face of such intransigence, what alternative did the barons have but to go to war.

12

THE WALLS BREACHED

B Y THE MIDDLE OF August 1215, the hotheads in the baronial party were in the ascendancy. When the king failed to attend a prearranged meeting at Oxford on August 15, and instead deployed the papal letters demanding that Stephen Langton and the other bishops excommunicate the rebels, the contentious decision was made to force John to abdicate. By early September, having divided up the kingdom between them, the barons declared John deposed and decided upon a replacement. Louis, son of King Philip of France, would be invited to be their new monarch.[1] In seeking to depose John, this radical group put themselves completely outside the law. They had even abandoned the tenets of their own agreement hammered out at Runnymede three months earlier. And it is plain to see that John had achieved a remarkable feat. He had turned a representative group of barons complaining about the malpractices of their king into an extremist group of excommunicates with neither the support of the pope nor that of the political community of the realm.[2]

In September 1215, John spent his time at Dover, recruiting mercenaries and perhaps also looking anxiously for any sign of French military activity that might suggest another attempt at invasion by King Philip. In London, the rebels looked anxiously toward Dover, expecting the king to march on them at any moment. In order to prevent, or at least delay, an attack on London, they decided to arm Rochester Castle.

The custody of Rochester Castle belonged by right to the archbishops of Canterbury, but, by an agreement entered into by Stephen Langton in the spring of 1215, control had been ceded to the sheriff of Kent, Reginald of Cornhill. This ought to have worked in John's favor. Reginald's father, Reginald the elder, had been one of John's must trusted men, who acted as purveyor of luxuries to the royal household. When Reginald the elder died in 1210, his son slipped effortlessly into his father's role, maintaining the family's hold over the shire of Kent and its central place in the acquisition of fine wares for the king's use.[3] But in late May 1215, Reginald had come under suspicion as pressure built not only on the king, but also on his servants. Some men cracked under the strain, and it looks as though Reginald was one of those royalists who began to think of joining the rebellion. John requested Stephen Langton to order Reginald to relinquish Rochester Castle to him, but his entreaty fell on deaf ears. In mid-August, John made another attempt to persuade the archbishop to force Reginald to surrender Rochester. When Reginald admitted the military might of the barons to the castle, therefore, the king was furious. It was this event that precipitated the outbreak of open war.[4]

For John, Rochester became indicative of the treachery of his archbishop, and he denounced him roundly. It also became symbolic of the treachery of his barons and of those he trusted within his government. As soon as he heard that Rochester had been fortified against him, he determined to bring it under his control. He set up his siege engines outside the castle and for the next seven weeks he bombarded its walls, finally undermining the southern corner of the keep, the collapse of which signaled the moment of surrender.

The opening of the Rochester campaign marked the moment when peace ended. The rebels had invited Louis of France to bring his forces to England and to replace John as its king; John returned the compliment by beginning the process of redistributing the rebels' lands to his loyal supporters.*[5] The first of the letters granting these lands was issued on October 12, which seems to be the point at which John made the decision to increase the stakes and treat the rebels as though they were traitors.

---

* The evidence is on every page of the close rolls from this point in time.

From this moment onward, and for the next twelve months, John issued a steady stream of orders to his officials, instructing them to release to named beneficiaries the lands of his enemies. On one day alone, November 10, 1215, John confiscated the lands of no fewer than twenty individuals in the counties of Kent, Oxfordshire, Hampshire, Lincolnshire, Northamptonshire, Warwickshire, Buckinghamshire and Dorset.

The fact that John knew the names of the men whose lands he ordered to be confiscated and what lands they held is a reminder that early thirteenth-century England was a highly (by the standards of the day) bureaucratized kingdom. John ordered his men in the localities to make inquiries and report back to him about who was in rebellion, and two of those inquiries survive, both made by members of the band of household knights that the king employed to provide the military and administrative weight that underpinned his regime. In Herefordshire, the man on the ground was Walter de Clifford, a member of a powerful Anglo-Norman dynasty that had held land on the border between England and Wales since the eleventh century. Walter reported that most of the county had been in opposition to John until Giles de Briouze, the bishop of Hereford and the second son of William de Briouze and Matilda de St. Valéry, "had made his peace with the king."[6] Three men were identified as still being against the king, one of whom certainly had his lands confiscated as a result of Walter's report.*[7]

Geoffrey de Serland, another of the king's household knights and custodian of Sauvay Castle in Lincolnshire, was required to report the names of rebels in his bailiwick who held lands in the counties of Rutland and Leicestershire. Geoffrey named twenty knights and eight serjeants in Rutland and a further six knights and four serjeants in Leicestershire. He ended by saying that he would make further inquiries and, if there were any other men in rebellion who came to his attention, he would forward their names to the king.[8] Although his letter is undated, the fact that the first confiscation relating to an individual he named, Hamo Falconer, was

---

* Walter of Stokes's land was given to Stephen of Evreux.

issued on October 31, suggests that Geoffrey's inquiry was conducted shortly after the siege of Rochester had begun.[9]

There must have been two further stages in the process of confiscation, since neither of the surviving reports lists the rebels' lands, and yet, when the orders were put into action, invariably the land to be taken was identified by name. The letter ordering the sequestration of Hamo Falconer's estate in Rutland was, for example, identified as Braunston-in-Rutland. In 1212, John had ordered an inquisition into lands held through knight service and serjeanty. The evidence, once gathered, was to be returned to the king and to the Exchequer, where it was to be enrolled on parchment for future reference.[10] This was, it seems, intended to provide the king with up-to-date information on the military (and therefore financial) capacity of his tenants as he prepared for his return to the continent that year. The writs authorizing the inquests were issued on 1 June, and the returns started to come in by the end of that month, so it was plainly conducted with all speed. It was, presumably, the results of this inquiry that were used to identify the lands of those branded by the king's officials as being in rebellion.[11]

The third stage in the process of confiscation was the allocation of rebel lands to the king's friends and adherents. These were distributed immediately rather than swelling John's royal landholdings. Each individual confiscation generated a writ addressed to the sheriff or bailiff in whose lands the miscreant lay, together with the name of the person to whom the estate was to be given "for as long as it is pleasing to the king." It is unclear exactly how this third stage worked, though there must have been some petitioning of the king for control of certain lands. William de Forz, for example, obtained custody of the lands of his sister, Alice, the wife of the younger William Marshal, who was in rebellion.[12]

Evidently there was also an incentive for men to come forward with accusations of disloyalty. In what must be one of the most remarkable of writs issued that autumn, on October 28, 1215, the lands of William Brewer in Somerset were ordered to be given to William's squire, Thomas Marsh, "because Thomas testified in the Justiciar's court that

William was with the king's enemies." William Brewer was a stalwart of the regime who had a long career in royal service and would continue to serve John loyally to the bitter end, acting as a witness to the king's final testament. That William should come under suspicion and that, temporarily at least, his loyalty was in doubt, is evidence of the confusion that prevailed in the early days of the war.[13]

The evidence also shows that John intended this redistribution of lands to go beyond his tenants in chief to the subtenants; indeed, he intended that rebels at all levels of society should lose their lands. Since 1204, John had been keen to bind all his free subjects to him by oaths of fealty and the performance of homage. Accordingly, the lands of freemen in general were also forfeit if they went into rebellion. William, earl of Ferrers, and Ranulf, earl of Chester, for example, were both given license to confiscate the lands of their tenants who had been identified as being in rebellion.[14] Nor was the confiscation to happen indiscriminately. When the order was issued for the sequestration of the lands of Robert de Crevequer, it was made clear that the action was to affect "all but the tenants [of Robert] who are not against us."[15]

From our perspective, the thousands of writs naming individuals whose land was to be taken provides a wealth of evidence about the last years of John's reign. But for those involved in the drama of the moment, it must have seemed as though the king intended a redistribution of property rights on an unprecedented scale. For a span of a whole year, hardly a day went by without an order (usually more than one) being issued to remove an estate from the hands of one man and to place it in the hands of another. High-born and low-born alike were to be broken on the wheel of poverty and their property rights dismissed by the king's actions. It seems that John's reaction to rebellion was to impose a tenurial revolution intended to radically realign the structure of landholding in the kingdom. Nothing like it had been seen in England since 1066.

Of course we do not know whether the redistribution of lands worked in every single instance. It must have been difficult to serve a writ on a tenant who held land in parts of Norfolk, for example, which for much of the remaining year of John's life, was off limits to royalist forces. But that many of these writs were effective is evidenced by the thousands issued by the Minority government in the wake of the civil war that returned confiscated lands to former rebels.

FOR THE KING, THE fall of Rochester Castle on November 30, 1215, was a high point in the war. News of the castle's capture spread rapidly, and the Barnwell chronicler reported that more than one baronial castellan considered with trepidation the task of standing up to a determined king. The king's immediate reaction had been to hang the whole garrison, but he was prevailed upon by wiser counsel to avoid the bloodletting that would inevitably follow such a draconian move.*

In an odd twist of fate, Rochester Castle was captured on the very day on which, in Rome, Innocent III declared the rebel barons excommunicate. It was the last day of one of the greatest Church councils of the Middle Ages and fittingly capped the pontificate of one of the most remarkable of the medieval popes. The Fourth Lateran Council, which met in November 1215, witnessed the gathering together of the greatest concentration of prelates and representatives of secular rulers. Innocent III had sent out the summonses for it in April 1213, with the express purpose of "rooting up vices and implanting virtues, correcting abuses and reforming morals, eliminating heresies and strengthening the faith . . . and to persuade Christian princes to provide succour to the Holy Land."[16] The English and Welsh contingent consisted of eleven bishops: only Peter des Roches (Winchester), Jocelin of Wells (Bath and Wells), William of Sainte-Mère-Église (London) and Herbert Poore (Salisbury) stayed at home; the first three were important royal officials while the fourth, Herbert of Salisbury, may well have been too decrepit to travel. As well as heads of religious houses and representatives of cathedral communities, also present at the council were the proctors of both King John and of the

---

* The man given credit for persuading John to hold his hand against his enemies was none other than Savaric de Mauléon, who had himself been the victim of John's anger in the wake of the capture of Mirebeau. He languished in prison for two years.

baronial opposition. The focus of the council was the great business of Christendom, of no less importance than the very salvation of the souls of the faithful; but since Innocent was John's overlord, it was in his court that matters had to be resolved. The conflict between John and his barons was to be aired before the whole of Christendom. It was a grand stage on which to have one's dirty laundry displayed and inspected.

John's representatives made their accusations against the barons and especially against the archbishop of Canterbury, Stephen Langton, at whose feet they laid much of the blame for the resistance of the other English prelates to Innocent's plans for the punishment of the recalcitrant barons. Innocent's response was to issue letters suspending Langton from office, dated November 4.[17] This was a powerful blow against the rebels, since it had been Stephen Langton who had provided much of the direction behind the articulation of the baronial position. It is unclear whether Langton appealed directly to the pope after his suspension, but by early January, according to Roger of Wendover, he was reinstated on condition that he not return to England until hostilities ceased. He did not step foot in England again until May 1218.

A further blow was delivered to the baronial party when its proctors were refused a hearing on the grounds that they were excommunicates, and then, on November 30, at the final plenary session, Innocent declared "all the barons of England and everyone who aided them" excommunicate because they impeded John's promised participation in Innocent's planned crusade. For good measure, Innocent also laid the barons' lands under an interdict. The news of the excommunication reached England just before Christmas 1215, by which time Rochester had fallen and John was free to turn his military superiority against the rebel strongholds in the north.[18]

T HE ARRIVAL IN ENGLAND of letters of support from Pope Innocent prompted John to gather his forces at St. Albans, which was, like Bury St. Edmunds, one of the great monasteries of medieval England. There, in the chapter house, before the monks of the community, he had the sentence of excommunication read aloud, and then ordered the monks to write to the other religious houses of England making known the pope's decision. The sentence against the barons was to be declared from the pulpit of every church in the land and repeated each Sunday, as Innocent had threatened against John only a few years before. John then decided to split his army in two, one part to remain in the south to occupy the barons in London, while he led the other to hound the northerners who were at the center of the baronial opposition to him. He was going to attack the rebels in their homesteads.

The meeting at St. Albans took place on December 20, by which time John would have received certain intelligence that Louis was planning to invade England. The barons had offered him the throne in September, and while the French court had prevaricated (hardly surprisingly given the outcome of the 1213 invasion plan), Louis had now made up his mind to accept their offer. Military preparations went ahead over the winter of 1215–16, during which time French knights, under the leadership of the marshal of France, had been sent to bolster London's defenses. The question of why John went northward, instead of heading for London to put the rebel barons under direct pressure, puzzled contemporaries. The most plausible explanation is that John simply did not feel confident that he could take the city. The men of London alone could put a large and effective army into the field. Since the barons were ensconced within the city walls and their numbers had been bolstered by the arrival of the Marshal of France with his troops, it seems that John judged that he had a better chance of winkling the barons out of London if he first deprived them of their estates in the north.[19]

The campaign that John waged in the north of England was extremely successful. His presence gave encouragement to those of his supporters who had been placed in strategic strongholds, and his enhanced reputation in the wake of the capture of Rochester meant that few were willing to hold their castles against him even if they had been so inclined. John's troops harried the countryside, reaching as far north as Berwick before returning southward. By springtime, John was back in the south-east, laying siege to Colchester Castle, which fell quickly to him, and he then proceeded to Dover, there to await the expected arrival of Louis and his army. Once again, John did not dare to approach London, much to the confusion of the Barnwell chronicler.[20]

L OUIS OF FRANCE ARRIVED in England on May 21, 1216, stepping ashore on the Isle of Thanet, watched, so we are told, by John himself, who, despite seeing the landing operation, made the decision not to confront the invader on the beaches. According to the author of the *History of the Dukes of Normandy*, the king was concerned that the majority of the knights in his pay were subjects of the king of France and might, therefore, be unwilling to attack Philip's son.[21] John, though, had not been supine. He had attempted to blockade Calais to prevent the sailing of Louis' ships, but the English fleet had been dispersed by a storm.[22]

Once Louis was on English soil, however, John withdrew to Winchester, where he met the papal legate, Guala Bicchieri, who had been appointed by Innocent III to defend John against the French. The legate had landed in England on May 20, but despite his arguments and the threat of dire sanctions, he had failed to prevent the invasion. John faced not only the rebel barons but also a man who had a rival claim to the throne and was backed by all the resources of the French monarchy. John was now battling for the very survival of the Angevins. And it did not help his cause that at exactly this point some of the pillars of his regime turned against him. Most notably, the king's half-brother, William Longspee, earl of Salisbury, hero of the victory at Damme, the leader of the king's troops at Bouvines and a constant source of support, went over to the rebel side. It must have been a bitter blow to King John, who could not but have noticed the irony that he had been deserted by his own half-sibling but not his Flemish mercenaries, who remained steadfastly by his side.

From Kent, John moved to the ancient English capital of Winchester, while Louis went to London to a rapturous reception from the rebels. On June 5, perhaps receiving intelligence that Louis was heading to

Winchester with his siege engines in an attempt to bring matters to a swift conclusion,[23] John retreated into Wiltshire, heading first to Devizes and then to Wilton. A few days later, John withdrew into Dorset and made his way to the stronghold at Corfe. He arrived there on June 23; the next day Winchester fell to the French.[24] John remained at Corfe while he prepared his forces. The castle itself was one on which he had lavished huge sums of money, and which made a very comfortable residence for the king. The same artisans and craftsmen who had worked on the recently built Wells Cathedral had also sumptuously decorated the king's house at Corfe.[25] Corfe was, too, a formidable castle, that could, if the need arose, make a good place for a last stand. With the royal family in the west of the country out of harm's way, John could concentrate on the business of fighting for his very existence.[26]

It must have taken considerable nerve to wait at Corfe while allowing Louis and his forces the freedom to march through southern England. In 1066, King Harold had felt the need to confront Duke William in battle precisely because the duke harried his lands and forced the king to defend his people at the earliest moment. John, too, must have felt the need to demonstrate his resilience to his people by bringing Louis to an armed confrontation, but he resisted that urge. Instead, John stayed at Corfe for a full month, from where he issued a stream of instructions for the continuation of the war. By the third week in July, it became evident that John was waiting for a sign that it was time to come out of his lair: on July 19, he received it.

John learned that Louis was taking his siege engines to Dover in a determined effort to take the castle. As John well knew, and as its castellan would later tell the chronicler Matthew Paris, Dover "was the key to England."[27] If Louis wanted a bridgehead through which he could bring more troops from the continent, he had to take the castle. John understood very clearly the importance of Dover to his survival, and so placed within its walls his most resolute servant, Hubert de Burgh, along with an elite troop of royal household knights and Flemish mercenaries.

When Louis himself arrived to supervise matters on July 22, the scene was set for a struggle that would go on for the next three months.

Once John knew that Louis was tied down outside Dover, he emerged from Corfe to direct the war from horseback. He went into the faithful heartlands of the west of England, touring the key castles of Bristol, Gloucester, Tewkesbury and Hereford. Throughout August he shuttled between Leominster and Corfe, stopping off at Worcester, Bridgnorth and Bristol, amongst other places, shoring up their defenses, and issuing dozens of letters redistributing his enemies' lands to his supporters. In September, John turned his attentions to the midland and eastern counties. He was to be found at Oxford and Wallingford until the middle of the month and then Bedford, Cambridge, Hedingham and Clare in Suffolk, ravaging the countryside as he went, before turning northward to arrive at Lincoln by the end of September. The close rolls for September, as they were for August, are littered with letters confiscating rebels' lands. By October 9, John was in East Anglia, where he was received by the men of Lynn and feasted royally. And it was here that he contracted the dysentery from which, ten days later, he would die.

Leaving Lynn on the morning of October 12, John made his way toward Wisbech and from there on to the nunnery of Swineshead, where he received news that a portion of his baggage train had been lost in the quicksands of the Wellstream estuary. It seems unlikely that much was lost, a few relics belonging to the chapel royal and some packhorses, although the story was later embroidered to turn it into one in which great treasures were consumed by the sands.[28] Here, according to one partisan account, John feasted on peaches and new cider, which merely exacerbated his symptoms.

He rested at Swineshead for a day, ministered to, presumably, by the nuns, before struggling on to Sleaford, where he was on the 14th and 15th. No business was transacted on the 14th as the king lay in his sickbed, and only three letters were issued by John on the 15th, the most important to Pope Honorius III (who had been elected after Innocent's death in July).[29] In it, John explained to the new pope that he was hindered by a grave illness and despaired for his life. He acknowledged that England was under the pope's authority, and he humbly begged Honorius to place the kingdom and his heir under papal protection to help his son gain his inheritance. Since England had been a fief of the papacy since 1213, Honorius was the obvious person to ask for aid in John's hour of greatest need. That he should commend his sons and his kingdom into the pope's hands equally meant that John feared that he was going to die.

On October 16, John was too weak to ride, so he was placed on a litter and carried the twenty-five miles to Newark. There he was bled by the abbot of Croxton, a noted physician, but to no avail. Only two pieces of business were transacted that day, the one a safe conduct for Gerard de Furnivall, the other an instruction to pay wages to the castle garrison at Northampton. The following day, John rallied a little, issuing two letters close and a letter patent granting custody of Wallingford Castle to his illegitimate son, Richard fitz Roy. On the 18th, the last full day of his life, the king burst into a flurry of activity, issuing a further seven letters, each of which looked forward to the forthcoming succession struggle. Letters of credence were given to the king's right-hand men, Savaric de Mauleon, Falkes de Bréauté and the earl of Aumale as they all went to Hervey Belet, the constable of the royalist stronghold of Norwich Castle, to put pressure on him to return to John's cause. Letters of safe conduct were given to all of those prepared to make peace with the king through Savaric, and especially mentioned by name was William of Buslingthorpe, a rebel Lincolnshire knight. John also made provision for Nicola de Hay, holding Lincoln Castle, and for Hubert de Burgh, the castellan of Dover, who was still keeping Louis and the French army at bay. And finally, he made out the terms of his last testament.

In considerable pain from the effects of the dysentery that was killing him, John's first thought was to the fate of his immortal soul: he begged those who were entrusted with the task of acting on his last wishes to give reparation to God in sufficient quantity to make amends for the damage he had done to the Church during his lifetime. It is unlikely, however, that there was enough money in the king's coffers to meet such a huge demand on its resources. John had pillaged the Church and spent his savings on a disastrous overseas campaign, a desperate civil war and the defense of the realm against the invasion of the French. John was about to meet the God whose earthly property he had wasted.

John also gave thought to the future of his sons. He urged those whom he had appointed as his executors to help his heir, Henry (then aged nine), and his second son, Richard (aged seven), to realize their inheritances. That, too, was going to be far from easy. John's kingdom was in ruins, and a foreign prince held sway over large swathes of England, including London and, importantly, Westminster, the seat of much government and where the next king would have to be crowned. John must have contemplated the end not only of his own life but also the end of his dynasty.[30]

John was two months away from his fiftieth birthday and he was, without any doubt, a catastrophic failure. As a king, as a leader of his army, as defender of his inheritance, as protector of his people and of his Church, he had failed, and his reputation as one of the most hapless of English kings was well on the way to being established. No king can leave a legacy like John's and expect to be remembered kindly by posterity. We know, too, that at his very last moment, John understood what he had done because he made a testament on the very evening of his death. The text was written in the first person singular, rather than the first person plural that was usual in royal documents, making it clear that John was a penitent individual facing his mortal end.[31] This is the authentic voice of John the man, not John the king, as he lay in extremis.

> I, John, by the grace of God king of England, lord of Ireland, duke of Normandy and Aquitaine, count of Anjou, hindered by grave infirmity . . . commit the arbitration and administration of my testament to . . . my faithful men whose names are written below . . . so that they will faithfully arrange and determine concerning my things as much as in making satisfaction to God and to holy church for damages and injuries done to them as in

> sending succour to the land of Jerusalem and in providing support
> to my sons towards obtaining and defending their inheritance and
> in making reward to those who have served us faithfully and in
> making distribution to the poor and to religious houses for the
> salvation of my soul . . .

The text was not copied onto the Chancery enrolments, but made its way with the king's body to Worcester where, at his request, he was interred and where, to this day, he still lies.

John's death did not bring about the end of the civil war. When Louis of France heard that his rival had died, he sought first to call out Hubert de Burgh from Dover Castle for a parley. "Your master is dead," Louis is reported to have said, "therefore give up the castle and become faithful to me, and I will enrich you with honours." Hubert refused to surrender Dover, whereupon Louis raised the siege and departed to "besiege smaller castles."[32] Meanwhile, after John's body had been placed in its tomb, on October 27, those whom he had appointed to help his sons gain their inheritances gathered together at Gloucester.* There they made preparations for the next step.

The first priority was to have John's son and heir, Henry, crowned king. The anointing with holy oil was crucial in the race to become the next monarch, and so those whose task it was to support Henry decided to move with such rapidity that they were prepared to completely discard convention. They decided to have Henry crowned the very next day, October 28, a Friday (rather than waiting until Sunday 30th) and on a day of no great religious significance (the feast of Saints Simon and Jude); they decided that the ceremony would be conducted by the papal

---

* According to John's testament, his executors were to be: the lord Guala, by the grace of God, cardinal-priest of the title of St. Martin and legate of the apostolic see; the lord Peter, bishop of Winchester; the lord Richard, bishop of Chichester; the lord Silvester, bishop of Worcester; Brother Aimery de St.-Maur; William Marshal, earl of Pembroke; Ranulf, earl of Chester; William, earl Ferrers; William Brewer; Walter de Lacy and John of Monmouth; Savaric de Mauléon; Falkes de Bréauté.

legate, Guala Bicchieri, who had been appointed by Pope Honorius III to provide on-the-ground support for John's cause against the French invasion (the right of consecration was reserved for the archbishop of Canterbury)[33]; and they decided that the ceremony should take place at Gloucester (Westminster was the coronation church of the English kings). This was all unprecedented and was a consequence of the fear that Louis, who controlled Westminster and (possibly, no one was quite sure) the archbishop of Canterbury, might have himself crowned king with all the correct forms on Sunday, October 30. Henry's guardians were taking no chances.

There were further problems with Henry's coronation. No child had been crowned king in England for very nearly 240 years. Early medieval polities generally eschewed the candidacy of minors on the grounds that the job of being a king was an energetic one requiring active rulership over aristocrats brought up to make war. The king needed to dominate those warrior aristocrats in order to maintain a level of control, and on the whole men raised for war do not fear children. Henry was just nine in October 1216.

In part, the solution to the problem of having a minor as king was to choose the right person to guide him during the minority years. In other contexts, that person might have been Henry's mother, Isabella of Angoulême. When minorities did occur in early medieval polities, the queen mother usually played a principal role in the young king's government.[34] There seems to have been no question of Isabella playing this role, and within nine months she had left England for her ancestral homelands, leaving Henry without any parental guidance. Instead, Henry's supporters turned to William Marshal, by 1216 seventy years old and with a reputation (not always deserved) of having an unimpeachable record of honorable service to two generations of Angevins. Unanimously, those gathered at Gloucester chose William who, after some hesitation, agreed to take up the challenge of becoming the king's guardian.[35]

The situation in the country was dire, and some expressed doubts as to whether the young Henry would ever be able to recover his kingdom; but the Marshal was resolute, and having considered the military situation, he decided to take the young king and his court to Bristol, where they would reissue Magna Carta (amended to remove some of the more objectionable clauses) in an attempt to break off the rebel barons from their allegiance to Louis. The charter was issued on November 12, 1216, at Bristol, where Savaric de Mauléon was castellan. The terms of the charter were granted by the counsel of the key individuals in the regime and were guaranteed by the fixing of the seals of William Marshal, as "our ruler and the ruler of our kingdom" ("rector noster et regni nostri"), and of the legate Guala.

This was the moment at which Magna Carta truly entered the political arena as a document of lasting consequence. While Magna Carta 1215 had been annulled by Pope Innocent III and comprehensively rejected by the participants in the civil war, Magna Carta 1216 emerged as a document of reconciliation between the new and blameless child-king Henry III and his rebellious barons. Magna Carta was now a "royalist manifesto"[36] that promised the king's faithful magnates that this king would rule according to the principles laid out in the charter. Magna Carta was, therefore, a primitive written constitution that could serve as a yardstick against which the actions of the king and his officers could be measured.

Magna Carta 1216 addressed the concerns of the rebel barons, but it made no attempt to bring Louis of France to the negotiating table. It produced precious few converts and in the end the conflict had to be resolved by battle. At Lincoln on May 20 and then again in a sea battle off the coast of Sandwich on August 24, 1217, Louis' forces were defeated. Afterward, as part of the peace process, Magna Carta was issued again, this time with a companion document, the Forest Charter. Again the seals of Guala and the Marshal authenticated these documents. The civil war and invasion provoked by John's actions were now officially at an end. All it remained to do was for the minority government to rebuild and secure royal rule ready for when Henry III eventually reached his majority.[37]

CONCLUSION

THE EFFIGY OF JOHN that sits on top of the sixteenth-century tomb (built at the same time as that built to house the remains of Prince Arthur, d. 1502, Henry VII's firstborn son) is a near contemporary representation of the king. It was almost certainly made in about 1228 and was commissioned by the monks of Worcester, who were engaged in a desperate struggle with John's Cistercian foundation of Beaulieu for control of the royal body. The abbot of Beaulieu, not without good cause, claimed that the king had intended to lie among the monks of his foundation and that only the circumstances of the war had dictated otherwise. In 1228, John's son, Henry III, was minded to agree with the Cistercians, and said as much in a letter to the pope. And yet, John's body remained, and remains, at Worcester.

In death, John's body was a valuable asset. His son sat on the throne of England, and the evidence shows that he looked upon his father's resting place with great affection. He sank vast sums of money into Worcester, which sustained a building program that lasted a half-century or more and resulted in the completion of an extraordinarily beautiful Gothic cathedral, much of which still stands today.[1] When, in 1228, it looked as though the monks might lose the precious commodity lying in the eastern part of their cathedral, they set out to show King Henry that Worcester was indeed a worthy place for his father's body. Quite evidently they succeeded, for in 1232 Henry and his sister were present on Ascension Eve, May 18, at a grand ceremony in which their father's remains were

243

reinterred at the very heart of the choir. The following day, the actual feast of the Ascension, Henry III gave to the monks at Worcester one hundred oak trees from which to build the roof that would sit above his father's tomb.

John had been crowned on Ascension Day 1199, and the reinterment of his remains at the same feast time thirty-three years later was no accident. The feast of the Ascension marks the day when Christ ascended into heaven to sit at the right hand of His Father. The focus of the feast is all about resurrection and salvation; it cannot have escaped the minds of those present that John's salvation was at the heart of the ceremony. The monks of Worcester were promising Henry that his father's soul was in good hands. And as well as their prayers, they sang, too. During the ceremony and, indeed, twice daily throughout the remainder of the Middle Ages, the monks of Worcester sang the *Laudes Regiae*. The chant "Christus Vincit," which had accompanied John in life, would serenade his soul throughout eternity.

The image of King John that the monks presented to his son and that won his heart and approval still survives. It shows the king as he would have appeared in life, dressed in his coronation regalia, while two saints, Oswald and Wulfstan, bearing censers, emerge from the Purbeck marble. The tomb would have been brightly painted (though this was subsequently removed), and the effigy was adorned with precious stones. It is a picture of majesty, and would have pleased John, since he enjoyed his pomp.

It is an image that is more than one of simple majesty, however. The king has his sword drawn. In iconographic terms, this is unique on the tombs of medieval English kings, who are all shown with their swords sheathed.[2] But the drawn sword is not the effigy's most significant feature. The artist has chosen to show the king standing on a lion, which represents the temporal world over which John had ruled while he lived. The lion is not supine; its head twists to seize the king's sword in its mouth and bend it. The world is in rebellion, resisting royal authority divinely appointed. This was the final judgment on John that was approved by his son, Henry III, no matter that history would tell a less sympathetic story.

BIBLIOGRAPHY

PRINTED SOURCES

Ancient Charters Royal and Private Prior to AD 1200, i, ed. J. H. Round (Pipe Roll Society, 10, 1888)

The Angevin Acta Project at the University of East Anglia, ed. N. C. Vincent, J. C. Holt, R. Mortimer, M. Staunton, J. Everard (forthcoming). This work includes the acts of Henry II, Count Richard, and Count John and until publication is accessible from Prof. Vincent at the University of East Anglia

Annales Monastici, 5 vols, ed. H. R. Luard, Rolls Series (London, 1864–9)

"The annals of Southwark and Merton," ed. M. Tyson, in *Surrey Archaeological Collections*, vol. 36 (1925), 24–57

Appendix to the 23rd Report of the Deputy Keeper of the Public Records in Ireland (London, 1891)

"The Articles of the Barons: Articles 1–48," The Magna Carta Project, trans. H. Summerson et al. http://magnacarta.cmp.uea.ac.uk/read/articles_of_barons/Articles

The Beaulieu Cartulary, ed. S. F. Hockey, Southampton Record Society (Southampton, 1974)

Bristol Charters, 1155–1373, ed. N. Dermott Harding (Bristol Record Society, 1, 1930)

Calendar of Ancient Correspondence Concerning Wales, ed. J. G. Edwards (Cardiff, 1935)

Calendar of Documents Relating to France, ed. J. H. Round (London, 1899)

Calendar of Documents Relating to Ireland, 1175–1251, ed. H. S. Sweetman (London, 1875)

Calendar of Ormond Deeds, 1172–1350, ed. E. Curtis (Dublin, 1932)

Calendar of the Carew Manuscripts Preserved in the Archiepiscopal Library at Lambeth, 6 vols, ed. J. S. Brewer and W. Bullen (London, 1867–73)

Calendar of the Gormanston Register c.1175–1397: From the Original in the Possession of the Rt. Hon. the Viscount of Gormanston, ed. J. Mill and M. J. McEnery (Extra Volume of the Royal Society of Antiquaries of Ireland, Dublin, 1916)

Calendar of the Liberate Rolls Preserved in the Public Record Office, 1226–1240 (London, 1916)

Cartae Antiquae Rolls 1–10, ed. L. Landon (Pipe Roll Society, new series, 17, 1939)

"Cartulaires de Hainaut," *Monuments pour servir à l'histoire des provinces de Namur, de Hainaut et de Luxembourg*, i, ed. De Reiffenberg (Brussels, 1844)

The Cartularies of St Mary's Abbey, Dublin: With the Register of its House at Dunbrody, and Annals of Ireland, 2 vols, ed. J. T. Gilbert, Rolls Series (London, 1884)

Cartulary of Cirencester Abbey, Gloucestershire, 3 vols, 1–2, ed. C. D. Ross (London, 1964), 3, ed. M. Devine (Oxford, 1977)

The Cartulary of Dale Abbey, ed. A. Saltman (London, 1967)

The Chancellor's Roll for the Eighth Year of the Reign of King Richard the First: Michaelmas 1196, ed. D. M. Stenton (Pipe Roll Society, new series, 45, 1930)

Chartae, Privilegia et Immunitates: Being Transcripts of Charters and Privileges to Cities, Towns, Abbeys, and Other Bodies Corporate, 1171–1395 (Irish Record Commission, 1829–30, 1889)

The Charters of Quarr Abbey, ed. S. F. Hockey (Isle of Wight County Record Office, 1991)

The Charters of the Anglo-Norman Earls of Chester, c.1071–1237, ed. G. Barraclough (Record Society of Lancashire and Cheshire, 126, 1988)

The Charters of the Duchess Constance and Her Family, ed. J. Everard and M. Jones (Woodbridge, 2000)

Charters of the Honour of Mowbray, 1107–1191, ed. D. E. Greenway (London, 1972)

The Charters of William II and Henry I: History from the writs and charters of two Norman kings, ed. R. Sharpe at http://actswilliam2henry1.wordpress.com

Chartes anciennes de l'abbaye de Zonnebeke, ed. C. Callewaert (Bruges, 1925)

The Chartulary of Cockersand Abbey of the Premonstratensian Order, 6 vols. ed. W. Farrer (Chetham Society, new series, 38–40, 43, 46–7, 1898, 1900, 1905)

Chronica Magistri Rogeri de Houedene, 4 vols, ed. W. Stubbs, Rolls Series (London, 1868–71)

The Chronicle and Historical Notes of Bernard Itier, ed. A. W. Lewis (Oxford, 2013)

The Chronicle of Battle Abbey, ed. E. Searle (Oxford, 1980)

The Chronicle of Richard of Devizes, ed. J. T. Appleby (London, 1963)

"The Chronicle of Robert of Torigny," *Chronicles of the Reigns of Stephen, Henry II, and Richard I*, 4 vols, ed. R. Howlett, Rolls Series (London 1884–89)

The Chronicle of the Election of Hugh Abbot of Bury St Edmunds and Later Bishop of Ely, ed. R. M. Thomson (Oxford, 1974)

Close Rolls of the Reign of Henry III Preserved in the Public Record Office, 1227–31 (London, 1902)

Correspondence of Thomas Becket, 2 vols, ed. A. Duggan (Oxford, 2000)

The Coucher Book of the Cistercian Abbey of Kirkstall, ed. W. T. Lancaster and W. Paley Baildon (Thoresby Society, 8, 1904)

Curia Regis Rolls of the Reigns of Richard I, John and Henry III Preserved in the Public Record Office (London, 1922–ongoing)

Diplomatic Documents preserved in the Public Record Office, 1101–1272, i, ed. P. Chaplais (London, 1964)

Documents Illustrative of English History in the Thirteenth and Fourteenth Centuries, ed. H. Cole (Record Commission, London, 1844)

Dugdale, W., *Monasticon Anglicanum*, 6 vols, ed. J. Caley, H. Ellis, and B. Bandinel (Record Commission, London, 1846)

Earldom of Gloucester Charters: The Charters and Scribes of the Earls and Countesses of Gloucester to AD 1217, ed. R. B. Paterson (Oxford, 1973)

Early Yorkshire Charters, 10 vols, 1–3, ed. W. Farrer (Edinburgh, 1914–16), 4–10, ed. C. T. Clay (Yorkshire Archaeological Society, Record series, extra series, 1935–55)

English Episcopal Acta 31: Ely 1109–1197, ed. N. Karn (Oxford, 2005)

English Historical Documents, ii, 2nd edn, ed. D. C. Douglas and G. Greenaway (London, 1981)

English Historical Documents, 1189–1327, iii, ed. H. Rothwell (London, 1975)

English Lawsuits from William I to Richard I, 2 vols, ed. R. C. van Caenegem (Selden Society, London, 1990–1).

Excerpta è Rotulis Finium in Turri Londinensi Asservatis, AD 1216–72, 2 vols, ed. C. Roberts (Record Commission, London, 1835–6)

Eye Priory Cartulary and Charters, 2 vols, ed. V. Brown (Suffolk Records Society, 12–13, 1992–3)

Foedera, Conventiones, Litterae et cuiuscunque generis Acta Publica, ed. T. Rymer, new edn, vol. I, part i, ed. A. Clark and F. Holbrooke (Record Commission, London, 1816)

Gesta Regis Henrici Secundi Benedicti Abbatis, 2 vols, ed. W. Stubbs, Rolls Series (London, 1867)

Giraldus Cambrensis, Expugnatio Hibernica. The Conquest of Ireland, ed. A. B. Scott and F. X. Martin (Dublin, 1978)

Giraldus Cambrensis, Opera, 8 vols, ed. J. S. Brewer, J. F. Dimock, and G. F. Warner, Rolls Series (London 1861–91)

Histoire des Ducs de Normandie et des Rois d'Angleterre, ed. F. Michel (Société de l'histoire de France, Paris, 1840)

The Historical Works of Gervase of Canterbury, 2 vols, ed. W. Stubbs, Rolls Series (London, 1879–80)

The Historical Works of Master Ralph de Diceto, 2 vols, ed. W. Stubbs, Rolls Series (London, 1876)

History of William the Marshal, 3 vols, ed. A. J. Holden, S. Gregory and D. Crouch, Anglo-Norman Texts Society (London, 2002–6)

Interdict Documents, ed. P. M. Barnes and W. R. Powell (Pipe Roll Society, new series, 34, 1960)

Irish Historical Documents, 1170–1922, ed. E. Curtis and R. B. McDowell (Dublin, 1943)

"The Irish pipe roll of 14 John, 1211–12," ed. O. Davies and D. B. Quinn, *Ulster Journal of Archaeology*, 4 (Supplement, July 1941)

Itinerarum Peregrinorum et Gesta Regis Ricardi in *Chronicles and Memorials of the Reign of Richard I*, ed. W. Stubbs, Rolls Series (London, 1864)

The Itinerary of King Richard I, ed. L. Landon (Pipe Roll Society, new series, 13, London, 1935)

John of Salisbury's Entheticus Maior and Minor, ed. J. van Laarhoven, 3 vols (Leiden, 1987)

Jordan Fantosme's Chronicle, ed. R. C. Johnston (Oxford, 1981)

Layettes du Trésor des Chartes, 4 vol. in 4°, tome I: *755–1223*, A. Teulet (Paris, 1863–1902)

Leges Henrici Primi, ed. L. J. Downer (Oxford, 1972)

Letters of Innocent III Concerning England and Wales (1198–1216), ed. C. R. Cheney and M. Cheney (Oxford, 1967)

Liber Feodorum. The Book of Fees Commonly Called Testa de Nevill, 3 vols (London, 1920–31)

List of Sheriffs for England and Wales (Public Record Office, Lists and Indexes 9, New York, 1963)

Magni Rotuli Scaccarii Normaniae sub Regibus Angliae, 2 vols, ed. T. Stapleton (Society of Antiquaries of London, 1840–4)

Magna Vita Sancti Hugonis, 2 vols, ed. D. L. Douie and D. H. Farmer (Oxford, 1985)

Matthaei Parisiensis, Monachi Sancti Albani, Chronica Majora, 7 vols, ed. H. R. Luard, Rolls Series (London, 1872–83)

The Memoranda Roll for the Michaelmas Term of the First Year of the Reign of King John, 1199–1200, ed. H. G. Richardson (Pipe Roll Society, new series, 21, 1943)

The Memoranda Roll for the Tenth Year of King John (1207–8), ed. R. Allen Brown (Pipe Roll Society, new series, 31, 1955)

Memoriale Fratris Walteri de Coventria, 2 vols. ed. W. Stubbs, Rolls Series (London, 1872–3)

Œuvres de Rigord et de Guillaume le Breton, ed. H. F. Delaborde, i (Paris, 1882)

The Parallel Lives by Plutarch, ix, trans. B. Perrin (Loeb Classical Library, 1920)

Petri Blesensis Archidiaconi Opera Omnia, 4 vols, ed. J. A. Giles, Rolls Series (London, 1846–7)

Pipe Roll 17 John and Praestita Roll 14–18 John, ed. R. Allen Brown and J. C. Holt (Pipe Roll Society, new series, 37, 1961)

Pleas Before the King or his Justices, 1198–1212, 2 vols, ed. D. M. Stenton (Selden Society, 83–4, 1966, 1967)

Pon, G., and Y. Chauvin, "Chartes de libertés et de communes de l'Angoumois, du Poitou et de la Saintonage (fin XIIᵉ-début XIIIᵉ siècle)," *Memoires de la Société des Antiquaires de l'Ouest*, 58 (2000), 25–149

Pontificia Hibernica: Medieval Papal Chancery Documents concerning Ireland, 640–1261, 2 vols, ed. M. Sheehy (Dublin, 1962–5)

Radulphi de Coggeshall Chronicon Anglicanum, ed. J. Stevenson, Rolls Series (London, 1875)

Reading Abbey Cartularies: British Library Manuscripts Egerton 3031, Harley 1708 and Cotton Vespasian E xxv, 2 vols, ed. B. R. Kemp (Camden Society, 4th series, 31, 33, 1986, 1987)

Recueil des Actes de Henri II, roi d'Angleterre et duc de Normandie, concernant les provinces françaises et les affaires de France, 4 vols, ed. L Delisle and E. Berger (Paris, 1916–66)

Red Book of the Exchequer, 3 vols, ed. H. Hall (Record Commission, London, 1896)

Register of St Thomas, Dublin, ed. J. T. Gilbert, Rolls Series (London, 1889)

Reports on the Lords Committees touching on the Dignity of a Peer of the Realm, Presented to the House 12 July 1819 (London 1820)

Richard fitz Nigel Dialogus de Scaccario and the Constitutio Domus Regis, ed. E. Amt and S. D. Church (Oxford, 2007)

Rogeri de Wendover, Chronica sive Flores Historiarum, 5 vols, ed. H. O. Coxe, English Historical Society (London, 1841–5)

Rotuli Chartarum in Turri Londinensi Asservati, ed. T. Duffus Hardy (Record Commission, London, 1837)

Rotuli Curiae Regis: Rolls and Records of the Court held before the King's Justiciars or Justices, 2 vols, ed. F. Palgrave (Record Commission, London, 1835)

Rotuli de Liberate ac de Misis et Praestitis Regnante Johanne, ed. T. Duffus Hardy (Record Commission, London, 1844)

Rotuli de Oblatis et Finibus in Turri Londinensi Asservati, ed. T. Duffus Hardy (Record Commission, London, 1835)

Rotuli Litterarum Clausarum in Turri Londinensi Asservati, 2 vols, ed. T. Duffus Hardy (Record Commission, London, 1833, 1844)

Rotuli Litterarum Patentium in Turri Londinensi Asservati, ed. T. Duffus Hardy (Record Commission, London, 1835)

Rotuli Normanniae in Turri Londinensi Asservati, ed. T. Duffus Hardy (Record Commission, London, 1835)

Royal and Other Historical Letters Illustrative of the Reign of Henry III, 2 vols, ed. W. W. Shirley, Rolls Series (London, 1862–6)

Select Charters and Other Illustrations of English Constitutional History, ed. W. Stubbs, 9th edn, ed. H. W. C. David (Oxford, 1913)

Selected Letters of Pope Innocent III Concerning England (1198–1216), ed. C. R. Cheney and W. H. Semple (London, 1953)

The Song of Dermot and the Earl, ed. G. H. Orpen (Oxford, 1892)

The Ruodlieb: The First Medieval Epic of Chivalry from Eleventh-Century Germany, trans. G. B. Ford (Leiden, 1965)

Tractatus de legibus et consuetudinibus regi Anglie qui Glanvilla vocatur, ed. G. D. G. Hall, rev. edn (Oxford, 1993)

La Vie du bienheureux Robert d'Arbrissel, patriarche des Solitaires de France, et institution de l'ordre de Fontevraud, ed. Balthazar Pavillon (Paris-Saumur, 1666)

Walter Map, De Nugis Curialium, ed. M. R. James, revised by C. N. L. Brooke and R. A. B. Mynors (Oxford, 1983)

William of Newburgh, Historia Rerum Anglicarum in *Chronicles and Memorials of the Reign of Richard I*, 2 vols, ed. ed. R. Howlett, Rolls Series (London, 1884)

SECONDARY WORKS

Alexander, J. W., *Ranulf of Chester: A Relic of the Conquest* (Athens, GA, 1983)

Appleby, J. T., *England Without Richard* (London, 1965)

Baldwin, J. W., *The Government of Philip Augustus: Foundations of French Royal Power in the Middle Ages* (Berkeley, 1986)

Bardsley, S., *Women's Roles in the Middle Ages* (Westport, CT, 2007)

Barlow, F., *The Feudal Kingdom of England, 1042–1216*, 4th edn (London, 1988)

Barratt, N., "The revenue of King John," *EHR*, 111 (1996), 835–55

Barrau, J., *Bible, lettres et politique. L'Écriture au service des hommes à l'époque de Thomas Becket* (Paris, 2013)

Bazelay, M., "The extent of the English forest in the thirteenth century," *TRHS*, 4th series, 4 (1921), 140–59

Bean, J. M. W., "'Bachelor' and Retainer," *Medievalla et Humanistica*, 3 (1972), 117–132

———, *From Lord to Patron: Lordship in Late Medieval England* (Manchester, 1989)

Benham, J. E. M., "Anglo-French peace conferences in the twelfth century," *Anglo-Norman Studies*, 27 (2005), 52–67

———, *Peacemaking in the Middle Ages: Principles and Practice* (Manchester, 2011)

Boase, T. S. R., "Fontevrault and the Plantagenets," *Journal of the British Archaeological Association*, 3rd series, 34 (1971), 1–10

Boivin-Champeaux, L., *Notice sur Guillaume de Long Champ* (Evreux, 1885)

Bolton, B., "Papal Italy," in *Italy in the Central Middle Ages*, ed. D. Abulafia (Oxford, 2004), 82–103

Bolton, J. L., "Inflation, economics, and politics in thirteenth-century England," in *Thirteenth Century England IV: Proceedings of the Newcastle upon Tyne Conference, 1991*, ed. P. R. Coss and S. D. Lloyd (Woodbridge, 1992), 1–14

———, "The English economy in the early thirteenth century," in *King John: New Interpretations*, ed. S. D. Church (Woodbridge, 1999), 27–40

Boorman, J., "The sheriffs of Henry II and the significance of 1170," in *Law and Government in Medieval England and Normandy*, ed. G. Garnett and J. Hudson (Cambridge, 1994), 255–75

Boutoulle, F., "L'apogée d'une 'bonne ville.' Saint-Emilion pendant les premiers temps de la jurade (1199–1253)," in *Fabrique d'une ville médiévale. Saint-Emilion au Moyen Age*, ed. F. Boutoulle, D. Barraud and J.-L. Piat (Bordeaux, 2011), 313–45

Bowie, C., *The Daughters of Henry II and Eleanor of Aquitaine: A Comparative Study of Twelfth-Century Royal Women* (Turnhout, 2014)

Brown, R. Allen, "Framlingham castle and Bigod, 1154–1216," *Proceedings of the Suffolk Institute of Archaeology*, 25 (1951), 127–48, and in his *Castles, Conquest and Charters: Collected Papers* (Woodbridge, 1989), 187–208

———, "A note on Kenilworth castle: the change to royal ownership," *Archaeological Journal*, 110 (1954), 120–4, and in his *Castles, Conquest and Charters: Collected Papers* (Woodbridge, 1989), 209–13

———, "Royal castle-building in England, 1154–1216," *EHR*, 70 (1955), 353–98, and in his *Castles, Conquest and Charters: Collected Papers* (Woodbridge, 1989), 19–64

———, "'The treasury' of the Later Twelfth Century," in *Studies Presented to Sir Hilary Jenkinson*, ed. J. Conway Davies (London, 1957), 35–49, and in his *Castles, Conquest and Charters: Collected Papers* (Woodbridge, 1989), 324–38

———, "A list of castles, 1154–1216" *EHR*, 74 (1959), 249–80, and in his *Castles, Conquest and Charters: Collected Papers* (Woodbridge, 1989), 90–121

———, *Rochester Castle, Kent* (London, 1969)

———, "The status of the Norman knight" in *War and Government in the Middle Ages: Essays in Honour of J. O. Prestwich*, ed. John Gillingham and J. C. Holt (Woodbridge, 1984), 18–32, and in his *Castles, Conquest and Charters: Collected Papers* (Woodbridge, 1989), 290–304

———, *Castles, Conquest, and Charters: Collected Papers* (Woodbridge, 1989)

Brown, R. Allen, H. M. Colvin, and A. J. Taylor, *The History of the King's Works: The Middle Ages*, 2 vols, general editor H. M. Colvin (London, 1963)

Brundage, J., *Law, Sex, and Christian Society in Medieval Europe* (Chicago, 1987)

Byrne, F. J., "The trembling sod," in *A New History of Ireland*, Vol 2: *Medieval Ireland 1169–1534*, ed. A. Cosgrave (Oxford, 1987)

The Cambridge History of the Book in Britain, Vol. 2, *1100–1400*, ed. Nigel J. Morgan and Rodney M. Thomson (Cambridge, 2008)

Carpenter, D. A., *The Minority of Henry III* (London, 1990)

———, *The Reign of Henry III* (London, 1996)

———, "Abbot Ralph of Coggeshall's account of the last years of King Richard and the first years of King John," *EHR*, 113 (1998), 1210–30

———, "'In testimonium factorum brevium': the beginnings of the English Chancery roll," in *Records, Administration and Aristocratic Society in the Anglo-Norman Realm*, ed. N. Vincent (Woodbridge, 2009), 1–28

————, *Magna Carta* (forthcoming)

Cawley, C., *Medieval Lands: A Prosopography of Medieval European Noble and Royal Families* at http://fmg.ac/Projects/MedLands/index.htm

Chaplais, P., *English Diplomatic Practice in the Middle Ages* (London, 2003)

Chaytor, H. J., *Savaric de Mauléon, Baron and Troubadour* (Cambridge, 1939)

Cheney, C. R., "King John's reaction to the Interdict in England,' *TRHS*, 4th series, 31 (1948), 129–50

————, "King John and the papal interdict,' *Bulletin of the John Rylands Library*, 31 (1948), 295–317

————, "The eve of Magna Carta,' *Bulletin of the John Rylands Library*, 38 (1955–6), 311–41

————, "The twenty-five barons of Magna Carta,' *Bulletin of the John Rylands Library*, 50 (1968), 280–307

————, *Pope Innocent III and England* (Stuttgart, 1978)

Church, S. D., "The knights of the household of King John: a question of numbers,' in *Thirteenth-Century England IV: Proceedings of the Newcastle upon Tyne Conference, 1991*, ed. P. R. Coss and S. D. Lloyd (Woodbridge, 1992), 151–65

————, "The earliest English muster roll, 18/19 December 1215," *Historical Research*, 67 (1994), 1–17

————, "The rewards of royal service in the household of King John: a dissenting opinion," *EHR*, 110 (1995), 277–302

————, "The 1210 campaign in Ireland: evidence for a military revolution?" *Anglo-Norman Studies*, 20 (1998), 45–57

————, *The Household Knights of King John* (Cambridge, 1999)

————, ed., *King John: New Interpretations* (Woodbridge, 1999)

————, "The care of the royal tombs in English cathedrals in the nineteenth and twentieth centuries: the case of the effigy of King John at Worcester," *Antiquaries Journal*, 89 (2009), 365–87

————, "King John's testament and the last days of his reign," *EHR*, 125 (2010), 505–28

Clanchy, M. T., *From Memory to Written Record*, 2nd edn (Oxford, 1993)

Constable, G., "Medieval letters and the letter collection of Peter the Venerable," in his *The Letters of Peter the Venerable* (Cambridge, MA, 1967)

Contamine, P., *War in the Middle Ages*, trans. Michael Jones (Oxford, 1984)

Coss, P. R., "Knighthood and the early thirteenth-century county court," in *Thirteenth Century England II: Proceedings of the Newcastle-upon-Tyne Conference, 1987*, ed. P. R. Coss and S. D. Lloyd (Woodbridge, 1988), 45–57

Cowdrey, H. E. J., "The Anglo-Norman *Laudes Regiae*," *Viator*, 12 (1968), 39–78

Crook, D., "The Forest eyre in the reign of King John," in *Magna Carta and the England of King John*, ed. J. S. Loengard (Woodbridge, 2010), 63–82

Crouch, D., *William Marshal: Court, Career and Chivalry in the Angevin Empire, 1147–1219* (London, 1990)

————, "The complaint of King John against William de Briouze (c. September 1210)," in *Magna Carta and the England of King John*, ed. J. S. Loengard (Woodbridge, 2010), 168–79

Dept, G., *Les Influences Anglais et Francais dans le comté de Flandre au début du xiiime siècle* (Paris, 1928)

De Sturler, J., *Les relations politiques et les eschanges commerciaux entre le duché de Brabant et l'Angleterre au moyen âge* (Paris, 1936)

Diggelmann, L., "Marriage as tactical response: Henry II and the royal wedding of 1160," *EHR*, 109 (2004), 954–64

Downham, C., "Living on the edge: Scandinavian Dublin in the twelfth century," *West over the Sea*, ed. B. B. Smith, S. Taylor and G. Williams (Leiden, 2007), 33–52

Duby, G., *William Marshal: The Flower of Chivalry*, trans. R. Howard (London, 1986)

———, *The Legend of Bouvines: War, Religion, and Culture in the Middle Ages*, trans. C. Tihanyi (Cambridge, 1990)

Du Chesne, André, *Histoire généalogique de la maison de Béthune* (Paris, 1639)

Duffy, S., "King John's expedition to Ireland, 1210: the evidence reconsidered," *Irish Historical Studies*, 30 (1996), 1–24

———, "Henry II and England's insular neighbours," in *Henry II: New Interpretations*, ed. C. Harper-Bill and N. Vincent (Woodbridge, 2004), 129–53

Dugdale, W., *The Baronage of England*, 2 vols (London, 1675–6)

Duggan, A., "The making of a myth: Giraldus Cambrensis, Laudabiliter, and Henry II's lordship of Ireland," *Studies in Medieval and Renaissance History*, 3rd series, 4 (2007), 107–70

———, "The power of documents: the curious case of *Laudabiliter*," in *Aspects of Power and Authority in the Middle Ages*, ed. B. Bolton and C. Meek (Turnhout, 2007), 251–75

Dunbabin, J., *France in the Making*, 2nd edn (Oxford, 2000)

Duncan, A. A. M., "John king of England and the kings of Scots," in *King John: New Interpretations*, ed. S. D. Church (Woodbridge, 1999), 247–71

Eales, R., "The game of chess: an aspect of knightly culture," in *The Ideals and Practice of Medieval Knighthood*, ed. C. Harper-Bill and R. Harvey (Woodbridge, 1986), 12–34

Engel, U., *Worcester Cathedral: An Architectural History* (London, 2007)

English, B., *The Lords of Holderness, 1086–1260: A Study in Feudal Society* (Oxford, 1979)

Evans, C., "Margaret of Scotland, Duchess of Brittany," in *Mélanges offerts à Szabolcs de Vajay . . . à l'occasion de son cinquantième anniversaire*, ed. Le comte d'Adhémar de Panat, X. de Ghellinck Vaernewyck and P. Brière (Braga, 1971), 187–191

Everard, J. A., *Brittany and the Angevins: Province and Empire, 1158–1203* (Cambridge, 2000)

Eyton, R. W., *Court, Household and Itinerary of King Henry II* (London, 1878)

Farrer, W., *Honors and Knights' Fees: An Attempt to Identify the Component Parts of Certain Honors and to Trace the Descent of the Tenants of the Same Who Held by Knight's Service or Sergeanty from the Eleventh to the Fourteenth Century*, 3 vols (London, 1923–5)

Flanagan, M. T., *Irish Society, Anglo-Norman Settlers, Angevin Kingship: Interactions in Ireland in the late Twelfth Century* (Oxford, 1989)

Foreville, R., "Le sacre des rois anglo-normands et angevins et le serment du sacre [XIᵉ–XIIᵉ siècles]," *Anglo-Norman Studies*, i (1978), 49–62

Frame, R., "Overlordship and Reaction c. 1200–c. 1450" in *The North Atlantic Frontier of Medieval Europe*, ed. J. Muldoon (Ashgate, 2009), 103–22

Fryde, N., "King John and the empire," in *King John: New Interpretations*, ed. S. D. Church (Woodbridge, 1999), 335–46

Fryde, N. and Reitz, D., *Bischofsmord im Mittelalter—Murder of Bishops* (Göttingen, 2003)

Galbraith, V. H., *Studies in the Public Records* (London, 1948)

————, "A draft of Magna Carta (1215)," *Proceedings of the British Academy*, 53 (1967), 345–60

Ganshof, F. L., "Note sur le premier traité Anglo-Flamand de Douvres," *Revue du Nord*, 40, no. 158, numéro spécial dédié à la mémoire de Raymond Monur (Lille, 1958), 245–57

Gillingham, J. B., *Richard the Lionheart* (London, 1978)

————, *Richard I* (New Haven, CT, 1999)

————, *The Angevin Empire*, 2nd edn (London, 2000)

————, *The English in the Twelfth Century* (Woodbridge, 2000)

————, "Doing homage to the king of France," in *Henry II: New Interpretations*, ed. N. Vincent and C. Harper-Bill (Woodbridge, 2007), 63–84

————, "Coeur de Lion in captivity," *Quaestiones Medii Aevi Novae* (2013), 59–85

Given-Wilson, C. and A. Curteis, *The Royal Bastards of Medieval England* (London, 1984)

Gold, P. S., *The Lady and the Virgin: Image, Attitude and Experience in Twelfth-Century France* (Chicago, IL, 1985)

Gransden, A., *Historical Writing in England c.550 to c.1307* (London, 1974)

Green, J., "The last century of Danegeld," *EHR*, 96 (1981), 241–58

Green, V., *An Account of the Discovery of the Body of King John in the Cathedral Church of Worcester, July 17, 1797* (London, 1797)

Handbook of British Chronology, ed. E. B. Fryde, D. E. Greenway, S. Porter and I. Roy (London, 3rd edn, 1986)

Handbook of Medieval Exchange, ed. P. Spufford, Royal Historical Society Guides and Handbooks 13 (London, 1986)

Hajdu, R., "Castles, castellans and the structure of politics in Poitou, 1152–1271," *Journal of Medieval History*, 4 (1978), 25–54

Harper, J., *The Forms and Orders of Western Liturgy from the Tenth to the Eighteenth Century* (Oxford, 1991)

Hatcher, J., "English serfdom and villeinage: towards a reassessment," *Past and Present*, 110 (1981), 3–39

The Heads of Religious Houses England and Wales, 940–1216, ed. D. Knowles, C. N. L. Brooke and V. London (Cambridge, 1972)

Heslin, A. J., "The coronation of the Young King in 1170," in *Studies in Church History*, ii, ed. G. J. Cuming (London, 1965), 165–85

Hill, M. C., *The King's Messengers, 1199–1377* (London, 1961)

Holden, B., *Lords of the Central Marches: English Aristocracy and Frontier Society, 1087–1265* (Oxford, 2008)

Holt, J. C., *The Northerners: A Study in the Reign of King John* (Oxford, 1961)

————, *Magna Carta*, 1st edn (Cambridge, 1965)

————, "The pre history of Parliament," in *The English Parliament in the Middle Ages*, ed. R. G. Davies and J. H. Denton (Manchester, 1981)

————, "The loss of Normandy and royal finance," in *War and Government in the Middle Ages: Essays in Honour of J. O. Prestwich*, ed. John Gillingham and J. C. Holt (Woodbridge, 1984), 92–105

————, *Robin Hood* (London, 1989)

————, *Magna Carta*, 2nd edn (Cambridge, 1992)

————, "King John and Arthur of Brittany," *Nottingham Medieval Studies*, 44 (2000), 82–103

Hoyt, R. S., *The Royal Demesne in English Constitutional History: 1066–1272* (Ithaca, NY, 1950)

Hyams, P., *Rancor and Reconciliation in Medieval England* (Ithaca, NY, 2003)

Jenkinson, H., "Financial records of the reign of King John," in *Magna Carta Commemoration Essays*, ed. H. E. Malden (London, 1917), 244–300

Johnson, P. D., *Equal in Monastic Professions: Religious Women in Medieval France* (Chicago, IL, 1991)

Jolliffe, J. E. A., "The Chamber and the castle treasuries under King John," in *Studies in Medieval History Presented to F. M. Powicke*, ed. R. W. Hunt, W. A. Pantin and R. W. Southern (Oxford, 1948), 117–42

———, *Angevin Kingship*, 2nd edn (London, 1963)

Jones, C. A., "The Chrism Mass in later Anglo-Saxon England," in *The Liturgy in the Late Anglo-Saxon Church*, ed. H. Gittos and M. Bradford Bedingfield (London, HBS Subsidia 5, 2005), 105–42

Kantorowicz, E., *Laudes Regiae: A Study in Liturgical Acclamations in Medieval Ruler Worship* (Oakland, CA, 1958)

Keen, M., *The Outlaws of Medieval Legend* (London, 1961)

Keene, D., "Roots and branches of power, 1000–1300," *The London Journal*, 26 (2001), 1–8

Kerr, B. M., *Religious Life for Women, c.1100–c.1350: Fontevraud in England* (Oxford, 1999)

King, E., *King Stephen* (New Haven, CT, 2010)

Lally, J. E., "Secular patronage at the court of King Henry II," *BIHR*, 49 (1976), 159–84

Latimer, P., "Early thirteenth-century prices," in *King John: New Interpretations*, ed. S. D. Church (Woodbridge, 1999), 41–73

Le Patourel, J. H., *The Medieval Administration of the Channel Islands, 1199–1399* (Oxford, 1937)

———, "The Plantagenet dominions," *History*, 50 (1965), 259–308

Lewis, A. W., "The birth and childhood of King John: some revisions," in *Eleanor of Aquitaine: Lord and Lady*, ed. B. Wheeler and J. C. Parsons (London, 2002), 159–75

Lindemann, R. H. F., "The English *esnecca* in northern Europe," *Mariner's Mirror*, 74 (1988), 75–82

Lyon, B., "The money fief under the English kings, 1066–1485," *EHR*, 66 (1951), 161–93

———, "The feudal antecedent of the indenture system," *Speculum*, 29 (1954), 503–11

———, *From Fief to Indenture* (Cambridge, MA, 1957)

Maddicott, J. R., *The Origins of Parliament, 924–1327* (Oxford, 2010)

———, "The Oath of Marlborough, 1209: fear, government and popular allegiance in the reign of King John," *EHR*, 126 (2011), 281–318

Martin, F. X., "John, lord of Ireland, 1185–1216," in *A New History of Ireland*, ii, *Medieval Ireland, 1169–1534*, ed. A. Cosgrove (Oxford, 1987), 127–55

———, "The sword on the stone: some resonances of a medieval symbol of power (the tomb of King John in Worcester cathedral)," *Anglo-Norman Studies*, 15 (1992), 199–241

———, "Diarmait Mac Murchada and the coming of the Normans," *A New History of Ireland*, ii, *Medieval Ireland, 1169–1534*, ed. A. Cosgrove (Oxford, 1987), 43–66

Martindale, J., *Status, Authority, and Regional Power* (Aldershot, 1997)

————, "Eleanor of Aquitaine: the last years," in *King John: New Interpretations*, ed. S. D. Church (Woodbridge, 1999), 137–64

Mason, E., "Maritagium and the changing law," *BIHR*, 49 (1976), 286–9

Milsom, S. F. C., "Inheritance by women in the twelfth and early thirteenth centuries," in *On the laws and customs of England: essays in honor of Samuel E. Thorne*, ed. M. S. Arnold et al. (Chapel Hill, NC, 1981), 61–89 and in his *Studies in The History of Common Law* (London, 1985), 231–60

Mitchell, S. K., *Studies in Taxation under John and Henry III* (New Haven, CT, 1914)

Morgan, N. J. and Thomson, R. M., ed, *The Cambridge History of the Book in Britain*, Vol. 2, *1100–1400* (Cambridge, 2008)

Morris, W. A., *The Medieval English Sheriff to 1300* (Manchester, 1927)

Mortimer, R., "The family of Rannulf de Glanville," *BIHR*, 54 (1984), 1–16

Nash, T. R., *Collections for the History of Worcestershire*, 2 vols (Worcester, 1781–99)

Nederman, C. J., "The liberty of the Church and the road to Runnymede: John of Salisbury and the intellectual foundations of Magna Carta," *Canadian Journal of Political Science*, 43 (2010), 457–61

Nederman, C. J. and Campbell, C., "Priests, kings, and tyrants: spiritual and temporal power in John of Salisbury's *Policraticus*," *Speculum*, 66 (1991), 572–90

Nelson, J., "Inauguration rituals," in her *Politics and Ritual in Early Medieval Europe* (London, 1986), 283–307

Norgate, K., *John Lackland* (London, 1902)

————, *The Minority of Henry the Third* (London, 1912)

O'Grady, S., "The last kings of Ireland," *EHR*, 4 (1899), 286–303

Orme, N., *From Childhood to Chivalry: The Education of the English Kings and Aristocracy, 1066–1530* (London, 1984)

Orpen, G. H., *Ireland under the Normans, 1169–1216* (Oxford, 1911)

Otway-Ruthven, A. J., *A History of Medieval Ireland*, 2nd edn (London, 1980)

Pafford, J. H. P., "King John's Tomb in Worcester Cathedral,' *Trans. Worcestershire Archaeological Society*, new series, 35 (1958), 58–60

Painter, S., *William Marshal: Knight Errant, Baron, and Regent of England* (Baltimore, MD, 1933)

————, *The Reign of King John* (Baltimore, MD, 1949)

————, "Castellans of the plain of Poitou in the eleventh and twelfth centuries," *Speculum*, 31 (1956), 243–57

————, "The lords of Lusignan in the eleventh and twelfth centuries," *Speculum*, 32 (1957), 27–47

Palmer, R. C., *The County Courts of Medieval England, 1150–1350* (Princeton, NJ, 1982)

Petit-Dutaillis, C., "Le déshéritement de Jean sans Terre et le meurtre d'Arthur de Bretagne," *Revue Historique*, 147 (1924), 161–203, *Revue Historique*, 148 (1925), 1–62, and reprinted as *Le déshéritement de Jean sans Terre et le meurtre d'Arthur de Bretagne* (Paris, 1925)

Poole, A. L., *From Domesday Book to Magna Carta*, 2nd edn (Oxford, 1955)

Powell, W. R., "The administration of the navy and the stannaries, 1189–1216," *EHR*, lxxi (1956), 177–88

Power, D., "French and Norman frontiers in the Middle Ages," in *Frontiers in Question*, ed. D. Power and N. Standen (London, 1999), 105–27

———, "The revolt at Alençon, 1203," *Historical Research*, 74 (2001), 444–64

———, *The Norman Frontier in the Twelfth and Early Thirteenth Centuries* (Cambridge, 2004)

Powicke, F. M., "The Angevin administration of Normandy," *EHR*, 22 (1907), 15–42

———, *King Henry III and the Lord Edward: The Community of the Realm in the Thirteenth Century*, 2 vols (Oxford, 1947)

———, *The Loss of Normandy, 1189–1204*, 2nd edn (Manchester, 1961)

———, "Richard I and John," *Cambridge Medieval History*, 6 (1968), 205–51

Reynolds, S. *Kingdoms and Communities in Western Europe, 900–1300* (Oxford, 1984)

———, "Magna Carta 1297 and the legal use of literacy," *Bulletin of the Institute of Historical Research*, 62 (1989), 233–44

———, *Fiefs and Vassals: the Medieval Evidence Reinterpreted* (Oxford, 1994)

Richard, A., *Histoire des comtes de Poitou* (Paris, 1903)

Richardson, H., "The morrow of the Great Charter," *Bulletin of the John Rylands Library*, 28 (1944), 422–43

———, "The marriage and coronation of Isabelle of Angoulême," *EHR*, 61 (1949), 289–314

Round, J. H., "An unknown charter of liberties," *EHR*, 8 (1893), 288–94

Rowlands, I. W., "King John, Stephen Langton, and Rochester Castle," in *Studies in Medieval History presented to R. Allen Brown*, ed. C. Harper-Bill, C. J. Holdsworth and J. L. Nelson (Woodbridge, 1989), 267–80

———, "King John and Wales," in *King John: New Interpretations*, ed. S. D. Church (Woodbridge, 1999), 273–87

Sayers, J., *Innocent III: Leader of Europe* (London, 1994)

Smith, J. B., "Magna Carta and the charters of the Welsh Princes," *EHR* 99 (1984), 344–62

Smith, R. J., "Henry II's heir: the charters and seal of Henry the young king, 1170–83," *EHR*, 106 (2001), 297–326

Stenton, D. M., "King John and courts of justice," *Proceedings of the British Academy*, 44 (1958), 103–28

———, *English Justice between the Norman Conquest and the Great Charter, 1066–1215* (Philadelphia, PA, 1964)

Strickland, M., "On the instruction of a prince: the upbringing of Henry, the young king," in *Henry II: New Interpretations*, ed. C. Harper-Bill and N. Vincent (Woodbridge, 2007), 184–214

Stringer, K. J., *Earl David of Huntingdon, 1152–1219: A Study in Anglo-Scottish History* (Edinburgh, 1985)

Stubbs, W., *Seventeen Lectures on Medieval and Modern History* (Oxford, 1887)

Swallow, R., "Gateways to Power: The castles of Ranulf III of Chester and Llywelyn the Great of Gwynedd," *Archaeological Journal*, 171 (2014), 289–311

Thompson, K., "The affairs of state: the illegitimate children of Henry I," *JMH*, 29 (2003), 289–98

Thompson, S., *Women Religious: The Founding of Nunneries after the Norman Conquest* (Oxford, 1991)

Tout, T. F., *Chapters in the Administrative History of Medieval England: The Wardrobe, the Chamber and the Small Seals*, 6 vols (Manchester, 1920–33)

———, *The Place of The Reign of Edward II in English History*, revised by H. Johnstone, 2nd edn (Manchester, 1936)

Treharne, R. F., "The Franco-Welsh treaty of alliance in 1212," *Bulletin of the Board of Celtic Studies*, 18 (1958), 74–5

Turner, G. J., "The justices of the forest south of the Trent," *EHR*, 18 (1903), 112–16

———, "The Minority of Henry III, part 1," *TRHS*, new series, 28 (1904), 245–95

———, "The Minority of Henry III, part 2," *TRHS*, 3rd series, 1 (1907), 205–62

Turner, R. V., *The English Judiciary in the Age of Glanville and Bracton, c.1176–1239* (Cambridge, 1985)

———, *Men Raised from the Dust: Administrative Service and Upward Mobility in Angevin England* (Philadelphia, PA, 1988)

———, *King John* (London, 1994)

———, "King John's concept of royal authority," *History of Political Thought*, 17 (1996), 157–78

van Cleve, T. C., *The Emperor Frederick II of Hohenstaufen: Stupor Mundi* (Oxford, 1972)

Veach, C., "A question of timing: Walter de Lacy's seisin of Meath, 1189–94," *Proceedings of the Royal Irish Academy*, 109 (2009), 165–94

———, "King and magnate in medieval Ireland: Walter de Lacy, King Richard and King John," *Irish Historical Studies*, 37 (2010), 179–202

———, "King John and the anglicisation of colonial Ireland: why William de Briouze had to be destroyed," *EHR* 129 (2014), 1051–1078

Vincent, N. C., *Peter des Roches, Bishop of Winchester 1205–38: An Alien in English Politics* (Cambridge, 1996)

———, ed., *The Letters and Charters of Cardinal Guala Bicchieri Papal Legate in England, 1216–1218*, Canterbury and York Society, 83 (1996)

———, "Isabella of Angoulême: John's Jezebel," in *King John: New Interpretations*, ed. S. D. Church (Woodbridge, 1999), 165–219

———, "Henry II and the Poitevins," in *La Cour Plantagenêt*, ed. M. Aurell (Poitiers, 2000), 103–36

———, *The Magna Carta*, Sotheby's Sale Catalogue (December 18, 2007)

———, "Stephen Langton, archbishop of Canterbury," in *Étienne Langton: prédicateur, bibliste, théologien*, ed. L.-J. Bataillon, N. Bériou, G. Dahan and R. Quinto (Turnhout, 2010), 51–123

Warren, W. L., *King John* (London, 1961)

———, *Henry II* (London, 1973)

———, "King John and Ireland," in *England and Ireland in the Later Middle Ages: Essays in Honour of Jocelyn Otway-Ruthven*, ed. J. Lydon (Dublin, 1987), 26–42

Waugh, S. L., *The Lordship of England: Royal Wardship and Marriages in English Society and Politics, 1217–1327* (Princeton, NJ, 1988)

Weiss, M., "The castellan: the early career of Hubert de Burgh," *Viator*, 5 (1974), 235–52

West, F. J., *The Justiciarship in England, 1066–1232* (Cambridge, 1966)

Wilkinson, B., "The government of England during the absence of Richard I on crusade," *Bulletin of the John Rylands Library*, 28 (1944), 485–509

Wilkinson, L. J., *Women in Thirteenth-Century Lincolnshire* (Woodbridge, 2007)

Wright, E. C., "Common law in thirteenth-century English forests," *Speculum*, 3 (1928), 168–91

Young, C. R. *The Royal Forests of Medieval England* (Leicester, 1979)

DISSERTATIONS AND THESES

Brand, J., "The Exchequer in the twelfth century," unpublished Polytechnic of North London PhD thesis (1989)

Hajdu, R., "A history of the nobility of Poitou, 1150–1270," unpublished Princeton University PhD thesis (1972)

Jones, M., "The *acta* of John, lord of Ireland and count of Mortain, with a study of his household," unpublished MA thesis, University of Manchester (1949)

Kanter, J. E., "Peripatetic and sedentary kingship: the itineraries of the thirteenth-century kings," unpublished University of London PhD thesis (2011)

Kaye, H., "The household of King John," unpublished University of East Anglia PhD thesis (2014)

Watson, R. C., "The counts of Angoulême from the ninth to the mid-thirteenth century," unpublished University of East Anglia PhD thesis (1979)

WEB PAGES

http://www.walesdirectory.co.uk/tourist-attractions/Gravestones_Memorials_Monuments_Effigies/Wales11356.htm

http://www.hrionline.ac.uk/normans/about.shtml

http://fmg.ac/Projects/MedLands/CONTENTS.htm

NOTES

Preface

1. *Walter of Coventry*, ii, 232.
2. *The Parallel Lives by Plutarch*, ix, trans. B. Perrin (Loeb Classical Library, 1920).
3. *Magna Vita Sanciti Hugonis*, ii, ed. D. L. Douie and D. H. Farmer (Oxford, 1985), 140–1.

Introduction

1. V. Green, *An Account of the Discovery of the Body of King John in the Cathedral Church of Worcester, July 17, 1797* (London, 1797).
2. Matthew Paris, *Chronica Majora*, ii, 559–64.
3. W. L. Warren, *King John* (London, 1961) is the best attempt in this regard. R. V. Turner, *King John* (London, 1994) claims only to "build upon the works of" Warren, S. Painter, *The Reign of King John* (Baltimore, MD, 1949), and K. Norgate, *John Lackland* (London, 1902). The best treatment of the reign is still to be found in J. C. Holt, *The Northerners: A Study in the Reign of King John* (Oxford, 1961), combined with his *Magna Carta*, 2nd edn (Cambridge, 1992), which will be superseded by D. A. Carpenter, *Magna Carta* (forthcoming).
4. R. Frame, "Overlordship and Reaction *c.* 1200–*c.* 1450" in *The North Atlantic Frontier of Medieval Europe*, ed. J. Muldoon (Ashgate, 2009), 103–22; R. Swallow, "Gateways to Power: The castles of Ranulf III of Chester and Llywelyn the Great of Gwynedd" *Archaeological Journal*, 171 (2014), 289–311.
5. John is given the appellation "*sine terra*" in a charter of Peter, count of Lara by which he granted land to his wife, Margaret de Bohun (PRO C115/K2/6683 (Llanthony cartulary) fo.25r, s.xiv ex. See also C. Evans, "Margaret of Scotland, Duchess of Brittany," in *Mélanges offerts à Szabolcs de Vajay . . . à l'occasion de son cinquantième anniversaire*, ed. Le comte d'Adhémar de Panat, X. de Ghellinck Vaernewyck and P. Brière (Braga, 1971), 187–191 at 188. Dated January 23, it must have been granted either in 1184, 1185 or 1186. This is the earliest reference to John's sobriquet.
6. J. C. Holt, *Robin Hood* (London, 1989), 29–40, 158–9.
7. R. Sharpe, "Charter of Liberties and Royal Proclamations," at http://actswilliam2henry1 .files.wordpress.com/2013/10/h1-a-liberties-2013-1.pdf.

8. E. King, *King Stephen* (New Haven, CT, 2010), chapter 9.

9. D. A. Carpenter, "'In testimonium factorum brevium': the beginnings of the English Chancery roll," in *Records, Administration and Aristocratic Society in the Anglo-Norman Realm*, ed. N. Vincent (Woodbridge, 2009), 1–28.

10. *Richard fitz Nigel Dialogus de Scaccario and the Constitutio Domus Regis*, ed. E. Amt and S. D. Church (Oxford, 2007).

11. H. Kaye, "The household of King John," unpublished University of East Anglia PhD thesis (2014).

12. *Rot. Litt. Claus.*, i, 89.

13. J. R. Maddicott, *The Origins of Parliament, 924–1327* (Oxford, 2010).

14. *John of Salisbury's Entheticus Maior and Minor*, ed. J. van Laarhoven, 3 vols (Leiden, 1987), 188, 190, 192.

15. C. J. Nederman and C. Campbell, "Priests, kings, and tyrants: spiritual and temporal power in John of Salisbury's *Policraticus*," *Speculum*, 66 (1991), 572–90.

16. On the king's will, J. E. A. Jolliffe, *Angevin Kingship*, 2nd edn (London, 1963) is still a profoundly important work. And see C. J. Nederman, "The liberty of the Church and the road to Runnymede: John of Salisbury and the intellectual foundations of Magna Carta," *Canadian Journal of Political Science*, 43 (2010), 457–61.

CHAPTER 1: LACKLAND

1. J. B. Gillingham, "Doing homage to the king of France," in *Henry II: New Interpretations*, ed. N. Vincent and C. Harper-Bill (Woodbridge, 2007), 63–84.

2. W. L. Warren, *Henry II* (London 1973), 108–10.

3. *Walter Map, De Nugis Curialium*, ed. M. R. James, revised by C. N. L. Brooke and R. A. B. Mynors (Oxford, 1983).

4. For John's supposed oblation at Fontevraud, see A. Richard, *Histoire des comtes de Poitou*, ii (Paris, 1903), 375, citing the Fontevraud epitaphs copied into Bibliothèque nationale de France, Latin 5480, part 1, 5. The epitaphs begin with that of Robert d'Arbrissel and are then followed by Fulk, count of Anjou and king of Jerusalem, kings Henry II, Richard, John, Henry III, Edward I, followed by Richard, earl of Cornwall, and Raymond, count of Toulouse. *La Vie du bienheureux Robert d'Arbrissel, patriarche des Solitaires de France, et institution de l'ordre de Fontevraud*, ed. Balthazar Pavillon (Paris-Saumur, 1666), 585, no. 90. John's sister, Joanna, was educated with him "for a short time" (588, no. 96). The abbey, by the time the necrology was written, boasted the fact that it watched over the remains of Henry II, Richard I, Eleanor of Aquitaine and John's widow, Isabella of Angoulême, and it may well have been that the monks wished to make their claim over John's remains (lying at Worcester and at Croxton Abbey). But that John was educated at Fontevraud ("*a nobis per 5 annorum spatium nutritus*") we need not doubt.

5. W. L. Warren took the view that John's Fontevraud years occurred from the ages of one to six "perhaps in the vain hope that he would become a novice" (W. L. Warren, *King John* (London, 1961), 26). The bad blood, so evident in Warren's biography of John, is here at the start of Warren's life of John. Ralph V. Turner thought that John had been deposited at Fontevraud shortly after his birth with his sister Joanna, "perhaps to prepare him for an ecclesiastical career, often the fate of younger sons in great families" (R. V. Turner, *King John* (London,

1994), 23). Here Turner is getting into his psychoanalytic stride as he searches for the origins of John's unpleasant character. For him, these are to be found in John's issues of abandonment.

6. *La Vie du bienheureux Robert d'Arbrissel* (Paris-Saumur, 1666), 582–3. See also J. Martindale, "Eleanor of Aquitaine," in her *Status, Authority, and Regional Power* (Aldershot, 1997), XI, 17–50.

7. P. S. Gold, *The Lady and the Virgin: Image, Attitude and Experience in Twelfth-Century France* (Chicago, IL, 1985), 93–115.

8. B. M. Kerr, *Religious Life for Women, c.1100–c.1350: Fontevraud in England* (Oxford, 1999).

9. It is striking that uniquely in twelfth-century western Christendom, the Angevins came to rest amongst women rather than men. Rulers generally did not choose to lie in eternity looked over by nuns; the Angevins did. (T. S. R. Boase, "Fontevrault and the Plantagenets," *Journal of the British Archaeological Association*, 3rd series, 34 (1971), 1–10).

10. At least one man remembered that he had been nurtured by the nuns of Notre-Dame de Saintes (P. D. Johnson, *Equal in Monastic Professions: Religious Women in Medieval France* (Chicago, 1991), 55).

11. S. Bardsley, *Women's Roles in the Middle Ages* (Westport, CT, 2007), 115.

12. *Gesta Regis Henrici Secundi*, i, 7.

13. N. Orme, *From Childhood to Chivalry: The Education of the English Kings and Aristocracy, 1066–1530* (London, 1984), 62–5.

14. M. Strickland, "On the instruction of a prince: the upbringing of Henry, the young king," in *Henry II: New Interpretations*, ed. C. Harper-Bill and N. Vincent (Woodbridge, 2007), 184–214.

15. C. Bowie, *The Daughters of Henry II and Eleanor of Aquitaine: A Comparative Study of Twelfth-Century Royal Women* (forthcoming).

16. For the family of Humbert see C. Cawley, *Medieval Lands: A Prosopography of Medieval European Noble and Royal Families* at http://fmg.ac/Projects/MedLands/SAVOY.htm #_Toc223264723.

17. The text of the agreement is transcribed into *Chronica Magistri Rogeri de Houedene*, ii, 41–5.

18. "La crut guerre senz amur" ("therein grew war without love"): *Jordan 'Fantosme's Chronicle*, ed. R. C. Johnston (Oxford, 1981), line 20.

19. K. Thompson, "The affairs of state: the illegitimate children of Henry I," *JMH*, 29 (2003), 289–98, at 143–6.

20. S. L. Waugh, *The Lordship of England: Royal Wardship and Marriages in English Society and Politics, 1217–1327* (Princeton, NJ, 1988), 146.

21. J. C. Holt, *Magna Carta*, 2nd edn (Cambridge, 1992), 448–53.

22. "The Chronicle of Robert of Torigny," *Chronicles of the Reigns of Stephen, Henry II, and Richard I*, 4 vols, ed. R. Howlett, Rolls Series (London 1884–89), iv, 268 ("*totam terram, quam habebat tam in Anglia quam in Normannia et in Walis, retinuit rex in manu sua, ad opus Johannis filii sui junioris, excepta parva portione, quam dedit filiabus ipsius comitis*").

23. S. F. C. Milsom, "Inheritance by women in the twelfth and early thirteenth centuries," in his *Studies in The History of Common Law* (London, 1985), 231–60. In 1186, for example,

Richard fitz Roger fined in £15 3s to recover his land having had it confiscated after making his daughter his heir "without the king's license" (*Pipe Roll 32 Henry II*, 143).

24. *Gesta Regis Henrici Secundi*, i, 124–5.

25. *Chronica Magistri Rogeri de Houedene*, ii, 133–5; S. Duffy, "Henry II and England's insular neighbours," in *Henry II: New Interpretations*, ed. C. Harper-Bill and N. Vincent (Woodbridge, 2004), 129–53, at 148.

26. "The Chronicle of Robert of Torigny," *Chronicles of the Reigns of Stephen, Henry II, and Richard I*, 4 vols, ed. R. Howlett, Rolls Series (London 1884–89), iv, p. 186; cf. M. T. Flanagan, *Irish Society, Anglo-Norman Settlers, Angevin Kingship: Interactions in Ireland in the late Twelfth Century* (Oxford 1989), 305–7.

27. A. J. Duggan, "The making of a myth: Giraldus Cambrensis, Laudabiliter, and Henry II's lordship of Ireland," *Studies in Medieval and Renaissance History*, 3rd series, 4 (2007), 107–70 is the fundamental work on the text of the bull that, as it stands, is an outrageous forgery. Duggan argues that the original bull did not give Henry lordship of Ireland but in fact advised him to seek the counsel of the Irish before acting precipitately (see also Duggan's "The power of documents: the curious case of *Laudabiliter*," in *Aspects of Power and Authority in the Middle Ages*, ed. B. Bolton and C. Meek (Turnhout, 2007), 251–75).

28. *Pontificia Hibernica: Medieval Papal Chancery Documents concerning Ireland, 640–1261*, 2 vols, ed. M. Sheehy (Dublin, 1962–5), i, nos 5–7, 19–23, and see *Irish Historical Documents, 1170–1922*, ed. E. Curtis and R. B. McDowell (Dublin, 1943), no. 3 for English translations.

29. *Chronica Magistri Rogeri de Houedene*, ii, 100 (placed in 1176 by Howden, but mistakenly).

30. *Gesta Regis Henrici Secundi*, i, 161–5.

31. *Gesta Regis Henrici Secundi*, i, 131.

32. *Pipe Roll 23 Henry II*, 105.

33. *Gesta Regis Henrici Secundi*, i, 221.

34. *Pipe Roll 25 Henry II*, 101. 14s 10d was also expended on a cart cover and a saddle set for John (*Pipe Roll 25 Henry II*, 125). At fourteen, John already had around him the nucleus of a personal household containing at least two chamberlains (Reginald and Alard fitz William), two washerwomen (Millicent and Isabelle) and three knights, and possibly also William Franceis. *Angevin Acta Project: Count John*, nos 162; 465; 520; 525; 529; 567; 583; 609; 611; 881; 2116; 2119; 2123; 2124; 3239.

35. He was being associated with the justiciar by Michaelmas 1180, covering the financial year September 29, 1179, to September 28, 1180 (*Pipe Roll 26 Henry II*, 9); under Northamptonshire, Alard fitz William was given 20 marks for the maintenance of John. The Higham Ferrers estate, at that time escheated to the crown and being farmed by the sheriff, Thomas fitz Bernard, gave 20 marks to Alard fitz William for the maintenance of John. The entry before this one is for Ralph fitz Stephen, also for 20 marks, authorized by Ranulf de Glanville's writ (*Pipe Roll 26 Henry II*, 82); *Pipe Roll 27 Henry II*, 15, 132; *Gesta Regis Henrici Secundi*, i, 304–5.

36. *Richard fitz Nigel Dialogus de Scaccario and the Constitutio Domus Regis*, ed. E. Amt and S. D. Church (Oxford, 2007), 22–3; F. J. West, *The Justiciarship in England, 1066–1232* (Cambridge, 1966), 55–6.

37. Best followed in *English Lawsuits*, ii, 605–6; *Gesta Regis Henrici Secundi*, i, 314–16; *Chronica Magistri Rogeri de Houedene*, ii, 286.

38. *Leges Henrici Primi*, ed. L. J. Downer (Oxford, 1972), 28.2, 30.1.

39. *Tractatus de legibus et consuetudinibus regi Anglie qui Glanvilla vocatur*, ed. G. D. G. Hall rev. edn (Oxford, 1993).

40. *Glanvilla*, xv, xxxiii.

41. *The Ruodlieb: The First Medieval Epic of Chivalry from Eleventh-Century Germany*, trans. G. B. Ford (Leiden, 1965), 28–30.

42. R. Eales, "The game of chess: an aspect of knightly culture," in *The Ideals and Practice of Medieval Knighthood*, ed. C. Harper-Bill and R. Harvey (Woodbridge, 1986), 12–34.

43. *Giraldus Cambrensis, Opera*, viii, chapter 28, 309–11.

44. *Giraldus Cambrensis, Opera*, i, 72–3. *Giraldus Cambrensis, Opera*, viii, preface, 6–7 and chapter 9, 173–5.

45. *Giraldus Cambrensis, Opera*, viii, chapter 10, 175–7; chapter 28, 309–11.

46. *Rot. Litt. Claus.*, i, 108b.

47. *Rot. Litt. Claus.*, i, 108.

48. *The Cambridge History of the Book in Britain*, Vol. 2, *1100–1400*, ed. Nigel J. Morgan and Rodney M. Thomson (Cambridge, 2008), 163–4; W. Stubbs, *Seventeen Lectures on Medieval and Modern History* (Oxford, 1887), 132–78.

49. *Gesta Regis Henrici Secundi*, i, 291.

50. The best modern account is in Gillingham, *Richard I*, 68–71.

51. *Gesta Regis Henrici Secundi*, i, 295.

52. *Gesta Regis Henrici Secundi*, i, 304–5; *Pipe Roll 29 Henry II*, 160 shows the cost of transporting John, Ranulf and their associates by ship (£15 4s); W. L. Warren, *Henry II* (London, 1973), 596.

53. N. C. Vincent, "King Henry II and the Poitevins," in *La Cour Plantagenêt*, ed. M. Aurell (Poitiers, 2000), 103–36; on 131–2 he notes that in three of Richard's charters, dated to 1181, 1184 and 1188, the name of Philip Augustus takes precedence over that of Henry II and at least one community was commended to the protection of the French king should Richard die. See also the articles by S. Painter, "Castellans of the plain of Poitou," *Speculum*, 31 (1956), 243–57; "The lords of Lusignan in the eleventh and twelfth centuries," *Speculum*, 32 (1957), 27–47.

54. *Gesta Regis Henrici Secundi*, i, 308; *Chronica Magistri Rogeri de Houedene*, ii, 282. Gillingham, *Richard I*, 76–9; Kate Norgate, *John Lackland* (London, 1902), 9, put it succinctly: "Richard had no mind to give up substance for shadow."

55. *Gesta Regis Henrici Secundi*, i, 311.

56. *Gesta Regis Henrici Secundi*, i, 320–1.

57. Gillingham, *Richard I*, 79.

58. *Gesta Regis Henrici Secundi*, i, 333–4.

CHAPTER 2: IRELAND, 1185

1. *Expugnatio Hibernica*, 198–9.

2. F. J. Byrne, "The trembling sod," in *A New History of Ireland, Vol 2: Medieval Ireland 1169–1534*, ed. A. Cosgrave (Oxford, 1987), 5 (citing with approval the words of Standish O'Grady, "The last kings of Ireland," *EHR*, 4 (1899), 286–303).

3. "The traditional five-fifths of Ireland (Ulster, Munster, Leinster, Connacht and Meath) may have been more of a cosmological scheme than a political reality" (Byrne, "The trembling sod," *A New History of Ireland*, 13); C. Downham, "Living on the edge: Scandinavian Dublin

in the twelfth century," *West over the Sea*, ed. B. B. Smith, S. Taylor and G. Williams (Leiden, 2007), 33–52, esp. 37.

4. The standard overview of Lacy's career is G. H. Orpen, *Ireland under the Normans*, ii (Oxford, 1911), 51–70; 75–90 in "the sub-infeudation of Meath"; M. T. Flanagan, *Irish Society*, 167–304.

5. *Pipe Roll 27 Henry II*, 122.

6. *Gesta Regis Henrici Secundi*, i, 336; *Chronica Magistri Rogeri de Houedene*, i, 302.

7. *Expugnatio Hibernica*, 236–7.

8. F. X. Martin, "Diarmait Mac Murchada and the coming of the Normans," *A New History of Ireland*, ii, *Medieval Ireland, 1169–1534*, ed. A. Cosgrove (Oxford, 1987), 60–1; A. Duggan, "The power of documents: the curious case of *Laudabiliter*," in *Aspects of Power and Authority in the Middle Ages*, ed. B. Bolton and C. Meek (Turnhout, 2007), 251–75.

9. J. B. Gillingham, "The English invasion of Ireland," in his *The English in the Twelfth Century* (Woodbridge, 2000), 145–60 is a good place to begin reading on English attitudes to the Irish, and explains why we should call the incomers English. *Expugnatio Hibernica*, 234–5.

10. Henry II had filled the Young King's household with his own men, too. He was an overbearing father.

11. R. H. F. Lindemann, "The English *esnecca* in northern Europe," *Mariner's Mirror*, 74 (1988), 75–82.

12. *Pipe Rolls 21 Henry II*, 193; *24 Henry II*, 105; *Angevin Acta Project: Henry II*, no. 1020 (PRO E368/123 (LTR Memoranda Roll 25 Edward III) m.53d). In 1212, Alard's daughter and heir was in the custody of Baldwin de Cantilupe by the grant of King John when the land was valued at 100s (*Liber Feodorum*, 106). By 1242–3, this service had become that of finding a serjeant to perform the duty of holding a rope whenever the queen wished to cross the sea; the serjeanty was still valued at 100s (*Liber Feodorum*, 863, 1383).

13. Gilbert witnessed twenty-one of Henry II's charters (*Angevin Acta Project: Henry II*, nos 87, 236, 280, 802, 1020, 1090, 1192, 1280, 1332, 1747, 1888, 1933, 1976, 1977, 2019, 2259, 2380, 2434, 2762, 2763, 2830).

14. *Pipe Rolls 13 Henry II*, 141 (cf. *Angevin Acta Project: Henry II*, no. 1197); *14 Henry II*, 120; *15 Henry II*, 112; *16 Henry II*, 74; *17 Henry II*, 83; *18 Henry II*, 1; *19 Henry II*, 38; *22 Henry II*, 144, 152; *23 Henry II*, 43; *26 Henry II*, 36, 52, 59, 85, 88, 100.

15. *Pipe Roll 25 Henry II*, 89.

16. *Pipe Rolls 28 Henry II*, 148; *29 Henry II*, 151.

17. John, constable of Chester had been involved in the pacification of Ireland in the early 1180s (*Expugnatio Hibernica*, 194–5).

18. *The Song of Dermot and the Earl*, ed. G. H. Orpen (Oxford, 1892), lines 2601–10.

19. J. Boorman, "The sheriffs of Henry II and the significance of 1170," in *Law and Government in Medieval England and Normandy*, ed. G. Garnett and J. Hudson (Cambridge, 1994), 255–75). He held these counties as sheriff for the next fifteen years (Pipe Rolls *16 Henry II*, 86; *30 Henry II*, 43). For the sheriff in general, see W. A. Morris, *The Medieval English Sheriff to 1300* (Manchester, 1927).

20. *Pipe Roll 19 Henry II*, 99 and each year until the end of the reign (*Pipe Roll 1 Richard I*, 171).

21. R. Mortimer, "The family of Rannulf de Glanville," *BIHR*, 54 (1984), 1–16.

22. *Calendar of Ormond Deeds, 1172–1350*, ii, 321–2, no. 426. G. H. Orpen, *Ireland under the Normans, 1169–1216* (Oxford, 1911), ii, 97–103.

23. *Gesta Regis Henrici Secundi*, i, 339; *Chronica Magistri Rogeri de Houedene*, ii, 307.

24. *Expugnatio Hibernica*, note 480 gathers together all the evidence for Hugh's murder.

25. W. L. Warren, *Henry II*, 621–2.

26. D. M. Stenton, *English Justice between the Norman Conquest and the Great Charter, 1066–1215* (Philadelphia, 1964) transcribes and translates the case as appendix V, 148–211.

27. *The Chronicle of Battle Abbey*, ed. E. Searle (Oxford, 1980), 310–13 gives a vivid account of the process by which a confirmation charter might be acquired and the role that it played in providing title to land.

28. *Chronica Magistri Rogeri de Houedene*, iii, 5.

29. *Gesta Regis Henrici Secundi*, ii, 72–3.

30. T. R. Nash, *Collections for the History of Worcestershire*, 2 vols (1781–99), ii appendix 137; *Earldom of Gloucester Charters: The Charters and Scribes of the Earls and Countesses of Gloucester to AD 1217*, ed. R. B. Paterson (Oxford, 1973), nos 48 and 92.

31. *Chronicle of Richard of Devizes*, 6.

32. "Itinerarum Regis Ricardi," in *Chronicles and Memorials of the Reign of Richard I*, ed. W. Stubbs, Rolls Series (London, 1864), 142.

33. *Chronica Magistri Rogeri de Houedene*, iii, 13–15.

CHAPTER 3: BROTHER IN ARMS

1. B. Wilkinson, "The government of England during the absence of Richard I on crusade," *Bulletin of the John Rylands Library*, 28 (1944), 485–509, at 486.

2. *Annales Cambriae*, 57 s.a. 1189.

3. *Gesta Regis Henrici Secundi*, ii, 87–8; *Chronica Magistri Rogeri de Houedene*, iii, 23.

4. *Chronica Magistri Rogeri de Houedene*, iii, 25–6.

5. *Historical Works of Ralph de Diceto*, ii, 72–3.

6. *Epistolae Cantuarienses*, 322–3.

7. *English Episcopal Acta 31: Ely 1109–1197*, lxxxiii–lxxxvi.

8. *Roger of Wendover, Flores Historiarum*, iii, 27.

9. This detail is in *Gesta Regis Henrici Secundi*, ii, 106, but not *Chronica Magistri Rogeri de Houedene*, ii. 32.

10. *Chronicle of Richard of Devizes*, 14.

11. *Chronica Magistri Rogeri de Houedene*, iii, 63.

12. *William of Newburgh*, i, 336; *Chronicle of Richard of Devizes*, 29.

13. G. Constable, "Medieval letters and the letter collection of Peter the Venerable," in his *The Letters of Peter the Venerable*, (Cambridge, Mass, 1967), 11.

14. P. Chaplais *English Diplomatic Practice in the Middle Ages* (London, 2003), 45.

15. J. Barrau, *Bible, lettres et politique. L'Écriture au service des hommes à l'époque de Thomas Becket* (Paris, 2013), 149; "Becket asked the papal notary, Gratian, to make sure that the letters between Alexander III and Henry II were enrolled in the papal register to inform posterity" (*Correspondence of Thomas Becket*, ed. A. Duggan (Oxford, 2000), letter 301).

16. *Chronica Magistri Rogeri de Houedene*, iii, 148–50.

17. The chronology followed is that of Appleby in his edition of *Chronicle of Richard of Devizes*, appendix F.

18. *William of Newburgh*, 337–9.

19. *Ancient Charters Royal and Private Prior to AD 1200*, i, ed. J. H. Round (Pipe Roll Society, 10, 1888), no. 55; R. J. Smith, "Henry II's heir: the charters and seal of Henry the young king, 1170–83," *EHR*, 106 (2001), 297–326, no. 32, p. 325–6. For Nicola de Haye see L. J. Wilkinson, *Women in Thirteenth-Century Lincolnshire* (Woodbridge, 2007), 13–26.

20. *Epistolae Cantuarienses*, ii, no. 347.

21. *Epistolae Cantuarienses*, ii, no. 348.

22. *Gervase of Canterbury*, i, 493.

23. *Epistolae Cantuarienses*, i, no. 386 (dated 27 Nov. 1191).

24. *Historical Works of Ralph de Diceto*, ii, 90.

25. *Chronica Magistri Rogeri de Houedene*, 193.

26. That by *William of Newburgh* is deemed by Appleby to be faulty (*Chronicle of Richard of Devizes*, 93).

27. *Angevin Acta Project: Count John*, nos 6, 30, 39, 71, 90, 106, 130, 147, 177, 221, 291.

28. *William of Newburgh*, 341.

29. *Giraldus Cambrensis, Opera*, iv, 392.

30. *Giraldus Cambrensis, Opera*, iv, 396.

31. *Giraldus Cambrensis, Opera*, iv, 389 supplies the text of the writ by which the chancellor had authorized the arrest of the prelate should he have the temerity to land in England, issued on July 30, more than a month before the archbishop's return.

32. *Giraldus Cambrensis, Opera*, iv, 389.

33. N. Fryde and D. Reitz, *Bischofsmord im Mittelalter—Murder of Bishops* (Göttingen, 2003).

34. *Historical Works of Ralph de Diceto*, ii, 96–8.

35. A council that perhaps marks the beginnings of conciliar government in England, an experiment that was to lead to the creation of parliament in the later thirteenth century (J. R. Maddicott, *The Origins of Parliament, 924–1327* (Oxford, 2010), 110).

36. *Chronica Magistri Rogeri de Houedene*, iii, 140.

37. *Chronica Magistri Rogeri de Houedene*, iii, 140.

38. K. Norgate, *John Lackland* (London, 1902), 38; J. T. Appleby, *England Without Richard* (London, 1965), 76; Gillingham, *Richard I*, 119–20; W. L. Warren, *King John* (London, 1961), 43.

39. *Chronicle of Richard of Devizes*, 48–9.

40. *Gesta Regis Henrici Secundi*, ii, 214; *Rot. Cur. Reg.*, i, cv.

41. *Chronicle of Richard of Devizes*, pp. 59–60.

42. *Gesta Regis Henrici Secundi*, ii, 221–2.

43. *Gesta Regis Henrici Secundi*, ii, 222–3.

CHAPTER 4: TROUBLESOME BROTHER

1. J. B. Gillingham, "Doing homage to the king of France," in *Henry II: New Interpretations*, ed. N. Vincent and C. Harper-Bill (Woodbridge, 2007), 63–84, at 80; and again in 1195 (Rigord, 133).

2. *Gesta Regis Henrici Secundi*, ii, 236.

3. J. Martindale, "Eleanor of Aquitaine," in her *Status, Authority, and Regional Power* (Aldershot, 1997), XI, 17–50; and her "Eleanor of Aquitaine: The last years," in *King John: New Interpretations*, ed. S. D. Church (Woodbridge, 1999), 137–64.

4. *Chronica Magistri Rogeri de Houedene*, iii, 188.

5. Gillingham, *Richard I*, 222–53.

6. Gillingham, *Richard I*, 234–5.

7. *Gesta Regis Henri Secundi*, ii, 236; *Chronica Magistri Rogeri de Houedene*, iii, 204.

8. *Gervase of Canterbury*, i, 514–15.

9. *Chronica Magistri Rogeri de Houedene*, iii, 217–28.

10. J. B. Gillingham, "Coeur de Lion in captivity," *Quaestiones Medii Aevi Novae* (2013), 59–85.

11. *Layettes du Trésor des Chartes*, i, no. 412.

12. As reported by Richard of Devizes (*Chronicle of Richard of Devizes*, 60).

13. As reported in *Chronica Magistri Rogeri de Houedene*, iii, 198.

14. *History of William the Marshal*, lines 10409–28. The author of the *Itinerarium Regis Ricardi*, Richard de Templo, writing at about the same time has a similar tale (*Chronicles and Memorials of the Reign of Richard I*, ed. W. Stubbs, Rolls Series (London, 1864), i, 449).

15. *Itinerary of Richard I*, 102–6.

16. C. Veach, "A question of timing: Walter de Lacy's seisin of Meath, 1189–94," *Proceedings of the Royal Irish Academy*, 109 (2009), 165–94.

17. As William Marshal is said to have pointed out to Richard when Richard demanded from him homage for his lands in Ireland (*History of William the Marshal*, lines 10289–10340); for a full account see C. Veach, "King and magnate in medieval Ireland: Walter de Lacy, King Richard and King John," *Irish Historical Studies*, 37 (2010), 179–202, at 184–5, 187.

18. *Calendar of the Gormanston Register c.1175–1397: From the Original in the Possession of the Rt. Hon. the Viscount of Gormanston*, ed. J. Mill and M. J. McEnery (Extra Volume of the Royal Society of Antiquaries of Ireland, Dublin, 1916), 178.

19. *William the Breton*, 197 (cf. Gillingham, *Richard I*, 292–3, for Vaudreuil).

20. *Itinerary of Richard I*, 112, 113. *Chronica Magistri Rogeri de Houedene*, iv, 5; *Magni Rotuli Scaccarii Normaniae sub Regibus Angliae*, 2 vols, ed. T. Stapleton (Society of Antiquaries of London, 1840–4), viii.

21. *Chronica Magistri Rogeri de Houedene*, iv, 16. Gillingham, *Richard I*, 308.

22. N. Fryde, "King John and the empire," in *King John: New Interpretations*, ed. S. D. Church (Woodbridge, 1999), 337.

23. "Cartulaires de Hainaut," *Monuments pour servir à l'histoire des provinces de Namur, de Hainaut et de Luxembourg*, i, ed. De Reiffenberg (Brussels, 1844), 323–4, nos 10, 11; *Calendar of Documents Relating to France*, ed. J. H. Round (London, 1899), nos 1361, 1362.

24. *Gervase of Canterbury*, i, 544.

25. *Angevin Acta Project: Count John*, no. 436.

26. The importance of this site and the story of the exchange between Richard and the archbishop is in Gillingham, *Richard I*, 301–7.

27. Gillingham, *Richard I*, 312.

28. Throughout 1198, John was in Normandy and often at court (*Itinerary of Richard I*, 127–41) and also received a huge gift of £716 13s 4d out of the revenues of the city of Rouen and was

able to borrow from the revenues of Bayeux a further £1,300 by order of King Richard (*Magni Rotuli Scaccarii Normaniae sub Regibus Angliae*, 2 vols, ed. T. Stapleton (Society of Antiquaries of London, 1840–4), xxi, lxxix, lxxxvi, cxxxiii, clxi, clxxviii–clxxix).

29. *History of William the Marshal*, line 10326 (by the restored William de Longchamp of all people!).

30. *Angevin Acta Project: Count John*, no. 2164.

CHAPTER 5: WINNER TAKES ALL

1. *Chronica Magistri Rogeri de Houedene*, iv, 81.

2. *Itinerary of Richard I*, 144.

3. *Rot. Cur. Reg.*, i, lxxxiv–v.

4. *Memoranda Roll 1 John*, 12.

5. *History of William the Marshal*, lines 11868–11903. In this the London author the dean of St. Paul's, Ralph de Diceto, or his continuator, also agreed (*Historical Works of Ralph de Diceto*, ii, 166).

6. J. C. Holt, "The *Casus Regis* reconsidered," *Haskins Society Journal*, 10 (2001), 163–82.

7. *Chronica Magistri Rogeri de Houedene*, iv, 88.

8. *Layettes du Trésor des Chartes*, i, no. 488.

9. *The Charters of the Duchess Constance and Her Family*, ed. J. Everard and M. Jones (Woodbridge, 2000), 109–33, at 110.

10. J. A. Everard, *Brittany and the Angevins: Province and Empire, 1158–1203* (Cambridge, 2000).

11. *Chronica Magistri Rogeri de Houedene*, iv, 87.

12. *Histoire des Ducs de Normandie*, 90.

13. *Rot. Cur. Reg.*, i, lxxxvi–viii; *Chronica Magistri Rogeri de Houedene*, iv, 86.

14. C. A. Jones, "The Chrism Mass in later Anglo-Saxon England," in *The Liturgy in the Late Anglo-Saxon Church*, ed. H. Gittos and M. Bradford Bedingfield (London, HBS Subsidia 5, 2005), 105–42, at 105. See also J. Harper, *The Forms and Orders of Western Liturgy from the Tenth to the Eighteenth Century* (Oxford, 1991).

15. J. Nelson, "Inauguration rituals," in her *Politics and Ritual in Early Medieval Europe* (London, 1986), 283–307.

16. A. J. Heslin, "The coronation of the Young King in 1170," in *Studies in Church History*, ii, ed. G. J. Cuming (London, 1965), 165–85, at 177.

17. A detailed description (probably an eyewitness description, R. Foreville, "Le sacre des rois anglo-normands et angevins et le serment du sacre [XIᵉ–XIIᵉ siècles]," *Anglo-Norman Studies*, i (1978), 49–62) of Richard I's coronation service is preserved for us by Roger of Howden (*Gesta Regis Henrici Secundi*, ii, 79–83).

18. *English Episcopal Acta 31: Ely*, no. 132.

19. F. Boutoulle, "L'apogée d'une 'bonne ville.'" Saint-Emilion pendant les premiers temps de la jurade (1199–1253), *Fabrique d'une ville médiévale. Saint-Emilion au Moyen Age*, ed. F. Boutoulle, D. Barraud and J.-L. Piat (Bordeaux, 2011), 317.

20. C. Petit-Dutaillis, "Le déshéritement de Jean sans Terre et le meurtre d'Arthur de Bretagne," *Revue Historique*, 147 (1924), 161–203; *Revue Historique*, 148 (1925), 1–62 and reprinted as *Le déshéritement de Jean sans Terre et le meurtre d'Arthur de Bretagne* Paris 1925.

21. *Foedera*, 75–6.

22. *Rot. Chart.*, 30b, where John's mother, Eleanor, conceded the county of Poitou to John *"sicut recto heredi nostro."*

23. *Chronica Magistri Rogeri de Houedene*, iv, 93.

24. *Chronica Magistri Rogeri de Houedene*, iv, 94–5.

25. D. Power, "French and Norman frontiers in the Middle Ages," in *Frontiers in Question*, ed. D. Power and N. Standen (London, 1999), 105–27; D. Power, *The Norman Frontier in the Twelfth and Early Thirteenth Centuries* (Cambridge, 2004), 394.

26. J. E. M. Benham, "Anglo-French peace conferences in the twelfth century," *Anglo-Norman Studies*, 27 (2005), 52–67.

27. *William the Breton*, 202.

28. L. Landon, "Appendix H: The Vexin," *Itinerary of Richard I*, 219–34; L. Diggelmann, "Marriage as tactical response: Henry II and the royal wedding of 1160," *EHR*, 109 (2004), 954–64.

29. *Chronica Magistri Rogeri de Houedene*, iv, 79.

30. D. Power, *The Norman Frontier in the Twelfth and Early Thirteenth Centuries* (Cambridge, 2004), 224–62.

31. J. H. Le Patourel, "The Plantagenet dominions," *History*, 50 (1965), 259–308, at 295.

32. J. B. Gillingham, *The Angevin Empire*, 2nd edn (London, 2000), 73–4.

33. R. W. Eyton, *Court, Household and Itinerary of King Henry II* (London, 1878), 289–93.

34. D. Power, *The Norman Frontier in the Twelfth and Early Thirteenth Centuries*, 406–12.

35. D. Power, *The Norman Frontier in the Twelfth and Early Thirteenth Centuries*, 413–14 gives the details.

36. *Layettes du Trésor des Chartes*, i, no. 412.

37. S. Reynolds, *Kingdoms and Communities in Western Europe, 900–1300* (Oxford 1984), 170–2.

38. D. Power, *The Norman Frontier in the Twelfth and Early Thirteenth Centuries*, 432–8.

39. G. Pon and Y. Chauvin, "Chartes de libertés et de communes de l'Angoumois, du Poitou et de la Saintonage (fin XIIe–début XIIIe siècle)" *Memoires de la Société des Antiquaires de l'Ouest*, 58 (2000), 25–149 (at 61–4).

40. *Rot. Chart.*, 1; 5b.

41. *Foedera*, 75.

42. F. M. Powicke, *The Loss of Normandy, 1189–1204*, 2nd edn (Manchester, 1961), 210–12.

43. *Diplomatic Documents*, i, nos 1, 2, 3.

44. *Layettes du Trésor des Chartes*, i, nos 501 (the count of Auvergne), 502 (Hervey IV, the lord of Douzy en Nivernais), 503 (and his brother, Reginald), 504 (Andrew de Chauvigny).

45. *Chronica Magistri Rogeri de Houedene*, iv, 96–7.

46. *Chronica Magistri Rogeri de Houedene*, iv, 119.

47. H. Richardson, "The marriage and coronation of Isabelle of Angoulême," *EHR*, 61 (1949), 289–314; N. C. Vincent, "Isabella of Angoulême: John's Jezebel," in *King John: New Interpretations*, ed. S. D. Church (Woodbridge, 1999), 165–219.

48. For the daughters, see C. Bowie, *The Daughters of Henry II and Eleanor of Aquitaine: A Comparative Study of Twelfth-Century Royal Women* (forthcoming);

49. http://www.walesdirectory.co.uk/tourist-attractions/Gravestones_Memorials_Monu ments_Effigies/Wales11356.htm; C. Given-Wilson and A. Curteis, *The Royal Bastards of Medieval England* (London, 1984). Perhaps to be identified with Clemency de Fougères, the

second wife of Ranulf earl of Chester (see R. Swallow, "Gateways to Power: The castles of Ranulf III of Chester and Llywelyn the Great of Gwynedd," *Archaeological Journal*, 171 (2014), 299–300).

50. The best introduction to sex and the Church's teaching on this normal human activity is to be found in J. A. Brundage, *Law, Sex, and Christian Society in Medieval Europe* (Chicago, 1987).

51. *Royal and Other Historical Letters Illustrative of the Reign of Henry III*, 2 vols, ed. W. W. Shirley, Rolls Series (London, 1862–6), i, 114–15.

52. Henry, Richard, Joanna, Isabella and Eleanor.

53. *Letters of Innocent III to England and Wales*, no. 355. Though we do not know what lands it comprised.

54. *Layettes du Trésor des Chartes*, i, no. 494.

55. *The Chronicle and Historical Notes of Bernard Itier*, ed. A. W. Lewis (Oxford, 2013), 60–1.

56. *Foedera*, 79; *Rot. Chart.*, 30–1.

57. H. Richardson, "The marriage and coronation of Isabella of Angoulême," *EHR*, 61 (1949), 299.

58. Both Philip's copy (preserved in the English royal archives, *Diplomatic Documents preserved in the Public Record Office, 1101–1272*, i, ed. P. Chaplais (London, 1964), i, no 9) and John's copy (preserved *Layettes du Trésor des Chartes*, i, no. 578) call John "rectus heres regis Ricardi."

59. *Layettes du Trésor des Chartes*, i, no. 589.

60. *Selected Letters of Pope Innocent III*, no. 8, 24; *Letters of Innocent III to England and Wales*, no. 295.

61. *Rigord*, 133.

62. *Chronica Magistri Rogeri de Houedene*, iv, 114.

63. *Memoranda Roll 1 John*, 90; H. E. J. Cowdrey, "The Anglo-Norman Laudes Regiae," *Viator*, 12 (1968), 39–78; E. Kantorowicz, *Laudes Regiae: A Study in Liturgical Acclamations in Medieval Ruler Worship* (Oakland, CA, 1958).

64. *Rot. Chart.*, 69.

65. *Chronica Magistri Rogeri de Houedene*, iv, 124–5.

66. *The Chronicle and Historical Notes of Bernard Itier*, ed. A. W. Lewis (Oxford, 2013), 172.

67. *Rot. de Lib.*, 1; *Rot. Norm.*, 34.

68. *Rot. Norm.*, 36.

69. *Gervase of Canterbury*, ii, 92–3.

70. *Magna Vita Sancti Hugonis*, 2 vols, ed. D. L. Douie and D. H. Farmer (Oxford, 1985), ii, 224–5.

71. *Chronica Magistri Rogeri de Houedene*, iv, 140–2.

CHAPTER 6: RETREAT TO THE CITADEL

1. *Rot. Chart.*, 74–5; N. C. Vincent, "Isabella of Angoulême: John's Jezebel," in *King John: New Interpretations*, ed. S. D. Church (Woodbridge, 1999), 186–8.

2. J. Dunbabin, *France in the Making*, 2nd edn (Oxford, 2000).

3. *Gervase of Canterbury*, ii, 93; John referred to this event as his "third coronation" and it was used. It was this coronation that provided the limit for writs of Novel Disseisin (see *Curia Regis Rolls*, ii, 96, 133, 141, 146, 271, 314–15).

4. *Historical Works of Ralph de Diceto*, ii, 170.

5. *Coggeshall*, 63; D. A. Carpenter, "Abbot Ralph of Coggeshall's account of the last years of King Richard and the first years of King John," *EHR*, 113 (1998), 1210–30, at 1216.

6. *Rot. Chart.*, 102.

7. *Rot. Chart.*, 102b.

8. The comment comes from Abbot Ralph of Coggeshall (*Coggeshall*, 76).

9. *Chronica Magistri Rogeri de Houedene*, iv, 160–1.

10. *Rot. de Lib.*, 14.

11. *Historical Works of Ralph de Diceto*, ii, 172; *Annales Monastici*, i, 208.

12. *Rot. Chart.*, 102b–3.

13. *Rot. de Lib.*, 14.

14. *Chronica Magistri Rogeri de Houedene*, iv, 164.

15. *Rot. de Lib.*, 15–18.

16. *Rigord*, 150.

17. *Chronica Magistri Rogeri de Houedene*, iv, 176.

18. *Rot. Litt. Pat.*, 1, 2.

19. *Rot. Litt. Pat.*, 2b.

20. *Chronica Magistri Rogeri de Houedene*, iv, 175.

21. S. Painter, "Castellans of the plain of Poitou in the eleventh and twelfth centuries," *Speculum*, 31 (1956), 256.

22. S. Painter, "Castellans of the plain of Poitou in the eleventh and twelfth centuries," *Speculum*, 31 (1956), 243–57; J. Le Patourel, "The Plantagenet dominions," *History*, 50 (1965), 259–308.

23. N. Vincent, "Henry II and the Poitevins," in *La Cour Plantagenêt*, ed. M. Aurell (Poitiers, 2000), 103–36, esp. 117–20.

24. R. C. Watson, "The counts of Angoulême from the ninth to the mid thirteenth century," unpublished University of East Anglia thesis (1979), 111–38; Gillingham, *Richard I*, 62–75.

25. R. Hajdu, "Poitou, Castles and Castellans," p. 10.

26. R. C. Watson, "The counts of Angoulême from the ninth to the mid thirteenth century," unpublished University of East Anglia thesis (1979), 57.

27. *Gervase of Canterbury*, ii, 93.

28. *Rigord*, 151–2.

29. *Rot. Litt. Pat.*, 10b.

30. *Layettes du Trésor des Chartes*, i, no. 647.

31. *The Chronicle and Historical Notes of Bernard Itier*, ed. A. W. Lewis (Oxford, 2013), 62, 184.

32. The author of the *Histoire des Ducs de Normandie* agreed, 92.

33. *Coggeshall*, 138.

34. *History of William the Marshal*, lines 12405–36.

35. *History of William the Marshal*, lines 12501–6.

36. *Rot. Litt. Pat.*, 17.

37. *Rot. Litt. Pat.*, 17b.

38. *Rot. Litt. Pat.*, 17b, 18, 20, 20b, 22.

39. *Rot. Litt. Pat.*, 5.

40. *Selected Letters of Pope Innocent III*, no. 14, 40.

41. *Selected Letters of Pope Innocent III*, no. 410.

42. E.g. *Rigord*, 153–7.

43. *Rot. Litt. Pat.*, 3.

44. *Chronica Magistri Rogeri de Houedene*, iv, 188–9.

45. *Letters of Innocent III to England and Wales*, no. 38.

46. *Rot. Norm.*, 70–2

47. D. Power, "The revolt at Alençon, 1203," *Historical Research*, 74 (2001), 444–64.

48. *Annales Monastici*, i, 27.

49. *Coggeshall*, 139.

50. J. C. Holt, "King John and Arthur of Brittany," *Nottingham Medieval Studies*, 44 (2000), 82–103.

51. Matthew Paris, *Chron. Maj.*, ii, 479–80.

52. C. Petit-Dutaillis, "Le déshéritement de Jean sans Terre et le meurtre d'Arthur de Bretagne," *Revue Historique*, 147 (1924), 161–203.

53. *Rot. Litt. Pat.*, 28b; F. M. Powicke, "King John and Arthur of Brittany," in his *The Loss of Normandy, 1189–1204*, 2nd edn (Manchester, 1961), appendix 1, 309–28.

54. *Rigord*, 158.

55. *Selected Letters of Pope Innocent III*, no. 56–9.

56. *Rigord*, 158–9; *Histoire des Ducs de Normandie*, 96ff.

57. *William the Breton*, 212–20.

58. *History of William the Marshal*, lines 12698–13278.

59. *Rot. Chart.*, 113.

60. *History of William the Marshal*, lines 12721–12743.

61. *Rot. de Lib.*, 72.

CHAPTER 7: INSIDE THE CITADEL

1. *Rot. de Lib.*, 77; F. M. Powicke, *The Loss of Normandy, 1189–1204*, 2nd edn (Manchester, 1961), 256.

2. Matthew Paris, *Chron. Maj.*, ii, 484; *Pipe Roll 6 John*, passim, confirms the size of the scutage.

3. *Foedera*, 90.

4. *Rot. de Lib.*, 77.

5. *Rot. Litt. Pat.*, 40.

6. *Letters of Innocent III to England and Wales*, nos 506, 507, 508, 509, 510, 511, 512 (*Selected Letters of Pope Innocent III*, no. 20).

7. *Letters of Innocent III to England and Wales*, nos 555, 556 (*Selected Letters of Pope Innocent III*, no. 21), 569.

8. *Coggeshall*, 145.

9. *Foedera*, 90.

10. *William the Breton*, 220.

11. *Layettes du Trésor des Chartes*, i, no. 716.

12. *Rigord*, 161.

13. *Rot. Chart.*, 128. The charter, in the same words and with the same witnesses and the same dating clause, was re-enrolled on the close rolls in late July 1215.

14. *Roger of Wendover, Flores Historiarum*, iii, 174.

15. *History of William the Marshal*, lines 12921–32.

16. *Coggeshall*, 143–4.

17. *Gervase of Canterbury*, ii, 96.

18. This statute is often confused with the statute of April 3, 1205, enrolled in the Patent Rolls (*Rot. Litt. Pat.*, 55–55b) on the authority of Stubbs in his *Select Charters and Other Illustrations of English Constitutional History*, ed. W. Stubbs, 9th edn, ed. H. W. C. David (Oxford, 1913), 275–6, but I do not see why we should disbelieve Gervase, who seems like a first-rate authority for this period in John's reign.

19. *Layettes du Trésor des Chartes*, no. 724, 725; *Rigord*, 161; *William the Breton*, 220–1.

20. *Rot. Litt Pat.*, 44b.

21. *History of William the Marshal*, lines 12995–13090.

22. *History of William the Marshal*, lines 13099–102.

23. *Rot. de Lib.*, 47 (2), 70.

24. *The Beaulieu Cartulary*, ed. S. F. Hockey, Southampton Record Society (Southampton, 1974), 3–5.

25. http://www.hrionline.ac.uk/normans/about.shtml.

26. *Rot. Litt. Pat.*, 54b–55.

27. *Handbook of Medieval Exchange*, ed. P. Spufford, Royal Historical Society Guides and Handbooks 13 (London, 1986).

28. S. D. Church, "The care of the royal tombs in English cathedrals in the nineteenth and twentieth centuries: the case of the effigy of King John at Worcester," *Antiquaries Journal*, 89 (2009), 365–87.

29. *Rot. Litt. Claus.*, i, 33.

30. *Rot. Litt. Pat.*, 54b.

31. *Annales Monastici*, ii, 256.

32. The great manual on the Exchequer is Richard fitz Nigel's account of *c.*1177, *Dialogus de Scaccario*: see *Richard fitz Nigel Dialogus de Scaccario and The Constitutio Domus Regis*, ed. E. Amt and S. D. Church (Oxford, 2007). See also John Brand, "The Exchequer in the twelfth century," unpublished Polytechnic of North London PhD thesis (1989).

33. *Rot. Litt. Pat.*, 55–55b.

34. *Rot. Litt. Pat.*, 53 (2).

35. *Reports on the Lords Committees touching on the Dignity of a Peer of the Realm, Presented to the House 12 July 1819* (London, 1820), vol. 3, appendix 1 part 1, 1.

36. *Coggeshall*, 152.

37. *History of William the Marshal*, lines 13132–248.

38. P. Hyams, *Rancor and Reconciliation in Medieval England* (Ithaca, 2003), 111–54.

39. *Coggeshall*, 154.

40. *Rigord*, pp. 161–2.

41. *Rot. de Fin.*, 368.

42. *Gervase of Canterbury*, ii, 98–9.

43. *Rot. Litt. Pat.*, 56.

44. *Letters of Innocent III to England and Wales*, nos 699–702.

45. *Rot. Litt. Pat.*, 56.

46. *Rot. Litt. Pat.*, 58.

47. *Rot. Litt. Pat.*, 59.

48. *Rot. Litt. Claus.*, i, 74b.

49. M. Keen, *The Outlaws of Medieval Legend* (London, 1961).

50. *Rot. Litt. Pat.*, 65.

51. *Rot. Litt. Pat.*, 65b, 67.

52. *Histoire des Ducs de Normandie*, 107.

53. *Rot. Litt. Pat.*, 66–66b, 67b (the order for the process of his release was not issued until September 30).

54. *Rot. Litt. Pat.*, 67b–68. The order was issued at Niort on June 19.

55. *Annales Monastici*, iv, 394.

56. *Rot. Litt. Pat.*, 67.

57. *Rigord*, 164; *William the Breton*, 224.

58. *Histoire des Ducs de Normandie*, 109.

59. *Foedera*, 95.

60. *Rot. Litt. Pat.*, 67b.

61. *Annales Monastici*, iv, 394.

62. N. Barratt, "The revenue of King John," *EHR*, 111 (1996), 835–55 (at 837), notes that the Jews were also mulcted severely from 1207, though nothing remains of the record that might have told us how much revenue John realized from this source.

63. *Annales Monastici*, ii, 258–9.

64. *Gervase of Canterbury*, ii, lvii.

65. *Rot. Litt. Pat.*, 72–3.

66. S. K. Mitchell, *Studies in Taxation under John and Henry III* (New Haven, CT, 1914), 84–92; N. Barratt, "Revenues of King John," *EHR*, 111 (1996), 835–55 (at 839).

67. *Rot. Litt. Pat.*, 73.

68. *Rot. Litt. Claus.*, i, 81.

69. J. Green, "The last century of Danegeld," *EHR*, 96 (1981), 241–58 (at 242).

70. *Rot. Litt. Pat.*, 72–b.

71. J. E. A. Jolliffe, "The chamber and the castle treasuries under King John," in *Studies in Medieval History presented to F. M. Powicke*, ed. R. W. Hunt, W. A. Pantin and R. W. Southern (Oxford, 1948), 117–42.

72. J. L. Bolton, "The English economy in the early thirteenth century," in *King John: New Interpretations*, ed. S. D. Church (Woodbridge, 1999), 27–40.

CHAPTER 8: THE CITADEL UNDER SIEGE

1. B. Bolton, "Papal Italy," in *Italy in the Central Middle Ages*, ed. D. Abulafia (Oxford, 2004), 100–1.

2. N. C. Vincent, "Stephen Langton, archbishop of Canterbury," in *Étienne Langton: prédicateur, bibliste, théologien*, ed. L.-J. Bataillon, N. Bériou, G. Dahan and R. Quinto (Turnhout, 2010), 51–123.

3. *Rot. Litt. Pat.*, 74; *Gervase of Canterbury*, ii, lxiii.

4. *Rot. Litt. Pat.*, 76.

5. *Rot. Litt. Claus.*, i, 114b.

6. *Rot. Litt. Pat.*, 74–7.

7. *Rot. Litt. Pat.*, 76.

8. *Selected Letters of Pope Innocent III*, 94.

9. *Letters of Innocent III to England and Wales*, nos 765, 766.

10. *Gervase of Canterbury*, ii, lxxxix–xc; *Letters of Innocent III to England and Wales*, no. 764.

11. *Gervase of Canterbury*, ii, lxxxv; *Letters of Innocent III to England and Wales*, no. 769; *Selected Letters of Pope Innocent III*, 96.

12. *Selected Letters of Pope Innocent III*, 97.

13. *Selected Letters of Pope Innocent III*, 88.

14. *Annales Monastici*, i, 28.

15. *Rot. Litt. Claus.*, i, 89.

16. *Rot. Litt. Pat.*, 78b.

17. *Rot. Litt. Pat.*, 80.

18. *Rot. Litt. Pat.*, 81, 81b.

19. *Rot. Litt. Pat.*, 83b.

20. *Rot. Litt. Claus.*, i, 108.

21. *Letters of Innocent III to England and Wales*, no. 792; *Selected Letters of Pope Innocent III*, 104.

22. *Selected Letters of Pope Innocent III*, 107–9.

23. *Letters of Innocent III to England and Wales*, nos 800, 835, 839, 842–5; *Gervase of Canterbury*, ii, xcvi. *Letters of Innocent III to England and Wales*, no. 827.

24. N. C. Vincent, *Peter des Roches, Bishop of Winchester 1205–38: An Alien in English Politics* (Cambridge, 1996), 84.

25. *Letters of Innocent III to England and Wales*, nos 801, 805, 806, 807, 808, 809, 820, 822; *Selected Letters of Pope Innocent III*, no. 38; *Gervase of Canterbury*, ii, xcv; *Letters of Innocent*, no. 830–3.

26. *Letters of Innocent III to England and Wales*, nos 793–9; most easily accessed through *Gervase of Canterbury*, ii, xc–xci.

27. *Rot. Litt. Pat.*, 85 (2), 86.

28. *Rot. Litt. Pat.*, 80–80b.

29. *Rot. Litt. Claus.*, i, 110b, 111b.

30. *Rot. Litt. Claus.*, i, 108–111.

31. *Rot. Lit. Claus.* i, 88b, 95b, 102b, 108, 111b, 197; *Rot. Litt. Pat.*, 91b; *The Heads of Religious Houses England and Wales, 940–1216*, ed. D. Knowles, C. N. L. Brooke, V. London (Cambridge, 1972), 127.

32. *Rot. Litt. Claus.*, i, 108b.

33. C. R. Cheney, "King John's reaction to the Interdict in England," *TRHS*, 4th series, 31 (1948), 129–50, at 147–8.

34. *Rot. Litt. Claus.*, i, 109b, 111b.

35. *Rot. Litt. Claus.*, i, 110.

36. C. R. Cheney, "King John's reaction to the Interdict in England," *TRHS*, 4th series, 31 (1948), 129–50, at 131.

37. *Rot. Litt. Claus*, i, 111b, 112.

38. *Rot. Litt. Claus*, i, 113.

39. *Magna Vita Sancti Hugonis*, 2 vols, ed. D. L. Douie and D. H. Farmer (Oxford, 1985), ii, 155.

40. C. R. Cheney, "King John's reaction to the Interdict in England," *TRHS*, 4th series, 31 (1948), 129–50.

41. N. Barratt, "The revenue of King John," *EHR*, 111 (1996), 835–55 at 837–8.

42. *Pipe Roll 14 John*, 44–5.

43. *Rot. Litt. Pat.*, 85, 86.

44. *Roger of Wendover, Flores Historiarum*, iii, 224–5.

45. *Curia Regis Rolls*, iv, 98–9 (headed *"placita capta corma domino rege …"* "pleas taken by the view of the Lord King").

46. *Curia Regis Rolls*, iv, 115, 135, 176, 206.

47. C. Veach, "King John and the anglicisation of colonial Ireland: why William de Briouze had to be destroyed," *EHR* 129 (2014), 1051–1078.

48. A. J. Otway-Ruthven, *A History of Medieval Ireland*, 2nd edn (London, 1980), 173–4.

49. *Rot. Litt. Pat.*, 66b.

50. The National Archives, E36/274 fos 438–9; D. Crouch, "The complaint of King John against William de Briouze (c. September 1210)," in *Magna Carta and the England of King John*, ed. J. S. Loengard (Woodbridge, 2010), 168–79.

51. The best modern discussion of the politics around William's fate is now in C. Veach, "King John and the anglicisation of colonial Ireland: why William de Briouze had to be destroyed," *EHR* 129 (2014), 1051–1078.

52. *Rot. Litt. Pat.*, 199b; S. Thompson, *Women Religious: The Founding of Nunneries after the Norman Conquest* (Oxford, 1991), 50–2.

Chapter 9: Lord of the British Isles

1. *Selected Letters of Pope Innocent III*, 113.

2. *Letters of Innocent III to England and Wales*, nos 825–6.

3. *Letters of Innocent III to England and Wales*, nos 836–7.

4. *Letters of Innocent III to England and Wales*, no. 844.

5. *Rot. Litt. Pat.*, 91; A. A. M. Duncan, "John king of England and the kings of Scots," in *King John: New Interpretations*, ed. S. D. Church (Woodbridge, 1999), 247–71.

6. J. Hatcher, "English serfdom and villeinage: towards a reassessment," *Past and Present*, 110 (1981), 3–39.

7. *Gervase of Canterbury*, ii, 104.

8. J. R. Maddicott, "The Oath of Marlborough, 1209: fear, government and popular allegiance in the reign of King John," *EHR*, 126 (2011), 281–318.

9. *Foedera*, 140.

10. J. Sayers, *Innocent III: Leader of Europe* (London, 1994).

11. *Selected Letters of Pope Innocent III*, 123.

12. S. D. Church, "The 1210 campaign in Ireland: evidence for a military revolution?" *Anglo-Norman Studies*, 20 (1998), 45–57.

13. S. Duffy, "King John's expedition to Ireland, 1210: the evidence reconsidered," *Irish Historical Studies*, 30 (1996), 1–24.

14. A. A. M. Duncan, "King John of England and the kings of Scots," in *King John: New Interpretations*, ed. S. D. Church (Woodbridge, 1999), 247–71, at 259.

15. F. X. Martin, "John, lord of Ireland, 1185–1216," in *A New History of Ireland*, ii, *Medieval Ireland, 1169–1534*, ed. A. Cosgrove (Oxford, 1987), 127–55.

16. S. K. Mitchell, *Studies in Taxation under John and Henry III* (New Haven, CT, 1914), 105.

17. E. C. Wright, "Common law in thirteenth-century English forests," *Speculum*, 3 (1928), 168–91; M. Bazelay, "The extent of the English forest in the thirteenth century," *TRHS*, 4th series, 4 (1921), 140–59.

18. D. Crook, "The Forest eyre in the reign of King John," in *Magna Carta and the England of King John*, ed. J. S. Loengard (Woodbridge, 2010), 63–82.

19. *Rot. de Lib.*, 235–6.

20. B. Holden, *Lords of the Central Marches: English Aristocracy and Frontier Society, 1087–1265* (Oxford, 2008).

21. *Rot de Lib.*, 242.

22. J. B. Smith, "Magna Carta and the charters of the Welsh Princes," *EHR* 99 (1984), 344–62; I. W. Rowlands, "King John and Wales," in *King John: New Interpretations*, ed. S. D. Church, 273–87.

23. *Walter of Coventry*, ii, 203.

Chapter 10: The Enemy at the Gate

1. *Walter of Coventry*, ii, 208; *Coggeshall*, ii, 167.

2. S. D. Church, *The Household Knights of King John* (Cambridge, 1999), 58–60.

3. These documents, on which we rely for so much of our detail of John's personality, fail us for the years between 1208/9 and 1212.

4. *Foedera*, 104–5.

5. S. D. Church, "The earliest English muster roll, 18/19 December 1215," *Historical Research*, 67 (1994), 1–17, at 9.

6. R. F. Treharne, "The Franco-Welsh treaty of alliance in 1212," *Bulletin of the Board of Celtic Studies*, 18 (1958), 74–5, and translated in *English Historical Documents, 1189–1327*, iii, ed. H. Rothwell (London, 1975), 296–7.

7. I. W. Rowlands, "King John and Wales," in *King John: New Interpretations*, ed. S. D. Church (Woodbridge, 1999), 283–4.

8. *Rot. Litt. Claus.*, i, 130b.

9. *Rot. Litt. Claus.*, i, 131.

10. *Roger of Wendover, Flores Historiarum*, iii, 239; *Annales Monastici*, iii, 33.

11. K. Norgate, *John Lackland* (London, 1902), note II, 289–93.

12. K. J. Stringer, *Earl David of Huntingdon, 1152–1219: A Study in Anglo-Scottish History* (Edinburgh, 1985), 113.

13. *Rot. Litt. Pat.*, 94b.

14. *Rot. Litt. Claus.*, i, 122–b.

15. *Rot. Litt. Claus.*, 123.

16. *Rot. Litt. Claus.*, i, 124.

17. *Rot. Litt. Pat.*, 94.

18. *Rot. Litt. Claus.*, i, 122.

19. *Rot. Litt. Claus.*, i, 121b–2.

20. *Walter of Coventry*, ii, 207.

21. *Rot. Litt. Claus.*, i, 132.

22. *Rot. Litt. Claus.*, i, 132b.

23. *Foedera*, 109.

24. *Histoire des Ducs de Normandie*, 123.

25. *Rot. Litt. Claus.*, i, 126.

26. *Rot. Litt. Pat.*, 96b.

27. C. R. Cheney, "King John and the papal interdict," *Bulletin of the John Rylands Library*, 31 (1948), 295–317.

28. *Rot. Litt. Pat.*, 97.

29. *Rot. Litt. Claus.*, i, 133.

30. *William the Breton*, 245.

31. *Rot. Litt. Claus.*, 129b.

32. *Walter of Coventry*, ii, 209; *Annales Monastici*, ii, 274.

33. C. R. Cheney, *Pope Innocent III and England* (Stuttgart, 1978), 326.

34. *William the Breton*, p. 251; *History of William the Marshal*, ii, lines 14624–40.

35. *Rot. Litt. Claus.*, i, 146.

36. *Rot. Litt. Pat.*, 98–103.

37. C. R. Cheney, *Innocent III and England* (Stuttgart, 1978), 344.

38. C. R. Cheney, *Innocent III and England* (Stuttgart, 1978), 349.

39. *Rot. Litt. Claus.*, i, 145.

40. *Walter of Coventry*, ii, 212.

41. *Foedera*, 113, 114.

42. *Rot. Litt. Pat.*, 102b, 103, 115.

43. J. C. Holt, *The Northerners: A Study in the Reign of King John* (Oxford, 1961), 88–9.

44. *Walter of Coventry*, ii, 215.

45. J. C. Holt, "The pre history of Parliament," in *The English Parliament in the Middle Ages*, ed. R. G. Davies and J. H. Denton (Manchester, 1981), 1–28, at 5–6.

46. *Rot. Litt. Pat.*, 115.

47. *Rot. Litt. Pat.*, 107.

48. For his period of rule while John was in Poitou, see N. C. Vincent, *Peter des Roches, Bishop of Winchester 1205–38: An Alien in English Politics* (Cambridge, 1996), 89–113. Copies of the letters sealed by his authority were enrolled on a separate Close Roll, *Rot. Litt. Claus.*, i, 204–13; for his appointment, *Rot. Litt. Pat.*, 110.

49. J. C. Holt, *The Northerners: A Study in the Reign of King John* (Oxford, 1961), 97–8.

50. *Rot. Litt. Claus.*, i, 164.

51. J. C. Holt, *The Northerners: A Study in the Reign of King John* (Oxford, 1961), 100.

52. J. L. Bolton, "The English economy in the early thirteenth century," in *King John: New Interpretations*, ed. S. D. Church (Woodbridge, 1999), 27–40.

53. *Foedera*, 118.

54. *The Chronicle and Historical Notes of Bernard Itier*, ed. A. W. Lewis (Oxford, 2013), 96–7, 104–5.

55. *Roger of Wendover, Flores Historiarum*, iii, 280–1; the concord is preserved in *Rot. Chart.*, 197b–8.

56. *William the Breton*, 254–5.

57. *William the Breton*, 260.

58. *Foedera*, 123.

59. Collected together in G. Duby, *The Legend of Bouvines: War, Religion, and Culture in the Middle Ages*, trans. C. Tihanyi (Cambridge, 1990).

60. T. C. van Cleve, *The Emperor Frederick II of Hohenstaufen: Stupor Mundi* (Oxford, 1972), 94–8.

61. *Roger of Wendover, Flores Historiarum*, iii, 291–2.

62. *Rot. Litt. Claus.*, i, 202.

63. *Foedera*, 124.

64. *Layettes du Trésor des Chartes*, nos 1032, 1033. A truce that was to apply to the Emperor Otto and King Frederick of Sicily if they wished.

65. *Letters of Innocent III to England and Wales*, no. 981.

66. J. C. Holt, *The Northerners: A Study in the Reign of King John* (Oxford, 1961), 100.

67. S. K. Mitchell, *Studies in Taxation under John and Henry III* (New Haven, CT, 1914), 109–18.

68. *Pipe Roll 16 John*, xi–xii.

CHAPTER 11: THE GARRISON TURNS ON ITS LEADER

1. *Roger of Wendover, Flores Historiarum*, iii, 293–5. Further arguments in favor of the meeting can be found in *The Chronicle of the Election of Hugh Abbot of Bury St Edmunds and Later Bishop of Ely*, ed. R. M. Thomason (Oxford, 1974), appendix IV, 189–92.

2. R. Sharpe, "Charter of Liberties and Royal Proclamations," at http://actswilliam2henry1 .files.wordpress.com/2013/10/h1-a-liberties-2013-1.pdf, especially 45–53. I am grateful to Professor Sharpe for letting me have access to this file before general publication.

3. *Walter Coventry*, ii, 218.

4. *Foedera*, 126–7.

5. *Letters of Innocent III to England and Wales*, nos 1004, 1006; *Selected Letters of Innocent III*, nos 76, 77, 78; *Walter of Coventry*, ii, 216.

6. L. Landon, "The rate of travel in medieval times," in *Itinerary of Richard I*, 184–91.

7. *Walter of Coventry*, ii, 218.

8. *Rot. Litt. Pat.*, 128.

9. J. C. Holt, *The Northerners: A Study in the Reign of King John* (Oxford, 1961), 104.

10. *Rot. Litt. Pat.*, 129.

11. *Letters of Innocent III to England and Wales*, nos 1001–3.

12. *Walter of Coventry*, ii, 219.

13. *Walter of Coventry*, ii, 219. ("The annals of Southwark and Merton," ed. M. Tyson, in *Surrey Archaeological Collections*, vol. 36 (1925), 24–57, at 48; S. Reynolds, *Fiefs and Vassals: the Medieval Evidence Reinterpreted* (Oxford, 1994), 371).

14. J. H. Round, "An unknown charter of liberties," *EHR* 8 (1893), 288–94.

15. J. C. Holt, *Magna Carta*, 2nd edn (Cambridge, 1992), 418–28.

16. Magna Carta 1215, cap. 2.

17. "The Articles of the Barons: Articles 1–48," The Magna Carta Project, trans. H. Summerson et al., http://magnacarta.cmp.uea.ac.uk/read/articles_of_barons/Articles, accessed June 9, 2014.

18. J. C. Holt, *Magna Carta*, 2nd edition (Cambridge, 1992), 492–3.

19. *Foedera*, 129.

20. *Rot. Litt. Claus.*, i, 204.

21. "The annals of Southwark and Merton," ed. M. Tyson, in *Surrey Archaeological Collections*, vol. 36 (1925), 24–57, 49.

22. J. C. Holt, *Magna Carta*, 2nd edn (Cambridge, 1992), 429–32; C. R. Cheney, "The eve of Magna Carta," *Bulletin of the John Rylands Library*, 38 (1955–6), 311–41.

23. *Rot. Litt. Pat.*, 138b, 142.

24. *Rot. Litt. Pat.*, 142b–143.

25. D. A. Carpenter, "The dating and making of Magna Carta," in his *The Reign of Henry III* (London, 1996), 6 lists the differences.

26. V. H. Galbraith, "A draft of Magna Carta (1215)," *Proceedings of the British Academy*, 53 (1967), 345–60. (*Roger of Wendover, Flores Historiarum*, iii, 317).

27. Here I follow the interpretation offered by D. A. Carpenter, "The dating and making of Magna Carta," in his *The Reign of Henry III* (London, 1996), 1–16. For the difficulties of the chronology, Carpenter's article is central.

28. V. H. Galbraith, *Studies in the Public Records* (London, 1948), 129.

29. J. C. Holt, *Magna Carta*, 2nd edn (Cambridge, 1992), 446. S. Reynolds, "Magna Carta 1297 and the legal use of literacy," *Bulletin of the Institute of Historical Research*, 62 (1989), 233–44.

30. *Rot. Litt. Pat.*, 143b; 123, 127, 127b.

31. C. R. Cheney, "The eve of Magna Carta," *Bulletin of the John Rylands Library*, 38 (1955–6), 311–41, at 326; J. C. Holt, *Magna Carta*, 2nd edn (Cambridge, 1992), 253.

32. *Rot. Litt. Pat.*, 144.

33. This is most easily followed in *English Historical Documents*, ii, 2nd edn, ed. D. C. Douglas and G. Greenaway (London, 1981). The Latin text is in *Recueil des Actes de Henri II, roi d'Angleterre et duc de Normandie, concernant les provinces françaises et les affaires de France*, 4 vols, ed. L. Delisle and E. Berger (Paris 1916–66), I, 61.

34. J. C. Holt, *Magna Carta*, 2nd edn (Cambridge, 1992), 494–5.

35. N. C. Vincent, *The Magna Carta*, Sotheby's Sale Catalogue (December 18, 2007).

36. J. C. Holt, *Magna Carta*, 2nd edn (Cambridge, 1992), 493–5.

37. C. R. Cheney, "The twenty-five barons of Magna Carta," *Bulletin of the John Rylands Library*, 50 (1967–8), 280–307; J. C. Holt, *Magna Carta*, 2nd edn (Cambridge, 1992), 478–80.

38. S. D. Church, "The 1210 Campaign in Ireland: evidence for a military revolution?" *Anglo-Norman Studies*, 20 (1998), 45–57; 51 shows that John took a force of 800 knights to Ireland.

39. J. C. Holt, *Magna Carta*, 2nd edn (Cambridge, 1992), 493–4.

40. *Selected Letters of Innocent III*, nos 82, 83.

41. J. C. Holt, *Magna Carta*, 2nd edn (Cambridge, 1992), 474–7.

42. J. C. Holt, *Magna Carta*, 2nd edn (Cambridge, 1992), 254–5, does not make this distinction.

43. *Annales Monastici*, iii, 43.

44. *Walter of Coventry*, ii, 222.

45. J. C. Holt, *Magna Carta*, 2nd edn (Cambridge, 1992), 498. Following Holt's dating (260–6) rather than that of H. Richardson, "The morrow of the Great Charter," *Bulletin of the John Ryland's Library*, 28 (1944), 422–43.

46. *Selected Letters of Pope Innocent III*, no. 80.

47. *Selected Letters of Pope Innocent III*, no. 83.

CHAPTER 12: THE WALLS BREACHED

1. *Walter of Coventry*, ii, 223.

2. J. C. Holt, *The Northerners: A Study in the Reign of King John* (Oxford, 1961), 128.

3. H. Kaye, "The household of King John," unpublished University of East Anglia PhD thesis (2014), chapter 5.

4. R. Allen Brown, *Rochester Castle, Kent* (HMSO, 1969), 10–11; I. W. Rowlands, "King John, Stephen Langton, and Rochester Castle," in *Studies in Medieval History presented to R. Allen Brown*, ed. C. Harper-Bill, C. J. Holdsworth and J. L. Nelson (Woodbridge, 1989), 267–80.

5. *Rot. Litt. Claus.*, i, 231 ff.

6. *A Calendar of Ancient Correspondence Concerning Wales*, ed. J. G. Edwards (Cardiff, 1935) 1.

7. *Rot. Litt. Claus.*, 246.

8. *Foedera*, 144.

9. *Rot. Litt. Claus.*, i, 233b.

10. *Liber Feodorum*, 52–65. The returns are printed at 65–228.

11. *Red Book of the Exchequer*, ii, ccxxiii–iv, 535.

12. *Rot. Litt. Claus.*, i., 260b.

13. *Rot. Litt. Claus.*, i, 233b. For William's career see R. V. Turner, "William Briewerre," in his *Men Raised from the Dust: Administrative Service and Upward Mobility in Angevin England* (Philadelphia, PA, 1988), 71–90.

14. *Rot. Litt. Claus.*, 233b.

15. *Rot. Litt. Claus.*, 232.

16. C. R. Cheney, *Innocent III and England*, (Stuttgart, 1978), 43–9.

17. *Selected Letters of Pope Innocent III*, no. 84.

18. C. R. Cheney, *Innocent III and England* (Stuttgart, 1978), 389–90.

19. D. Keene, "Roots and branches of power, 1000–1300," *The London Journal*, 26 (2001), 1–8.

20. *Walter of Coventry*, ii, 229.

21. *Histoire des Ducs de Normandie*, 170.

22. *Coggeshall*, 181.

23. *Coggeshall*, 182.

24. *Annales Monastici*, ii, 82–3.

25. R. Allen Brown, H. M. Colvin and A. J. Taylor., *The History of the King's Works: The Middle Ages*, 2 vols, general editor H. M. Colvin (London, 1963), ii, 616–24.

26. *Rot. Litt. Claus.*, 274.

27. Matthew Paris, *Chronica Majora*, iii, 28.

28. The best summary is in W. L. Warren, *King John* (London, 1961), 278–85.

29. N. C. Vincent, ed., *The Letters and Charters of Cardinal Guala Bicchieri Papal Legate in England, 1216–1218*, Canterbury and York Society, 83 (1996), No. 140b.

30. S. D. Church, "King John's testament and the last days of his reign," *EHR*, 125 (2010), 505–28.

31. S. D. Church, "King John's testament and the last days of his reign," *EHR*, 125 (2010), 505–28.

32. *Roger of Wendover, Flores Historiarum*, iv, 4.

33. *Foedera*, 145.

34. For example, Blanche of Castile, wife of King Louis VIII of France and Henry's first cousin, would be her son's regent between 1226 and 1234.

35. D. A. Carpenter, *The Minority of Henry III* (London, 1990), 13–19; 268–9.

36. The phrase is W. L. Warren's, *King John* (London, 1961), 256.

37. For which still see D. A. Carpenter, *The Minority of Henry III* (London, 1990).

CONCLUSION

1. U. Engel, *Worcester Cathedral: An Architectural History* (London, 2007).

2. J. Martindale, "The sword on the stone: some resonances of a medieval symbol of power (the tomb of King John in Worcester cathedral)," *Anglo-Norman Studies*, 15 (1992), 199–241.

INDEX

This index has been organised by personal name except in the instance of modern commentators. For example, Savaric de Mauléon is indexed under "Savaric," but Anthony Mundy is to be found under Mundy. Cross-references are supplied where appropriate.